PENTECOST
TO THE
PRESENT

PENTECOST
TO THE
PRESENT

BOOK TWO: *REFORMATIONS AND AWAKENINGS*

JEFF OLIVER

BRIDGE
LOGOS

Newberry, FL 32669

Bridge-Logos
Newberry, FL 32669

Pentecost to the Present:
The Holy Spirit's Enduring Work in the Church
by Jeff Oliver

Printed in the United States of America.

Editing services by ChristianEditingServices.com

Cover/Interior design by Kent Jensen | knail.com

Cover photo: "Camp Meeting of the Methodists in N. America" by Jacques Gérard Milbert (c. 1819) aquatint engraving by M. Dubourg. Source: Library of Congress Prints and Photographs Collection.

International Standard Book Number: 978-0-91210-631-1

VP 03-13-17

DEDICATION

To the Spirit of God, whose tireless work through the centuries has gone largely unnoticed.

To Pastor Reggie Scarborough of Family Worship Center in Lakeland, Florida—the man who taught me "progressive Pentecost."

To my beautiful wife, Faith, without whose love and support I could not have completed this work.

And to our West Highland Terrier, Gracie Lou, who lay at my feet or on my lap through most of this writing.

A special thanks to Karen Burkett, Harold Helms, Glenn Gohr, Craig Keener, Douglas Jacobsen, Mark Nickens, Edward Harding, and all who contributed to the editing process.

CONTENTS

FOREWORD

After many years of study and research, Jeff Oliver has now published the fruits of his labor. *Pentecost to the Present: The Holy Spirit's Enduring Work in the Church* is a very readable and accurate history of charismatic Christianity from the days of the apostles to the present day. As Jeff said, he wrote this book to show the world that Pentecostalism has deep "roots in historic Christianity" contrary to what many have thought. He also shows that such spiritual gifts as speaking in tongues has recurred over the centuries before the advent of modern Pentecostalism.

This book is a popular history, "written in plain language" as a resource for Pentecostal and charismatic leaders and lay persons who may not know or understand their own heritage. *Pentecost to the Present* is useful for those who want to seek a better and deeper understanding of their own Pentecostal faith. Jeff has covered all the bases in the Pentecostal tradition from the New Testament church through the church fathers, the Reformation, the Wesleyan Holiness revival, the classical Pentecostal churches, and the charismatic movement in the mainline churches. Along the way he has included short biographies of most of the leaders he covers along with many wonderful portraits of them all.

This book is well written, easy to read, and tells the Pentecostal story in a narrative form that is easy to grasp. The questions at the end of each chapter will make this book useful in adult small groups, youth groups, family discussions, and as a classroom text in college classes.

Jeff Oliver knows whereof he speaks. Coming into Pentecostalism in the days of the charismatic renewal, he joined a number of Pentecostal and charismatic churches. Before writing this book he attended Rhema Bible Training College in Broken Arrow, Oklahoma, and served as a Christian Education Director and senior pastor for thirteen years. Most recently, he has joined the International Church of the Foursquare Gospel where he was ordained to the ministry, and is now helping to plant a Foursquare congregation in Charlotte, North Carolina. His desire is to help the many "Christian adults and youth who are unaware of their rich spiritual heritage in Christ dating back to Pentecost." He has done a great job.

VINSON SYNAN, PH.D.

DEAN EMERITUS, REGENT UNIVERSITY SCHOOL OF DIVINITY

INTERIM DEAN, ORAL ROBERTS UNIVERSITY COLLEGE OF THEOLOGY AND MINISTRY

INTRODUCTION

Jesus once spoke of a time when men would sleep and an enemy would come and sow tares among the wheat. The Renaissance, the Enlightenment, and the Modern Age was just such a time.

This second book in a series of three books covers the period from the Middle Ages to the early twentieth century, including the Renaissance and the Enlightenment and how they affected Christianity both in Europe and in the New World.

Book One: Early Prophetic and Spiritual Gifts Movements covers the period from the early church through the Middle Ages, when much of Northern Europe was converted through miracle-working missionary monks.

Book Three: Worldwide Revivals and Renewal brings us up to the present day, sparked by the 1904-05 Welsh Revival and the Azusa Street Revival in 1906, followed by the charismatic renewal and the global rise of Pentecostalism.

This current installment, *Book Two: Reformations and Awakenings*, demonstrates how:

- Supernatural signs and wonders played roles in the foundations of nearly every new state church, free church, and denomination.

- Catholicism countered with a reformation of its own that included a revival of mysticism, a new army of spiritual soldiers, and the discovery of the New World.

- Restorationist movements countered the intellectual revolutions of their day with revivals of faith in the supernatural.

- A decade-long prayer meeting shaped the future of revivalism affecting both England's Wesleyan Revival and America's First Great Awakening.

- The French Revolution replaced Christianity with liberalism as the world's dominant ideology and many Americans countered this new revolution with a Second Great Awakening.

- Phoebe Palmer began the modern Holiness movement and Jeremiah Lanphier launched a worldwide Layman's Prayer Revival.

- Many Americans reunited after the Civil War with a series of Holiness Camp Meetings, followed by a similar "Higher Life" movement in Britain, and later, a new stream of American healing ministries.

THE REFORMATION

(c. 1501 – 1650)

As Thomas Aquinas toured the palatial palace in Rome, Pope Innocent IV flaunted the vastness of the church's wealth before Thomas's eyes, remarking, "As you can see, the Church is no longer in an age in which she can say, 'Silver and gold have I none.'" Thomas replied, "True. Nor can she say to the lame man, 'Rise up and walk.'"[1]

In the course of time, every human institution is judged, and the papal ruled Catholic Church was no exception. Individuals are not judged so much as the institutions themselves. In time, Europeans grew increasingly skeptical that any single human or office could represent Christ, or for that matter, every Christian on earth. The Great Papal Schism had demonstrated all too clearly the abuses of power, and the seeds of the Reformation had been planted in the resulting council of national churches. The signs were also evident in early reformers like Bernard of Clairvaux, as well as dissenters like the Cathars and Waldensians.

---

1   Adam Clarke, *Commentary*, 705: Eddie L. Hyatt, *2000 Years of Charismatic Christianity* (Lake Mary, Fla.: Charisma, 2002), 51 [hereafter CC].

JOHN WYCLIFFE

Martin Luther was not the first reformer. He was simply the first to successfully challenge the Catholic Church. Among the earliest reformers was Englishman and Oxford University teacher John Wycliffe (1330–1384). Like Luther, Wycliffe destroyed the medieval barrier between God and humanity by teaching that everyone—priest and layman alike—had an equal place in the eyes of God. Like Calvin, he believed God had predetermined who would and would not be saved. Wycliffe stated, "No man, not even a pope, knows whether he is of the church."[2] And like most branded heretics, Wycliffe used the Scriptures as his standard for judging the church. One advantage Wycliffe had over his successors, however, was that Wycliffe had the Great Papal Schism as a backdrop for his arguments.

Wycliffe's doctrine of "dominion founded on grace" meant that everyone had been given the right to govern themselves through sanctifying grace—instead of one man living in sin being given the right to rule all others. Wycliffe detested the trappings of power and denounced the worldliness and luxury of the popes. In time, he came to believe the pope was "Antichrist," often drawing contrasts between the current state of the papacy and the simple faith of Jesus and his disciples: Christ was truth; the pope was the principle of falsehood. Christ lived in poverty; the pope labored for worldly magnificence. Christ refused temporal dominion; the pope sought it. Christ alone was the head of the church; the papal institution was full of poison. "It

---

2   K.B. McFarlane, *John Wycliffe and the Beginnings of English Nonconformity* (London: English University, 1952): Bruce L. Shelley, *Church History in Plain Language, Third Edition* (Nashville: Thomas Nelson, 2008), 227 [hereafter CH].

is Antichrist itself," he exclaimed, "the man of sin who exalts himself above God. Let judgment fall!"[3]

Though Wycliffe retained many Catholic beliefs, including purgatory, confession, and praying to saints, he also preached against the doctrine of transubstantiation—belief that the Eucharist or Communion elements actually transform into the body and blood of Christ. Of course, this opened the door for him to be labeled a heretic and the church eventually forbade him to lecture—but not until he had launched a new movement. Much like Waldo before him, Wycliffe led a group of scholars to translate the Bible into the language of craftsmen and peasants and sent out his "poor priests" into the byways and villages, armed with tracts, sermons, and pages ripped from his new Bible. Their enemies dubbed them "Lollards," which means "drunken babblers," because they lacked any formal academic background. However, Wycliffe had soon enlisted so many to his cause that one man cried out, "Every second man I meet is a Lollard!" The Lollards were hunted down and forced to recant or be expelled from the church. Wycliffe himself, having already gained enough popular support, was wisely left alone—except to be expelled from the university. But it was too late as Wycliffe's movement soon found even greater support elsewhere.

John Wycliffe, "the Morningstar of the Reformation," giving his "Poor Priests" his new translation of the Bible by William Frederick Yeames (1835-1918). The church dubbed them "Lollards," meaning "drunken babblers," and likened them to locusts with scorpion tails (Revelation 9:9–10) because they rejected the pope as head of the church and taught that the organized church was not necessary for salvation, believing instead that simple obedience to God and the Bible was sufficient. Source: www.bible-researcher.com. Photo: Wikimedia/Pimbrils.

---

3   Ibid.

JAN HUS

Jan Hus (1369–1415) was born of peasant parents in southern Bohemia (modern-day Czeck Republic), where he later studied theology at the University of Prague and was exposed to the writings of Wycliffe. After becoming pastor of the nearby 3,000-seat Bethlehem Chapel, Hus immediately adopted Wycliffe's views of the church as a company of believers with Christ (not the pope) as its true head. On the walls of Bethlehem Chapel hung paintings reflecting Wycliffe's teachings and contrasting the behavior of Christ and the popes. In one painting, the pope rode a horse; next to it, Christ walked barefoot. Another depicted the pope crowned in all of his glory; next to it, Christ wore a crown of thorns. In another, Jesus washed the disciples' feet; next to it, the pope was having his feet kissed. Student riots—both for and against—broke out in the streets. The archbishop of Prague complained to the pope, and the pope replied, "Root out that heresy!" Then when the archbishop excommunicated Hus, an even greater tumult erupted as Hus fled into exile. On November 1, 1414, Hus was summoned to appear before the Council of Constance. Considering it an opportunity to present his views to the court and being granted safe travel there and back, Hus agreed. However, upon arrival, he found instead he was to be the next victim of the Inquisition. The process was simple—confess and renounce your errors and face life imprisonment, or be burned. Hus was willing to submit to the church's teachings, but only as they aligned with the truth of Scripture. Historian Bruce Shelley wrote, "Few scenes in church history are more touching than Hus's fidelity and refusal to swerve from absolute truth, even to save his life."[4] After refusing to recant, Hus lay in prison for eight months.

---

4   CH 232.

Jan Hus before the Council of Constance (detail) by Václav Brožík (1883) oil on canvas, Bethlehem Chapel, Prague, Czeck Republic. Source: AΩ institut. Photo: Wikimedia/Jedudedek.

On July 6, 1415, the day of his execution, Hus was given one final opportunity to recant and save his life. He replied, "God is my witness that the evidence against me is false. I have never thought nor preached except with the one intention of winning men, if possible, from their sins. In the truth of the gospel, I have written, taught, and preached; today I will gladly die."[5] Despite the pope's best efforts to put the Bohemian heresy to rest, yet another movement refused to die along with its leader, and an independent church was formed along doctrinal and ethnic lines called the "Unity of the Brotherhood." Though they would remain little more than a root in dry ground for a hundred years, the Moravian Church had been born.

Both Hus and the Moravians believed in miracles. *The History of the Persecutions of the Bohemian Church* states, "By one or more exiled Bohemians, we find mention of many signs, and divine prodigies, wrought on behalf of the Bohemians under persecution." And again, "We have here an extraordinary manifestation of Divine power, perceptible to unbelievers as well as believers."[6] Hus himself frequently had visions and dreams and foresaw future events even while in prison. On the day

---

5   *John Hus: A Biography* (N.J.: Princeton University, 1968): CH 232.

6   Boys, *Suppressed Evidence*, 72–85: Jeff Doles, *Miracles & Manifestations of the Holy Spirit in the History of the Church* (Seffner, Fla.: Walking Barefoot Ministries, 2008), 134-135 [hereafter MM].

of his execution, Hus prophesied, "This day you roast a goose, but a hundred years hence you shall hear a swan sing, that you shall not roast."[7] Exactly one hundred years later, in 1515, Martin Luther preached his message of reform from Wittenberg University and two years after that nailed his Ninety-Five Theses to the door of Wittenberg Castle, officially beginning the Protestant Reformation. Hus had been right. Another persecuted Bohemian prophesied this before his death: "The fury of the enemies of the truth has now the upper hand. But this will not always be so: for there will arise a people without display, without sword, and without power, whom they will not be able to resist."[8]

MARTIN LUTHER

Hans and Margarethe Luther's eldest son, Martin (1483–1546), was being groomed to become a lawyer until one night, in a thunderstorm while returning to the university on horseback, he was nearly struck by lightning. "Help!" he cried. "Save me, St. Anne, and I will become a monk!" (St. Anne is believed to be the mother of Mary, the grandmother of Jesus and the patron saint of miners, and Luther's father was a miner). Much to his father's dismay, Martin entered the priesthood. He wrote, "If ever a monk got to heaven by his sheer monkery, it was I."[9] Luther often fasted and slept without a blanket in winter, trying every means possible to obtain salvation. Martin's lifelong friend, mentor, and mystic Johann von Staupitz, trying to ease Martin's conscience, suggested he try loving God instead. Luther wrote, "Love God? I hated him!" But Staupitz had a better idea. Believing that Martin would find his love for God in the Scriptures,

---

7   Ibid: MM 132.

8   Ibid: MM 133.

9   Roland H. Bainton, *Here I Stand: A Life of Martin Luther* (Nashville: Abingdon, 1950): CH 238.

he gave him his position at Wittenberg University—and it worked! As Martin's eyes fell on Romans 1:17 for the first time, "For therein is the righteousness of God revealed from faith to faith: as it is written, the just shall live by faith," he gained a whole new perspective on God. "Night and day," he recalled, "I pondered until I saw the connection between the justice of God and the statement 'the just shall live by faith.' Then I grasped that the justice of God is that righteousness by which through grace and sheer mercy God justifies us through faith. Thereupon I felt myself to be reborn and to have gone through open doors into paradise."[10]

THE BIRTH OF THE REFORMATION

Luther's "justification by faith" doctrine would not only become his own salvation but would also soon lay the groundwork for a worldwide movement with enormous implications. If salvation came through faith alone, then the entire ecclesiastical structure of the church with its mediation of priests, popes, monks, Mass, prayers to saints, penance, confessions, and indulgences would no longer be necessary. Armed with this newfound understanding of salvation by faith, Luther began questioning and criticizing the church's sale of indulgences and other abuses. His malcontent was reinforced in 1517 when Dominican John Tetzel began preaching throughout Germany as part of his papal fundraising campaign for the reconstruction of St. Peter's Basilica in Rome. In exchange for a contribution, Tetzel promised that a loved-one's soul could be freed from purgatory (an intermediate place where those who die in grace are believed to be made ready for heaven). Tetzel even devised a jingle: "As the coin in the coffer rings, a soul from purgatory springs." The absurdity of Tetzel's antics led Luther to post

---

10   John Dillenberger, *Martin Luther: Selections from His Writings* (Garden City, N.Y.: Doubleday, 1961): CH 239.

his Ninety-five Theses to the door of Wittenberg's Castle on October 31, 1517. Luther argued that the issuance of indulgences provided a false sense of security by claiming to remove guilt or free loved ones from purgatory. This was the spark that ignited the Protestant Reformation.

"A WILD BOAR IN THE LORD'S VINEYARD"

The Dominicans quickly denounced Luther. A Roman theologian issued a series of counter theses arguing that anyone who criticized indulgences was guilty of heresy. In the same vein as Wycliffe, Hus, and others, Luther questioned their authority and insisted on scriptural proof. However, as Rome prepared to declare him a heretic, Luther wisely took his case to the German people and princes, publishing a series of pamphlets in which he called upon the princes to correct the abuses within the church, in effect lobbying for a national German church. In June of 1520, Pope Leo X issued a sealed document condemning Luther and giving him sixty days to return from his heretical course or face the consequences. The document described Luther as a "wild boar" who had invaded the Lord's vineyard and must be judged. Forty-one of Luther's theses were condemned as "heretical, scandalous, false, offensive to pious ears, seductive of simple minds, and repugnant to Catholic truth."[11] Luther responded by leading a crowd of eager students outside Wittenberg to burn copies of the Canon Law and other theological works to which Luther personally added a copy of the papal bull condemning him. As bold and risky as this was, Luther later reported he was more pleased over this single act than any other act of his entire life. Indeed, many historians mark the Bonfire of 1520, instead of the posting of the Ninety-Five Theses, as the official beginning of the Protestant Reformation.

11   Bainton, *Here I Stand: A Life of Martin Luther.* CH 237.

Regardless, the pope responded predictably, declaring Luther a heretic and excommunicating him from the church.

Martin Luther with some of his university supporters on December 10, 1520, burning the papal bull and various other documents and theological works. Some historians mark this event as the official beginning of the Protestant Reformation. From the *Life of Martin Luther and Heroes of the Reformation!* (detail) by H. Brückner, H. Breul, lithographer (c. 1874). Source: Library of Congress Prints & Photographs Division. Photo: Wikimedia/Alex:D.

The problem with what to do with Luther now fell on Germany's young emperor Charles V, who had sworn by oath to defend the church and to root out heresy wherever it may be found. The emperor summoned Luther to an imperial assembly at Worms. Again, Luther appealed to the Scriptures: "My conscience is captive to the Word of God. I will not recant anything, for to go against conscience is neither honest nor safe. Here I stand, I can do no other. God help me. Amen."[12] The emperor was not impressed. He declared Luther an outlaw and granted him twenty-one days' safe passage to Saxony before his sentencing. The sentencing never came. Luther was saved from arrest and death by Duke Frederick the Wise, Prince of Saxony—the province that surrounded Wittenberg. Luther was kidnapped and offered solitude at the Duke's Wartburg Castle, where he spent nine months translating the New Testament into German while disguised as a minor nobleman.

LUTHER'S REFORMS

Meanwhile, the revolt against Rome continued to spread as princes, dukes, and other elected officials—including more radical reformers—

12   Dillenberger, *Martin Luther: Selections from His Writings*. CH 242.

began lending their support to the new movement. In 1522, Luther returned to Wittenberg to put into effect his reforms, which would soon become a model for Germany and much of Western civilization. Among the first was to abolish the office of bishop, which he regarded as unscriptural. Priests also abandoned their celibacy as many monks and nuns—including Luther—married. Suddenly, a new image of ministry began to emerge—that of a married pastor living with his family like any other. The face of worship also changed dramatically from a liturgical service filled with ritual and ceremony to a celebration filled with music and preaching. Luther believed music propelled the gospel forward and, next to the Word of God, deserved the highest praise. Luther himself became an accomplished singer, musician, and hymn writer.[13]

THE PEASANT REVOLT

In 1524, taking their cues from the Reformation, Germany's peasant class began their own uprising against the noble classes. At first, Luther sympathized with their cause, but when they turned violent and began rebelling against authority, Luther sided with the princes who had once stood with him. In a letter written to Germany's nobility, he wrote, "Smite, strangle, and stab, secretly or openly, for nothing can be more poisonous, hurtful, or devilish than a rebel." In 1525, the princes and nobles responded by crushing the rebellion, and an estimated 100,000 lives were lost. Luther wrote a second letter to the princes, pleading for mercy for the peasants, but it was too late.

---

13   "Martin Luther, The Later Years and Legacy," Christian History Magazine 12,
       no. 3, issue 39 (Carol Stream, IL: Christianity Today), 10: Roberts Liardon, God's
       Generals: The Roaring Reformers (New Kensington, Pa.: Whitaker, 2003), 170
       [hereafter GGRR].

The peasants blamed Luther for their defeat, the nobles blamed Luther for instigating the rebellion, the emperor hated him, the pope hated him, and Catholics hated him—such was the life of a reformer. Then came the plague. Everyone who was well left Wittenberg while the Luthers stayed behind to care for the sick. The local monastery was turned into a hospital as Luther watched many of his friends die. It was there, at the lowest point of his life, that Luther penned the words of his most beloved hymn: "A mighty fortress is our God, a bulwark never failing; our helper He amid the flood of mortal ills prevailing." Once again, Luther turned to God for his help. Just before his death, Luther wrote to his wife, "I am fed up with this world, and it is fed up with me."[14] He died with his faith in the newly reformed church intact: "I entertain no sorry picture of our Church, but rather that of the Church flourishing through pure and uncorrupted teaching and one increasing with excellent ministers from day to day."[15]

Portrait of Martin Luther (detail) at the Coburg Fortress in Coburg, Germany, by Lucas Cranach the Elder (1528), court painter to the electors of Saxony in Wittenberg and a close friend of Martin's. Cranach also painted Martin's wife, Katharina Von Bora, and parents, Hans and Margarethe Luther. Source: Carol Gerten-Jackson. Photo: Wikimedia/Botaurus.

LUTHER ON MIRACLES

Luther resented how the Catholic Church often faked miracles—even demanding that he produce miracles of his own to prove his doctrine. He repeatedly replied that no sign would be given them other than the Word

14   Ibid, 35: GGRR 178.
15   Bainton, *Here I Stand*, 286: GGRR 179.

of God. Luther also believed the primary purpose of miracles was for the spreading of the gospel, and since the gospel had already spread into the entire world, there was no longer a need for miracles as in apostolic times. Nevertheless, Luther believed in and often dabbled in the supernatural, claiming the direct activity of the Holy Spirit as the source of all his teachings. In one of his earliest writings, he assured his readers that the truth he presented was "learned under the Spirit's guidance," and when asked by church officials at Worms to reveal the source of his authority, he said he "relied on the revelation of God to him through the Word, but via the Spirit in a personal manner."[16] Once when asked by a mystic if he had received revelations, Luther replied, "Yes."[17]

Thomas Müntzer (c. 1489–1525), an early disciple of Luther, who later joined the Radical Zwickau Prophets and led thousands to their deaths in the Peasant's War, took Luther's beliefs several steps further. Müntzer believed all Christians should experience the Holy Spirit as powerfully in their day as in the days of the apostles and prophets. He taught that an inward baptism of the Holy Spirit was necessary but outward (infant) baptism was not necessary. This Spirit baptism could be received only through inner turmoil, abandonment of worldly pleasures, and taking up one's cross daily to follow Jesus—all of which were necessary to become consciously aware of the Spirit's indwelt presence. Christians should seek not only to be possessed by the Holy Spirit but also to be guided by him through prophecy, visions, and dreams, which were considered evidence of the Spirit's descent. Müntzer placed great importance on direct revelation, which he called the "inner" word of God as opposed to

16   Martin Luther, *The Babylon Captivity of the Church*, vol. 36 of Luther's Works, eds. Helmut T. Lehman and Jaroslav Pelikan (Phila.: Muhlenberg, 1958), 77; John S. Oyer, *Lutheran Reformers Against the Anabaptists* (The Hague, Netherlands: Marinus Nijhoff, 1964), 231: CC 74.

17   Bengt Hoffman, *Luther and the Mystics* (Minneapolis: Augsburg, 1976), 190: CC 74.

the "outer" or audible word of God. Müntzer also believed in the soon and imminent return of Christ and taught radical social reforms, such as believers having all things in common, which would help lay the groundwork for the Swiss Brethren and other early Anabaptist groups.

LUTHER THE PROPHET

German church historian, T. Souer, described Luther as "a prophet, evangelist, speaker in tongues and interpreter, in one person, endowed with all the gifts of grace."[18] Luther spoke prophetically on a number of occasions. Some of his prophecies were fulfilled during his lifetime, and others later. Indeed, so frequent were Luther's prophecies that Philipp Melanchthon, his close friend and colleague, called him "Elijah."[19] One such prophecy stated, "As long as I live, there will, God willing, be no danger, and a good measure of peace will continue in Germany; but, when I am gone, pray. There will be need, truly, of prayers; and our children will be forced to seize their spears, so bad will be the state of Germany." After Luther's death in 1546, Lutheran princes took up arms against Imperial Catholic forces in a conflict that lasted until 1555. Then in 1618, the Thirty Years' War—Europe's longest and bloodiest—ensued. Germany was left devastated, depopulated, bankrupt, and riddled with famine and disease.

LUTHER ON HEALING

Luther once said, "Often has it happened, and still does, that devils have been driven out in the name of Christ; also by calling on His

---

18   T. Souer, *Geschichte der Christlichen Kirche für (History of the Christian Church)* vol. 3 (1959), 406: Gordon F. Atter, *The Third Force* (Peterborough, Ontario: College Press, 1962), 12.

19   John Horsch, "The Faith of the Swiss Brethren, II," *Mennonite Quarterly Review* 5, No. 1 (1931), 16: CC 74

name and prayer, the sick have been healed."[20] Melanchthon wrote, "I should have been a dead man had I not been recalled from death itself by the coming of Luther."[21] Friedrich Myconius, another of Luther's colleagues, was dying of tuberculosis when Luther wrote him, saying, "I command you in the Name of God to live because I still have need of you in the work of reforming the Church. The Lord will never let me hear that you are dead, but will permit you to survive me. For this I am praying, this is my will, and may my will be done because I seek only to glorify the Name of God."[22] Myconius was not only healed but also outlived Luther by two months.

Once when an eighteen-year-old demon-possessed girl was brought to him, Luther ordered the girl to recite the Apostles' Creed. But as she attempted to say, "and in Jesus Christ His only Son our Lord," she fell into convulsions. Luther said, "I know you, Satan. You would like for me to begin exorcising with great display, but I will do no such thing." The next day, she was again brought to him, and again fell prostrate and went into convulsions. After the students picked her up, Luther instructed them, saying it was not the season for casting out devils since the church had been established. He urged them not to follow popish ceremonies of exorcism but to simply pray patiently and perseveringly without assigning God a time or manner in which to cast out the demon. Luther then laid his hand on the girl's head, repeated the Apostle's Creed and the Lord's Prayer, and quoted John 14:12: "He who believes on me, the works that I do shall he do also, and greater works than these shall he do." Then he and the other ministers

---

20　Gordon, *The Ministry of Healing*, 92: CC 75.

21　Ibid., 94: CC 75.

22　*Change the World School of Prayer* (Studio City, N.Y.: Word Literature Crusade, 1976), C-35: CC 75.

prayed, asking God for Christ's sake to cast the devil out of the girl. Luther then touched the girl with his foot and repeated, "Proud devil, you would indeed like for me to proceed against you with great display, but I will do no such thing. I know that your head is crushed and that you lie prostrate at and under the feet of our Lord Jesus Christ."[23] Then he left, and the girl was taken home to her friends, where she was no more troubled by the devil.

In a collection of sermons taken from Luther's church and dated 1523, Luther again referred to John 14:12: "He who believes on me, the works that I do shall he do also; and greater works than these shall he do." He then commented, "Therefore, we must allow these words to remain and not gloss over them, as some have done who said that these signs were manifestations of the Spirit in the beginning of the Christian era and that now they have ceased. That is not right; for the same power is in the church still."[24]

ULRICH ZWINGLI

Ulrich Zwingli (1484–1531), pastor of the Grossmünster Church in Zurich, Switzerland, also preached a radical style of reform—not by posting theses or burning Canon Law but by simply teaching straight from the Bible, yet another revolutionary idea in the sixteenth century. As Zwingli taught from Matthew, Acts, and the Epistles, his followers began hearing of a different kind of church than the state-run churches they were used to. Instead of every newborn infant being baptized and automatically becoming a church member, the

---

23   Boys, *Suppressed Evidence*, 162–167 commenting on a passage from Seckendorf's History of Lutheranism: MM 136–137.

24   A Sermon by Martin Luther; taken from his Church Postil, 1523: MM 136.

community of believers they heard about freely chose to be baptized and become committed followers of Jesus. And while Luther had allowed for the continuance of any church practice not prohibited by the Bible, Zwingli felt it necessary to freely challenge anything not prescribed by the Bible. Thus, fasting at Lent, Mass, statues of saints, relics, icons, candles, infant baptism—they all had to go. But as Zwingli and his followers began introducing their reforms one by one, the local Zurich city council met to discuss them—allowing some while prohibiting others. However, for Conrad Grebel (1498–1526) and Zwingli's more radical wing of followers, this was not enough. As far as they were concerned, Luther "tore down the old house, but built no new one in its place," and though Zwingli "threw down all maladies as with thunder strokes," he "erected nothing better in its place."[25] Luther's churches were still part of an established church that looked to the state for support and considered the entire population of a territory to be their membership. Grebel's group wanted civil government completely out of church affairs so they could establish a congregation of the faithful, while Zwingli coveted the support of the city council and would hear none of it.

Ulrich Zwingli by Georg Osterwald (1803–1884). Ulrich, the founder of Swiss Protestantism and the first Reformed theologian, devoured the Greek New Testament, memorized Paul's epistles, and preached straight from Scripture, expounding its truths even when they differed from traditional church teachings—all before anyone in Switzerland had heard the name Martin Luther. Source: Bibliothèque publique et universitaire de Neuchâtel – BPUN. Photo: Wikimedia/gardenfriend.

25   Franklin H. Littell, *The Origins of Sectarian Protestantism* (New York: Beacon, 1964), 2: CC 79.

THE ANABAPTISTS

The matter came to a head in 1524 when the Zurich city council insisted that all newborn infants be baptized, which was a serious matter since Grebel's group believed water baptism was not for infants, but for believers only. And now that Grebel's wife had just given birth to a new baby, what were they to do? The Grebels refused to baptize their baby. Other parents followed suit. Zwingli met secretly with Grebel's group, hoping to talk them down off the ledge, but to no avail. Then Zwingli wrote an article accusing his own followers of causing rebellion and unrest. On January 17, 1525, the council sided with Zwingli, ordering anyone refusing to have their child baptized to be expelled. Four days later, on January 21, 1525, as Grebel's group met at Felix Manz's house, George Blaurock, a former priest, turned to Conrad Grebel and asked him to baptize him. The first adult water baptism was performed, and the first free church (free from state rule) in modern times was born.

The Catholic Church called them Anabaptists, meaning "rebaptizers," to label them as heretics and begin the process of persecution. They resented the title, preferring simply "Baptists." After all, since the ceremonial sprinkling of infants was unscriptural, theirs was not a rebaptism but the only baptism. In 1526, the Zurich city council released a mandate stating that anyone who rebaptized another did so under penalty of death by drowning. Evidently if these heretics wanted water, they decided to let them have it! In less than two years, Felix Manz, the man in whose house the first Anabaptist meeting took place, became the first Anabaptist martyr. George Blaurock fled east and was burned at the stake. Within four years, between 4,000 and 5,000 of the Swiss Brethren were executed by fire, water, or sword.

Others fled to Germany, Austria, or Moravia, where sympathetic and tolerant princes remained. Some of these groups later consolidated under Jakob Hutter and became known as Hutterites. Meanwhile, Ulrich Zwingli became embroiled in a controversy with Martin Luther over whether the Eucharist "represented the real presence of Christ" as Luther believed, or was purely symbolic as he believed. He was slain in 1531 in a civil war between Swiss Catholics and Protestants.

ANABAPTISTS ON THE HOLY SPIRIT

Early Anabaptists believed strongly in the restoration of apostolic Christianity and a return to the church of true believers, including baptism in the Holy Spirit and speaking in other tongues. Water baptism by immersion simply stood out as their most unusual practice. Because of intense persecution, however, the Anabaptists often met secretly in homes or in open-air meetings in forests and fields, where they read the Bible and prayed for that same Spirit and power that had come down on the early church to come upon them. It was not unusual for early Anabaptists to dance, fall under the power, speak in tongues, raise the dead, or experience healings.[26] Indeed, according to one Swiss Anabaptist document written in the 1530s, the main reason Anabaptists refused to attend state-run churches was because these churches did not allow their members to exercise spiritual gifts according to "the Christian order as taught in the gospel or the Word of God in 1 Corinthians 14."[27] The document also accused Luther and

---

26   Ibid., 19: CC 79.

27   Paul and Shem Peachey, trans., "Answer of Some Who Are Called (Ana) Baptists. Why They Do Not Attend The Churches," Mennonite Quarterly Review 45, No. 1 (1971), 10: CC 80.

Zwingli of transgressing their own "original teaching" and impeding "the rivers of living water" by not allowing the free exercise of spiritual gifts in their congregations. At their core, Anabaptists believed the Holy Spirit resided in every church member. Therefore, every member possessed one or more of his gifts for the edification of the body, and every member should have an opportunity to exercise those gifts for the building up of the congregation. Consequently, a Christian gathering dominated by one person was not controlled by the Holy Spirit: "When someone comes to church and constantly hears only one person speaking, and all the listeners are silent, neither speaking nor prophesying, who can or will regard or confess the same to be a spiritual congregation, or confess according to 1 Corinthians 14 that God is dwelling and operating in them through His Holy Spirit and His gifts, impelling them one after another in the abovementioned order of speaking and prophesying?"[28]

Anabaptists also believed in the illuminating presence of the Holy Spirit when they read the Bible. When Felix Manz was put on trial, for example, the fact that he claimed to have received special revelations outside of, or equal to, the Bible while reading Paul's epistles was considered undeniable proof he was a heretic and a blasphemer. Today such a revelation might warrant a new book or teaching, but in the sixteenth century, it warranted death.

THE MÜNSTER REBELLION

Much like every other charismatic movement in history, the Anabaptists believed strongly in the soon and imminent return of

28   Ibid., 8: CC 81.

Christ. When such strong eschatological views are mixed with large doses of intense persecution and prophetic activity, matters can quickly get out of hand. In the 1530s, a group of Anabaptists who had emigrated to Münster near the German-Holland border began claiming to be end-times apostles and prophets endowed by God with miraculous powers to usher in Christ's earthly kingdom. Melchior Hoffman, for example, who was prophesied to be "Elijah," ordained twelve apostles and then elevated himself to a special position above an apostle. One prophecy stated that Hoffman would be imprisoned in the city of Strasbourg for six months before departing with 144,000 true apostles who would be endowed with such miraculous powers that no one could resist them. Hoffman then moved to Strasbourg, where he preached publicly and was soon arrested and imprisoned, thus fulfilling the first part of the prophecy. However, as anticipation mounted for the second half of the prophecy to be fulfilled, six months came and went as Hoffman remained in prison. About the time Hoffman died in prison and had been forgotten, a new leader emerged, Jan Matthys, claiming to be "Enoch" and one of the two witnesses in Revelation. Then as Matthys took over the city of Münster, intending to make it the "New Jerusalem," yet another leader, Jan van Leiden, took several wives and declared himself to be "King David." When the regional bishop massed his troops (Catholics and Protestants) on the border to retake the city, the Anabaptists uncharacteristically took up arms to defend themselves but were quickly overpowered. The authorities wasted no time in executing Matthys and his followers, while the remains of three leaders were placed in cages and hoisted from the tower of Münster's Lambert Church for nearly fifty years as a warning against future and similar extremes. Many Catholics and Protestants alike never forgot the infamous Münster rebellion.

After the besiege of Münster, the remaining Anabaptist leaders—Jan van Leiden, Bernhard Knipperdolling, and former Catholic priest, Bernd Krechting—were tortured, executed, placed in cages, and hoisted high above the city in St. Lambert Church's steeple for nearly fifty years. Their cages remain as reminders to this day. Photo: Wikimedia/Rüdiger Wölk, Münster, Germany.

THE MENNONITES

Fortunately, these extremist groups did not represent the mainstream of Anabaptism. In 1536, Menno Simons, a former Catholic priest, was able to reorganize the Anabaptists of northern Europe through his moderate, yet inspirational, teaching and preaching. Though Menno and his followers suffered great persecution, often living as fugitives, and though he was not the movement's founder, his name eventually came to represent the movement's non-violent element as many Anabaptists became known as "Mennonites." Simons also reinforced the Anabaptist idea of water baptizing only Spirit-filled believers, noting that "Peter . . . refused to baptize the pious, noble and Godly centurion and his associates so long as he did not see the Holy Spirit was descended upon them, so that they spoke with tongues and glorified God. . . . Peter commanded that those only should be baptized who had received the Holy Ghost, who spoke with tongues and glorified God, which only pertains to the believing, and not to minor children."[29]

---

29 J.C. Wenger, ed., *Complete Writings of Menno Simons* (Scottsdale, Penn.: Herald, 1965), 276: CC 84.

Menno believed that just as the prophets of old foretold the future, performed miracles, had dreams and saw visions by the Spirit . . . and just as the Spirit had descended upon Christ at baptism and later to the apostles as cloven tongues of fire . . . in his day the Holy Spirit still converted those who became part of the true church. They were born from above, their minds were regenerated, they were freed from sin, and they accepted the Bible as God's "certain word"—all by the operation of the Holy Spirit.[30] The Spirit also adorned Christians with heavenly and divine gifts—especially gifts of speech, wisdom, and discernment, which were never to be exercised for personal influence or gain. Rather, in the Spirit each member assumed responsibility for the well-being of all. If any individual distorted the message of the Spirit, the united witness of the other members would recognize the error, creating an environment in which the prophetic and mystical elements of the church could be held in balance. While the united witness of the congregation protected believers from the excesses of any personal or skewed inspirations, the Spirit within the believer would free them from bondage to any stiff literalness concerning the written Word of God.[31]

As true reformers, Anabaptists believe strongly in freedom, discipleship, the priesthood of the believer, and love expressed through pacifism and communal living. Indeed, the Anabaptist idea of freedom would soon become a founding principle of Western

---

30 Leonard Verguin, trans., *The Complete Writings of Menno Simons* (Scottsdale, Penn.: Herald, 1956), 303, 496; Daniel Liechty, ed., *Early Anabaptist Spirituality: Selected Writings* (CWS; New York/Mahwah: Paulist, 1994), 259, 267: Stanley M. Burgess, *The Holy Spirit: Medieval Roman Catholic and Reformation Traditions* (Peabody, Mass.: Hendrickson, 1997), 213 [hereafter MCRT].

31 *Complete Writings*, 65, 496, 1039: MCRT 215–216.

society. George Williams, professor of Ecclesiastical History at Yale, wrote, "All who cherish Western institutions and freedoms, must acknowledge their indebtedness to the valor and vision of the Anabaptists."[32] Direct descendants of the Anabaptists include the Amish, Mennonites, Hutterites, and Church of the Brethren. More distant relatives include Quakers, Shakers, Baptists, and Congregationalists. Unfortunately, some of the founding Anabaptist characteristics were lost over the centuries, including their zeal for evangelism and for the Spirit of God, which eventually gave way to legalism. Today Anabaptists are simply known as good, quiet people and excellent farmers, but at their core, they were biblical literalists with charismatic gifts. Mennonite scholar John H. Yoder noted that Pentecostalism in the twentieth century is "the closest parallel to what Anabaptism was in the sixteenth."[33]

JOHN CALVIN

Like Luther, John Calvin's (1509–1564) parents hoped their son would become a lawyer. However, while pursuing humanist studies in Paris at age twenty-four, Calvin had a profound spiritual conversion experience that ultimately led him into ministry and out of the Catholic Church: "To this pursuit I endeavored faithfully to apply myself in obedience to the will of my father; but God, by the secret guidance of his providence, at length gave a different direction to my course. And first, since I was too obstinately devoted to the

---

32 George H. Williams, ed., *Spiritual and Anabaptist Writers*, vol. 25 of *The Library of Christian Classics* (London: SCM Press, 1957): CC 85.

33 Kenneth R. Davis, "Anabaptism as a Charismatic Movement," *Mennonite Quarterly Review* 53, no. 3 (1979), 221: CC 85.

superstitions of Popery to be easily removed from so profound an abyss of mire, God by a sudden conversion subdued and brought my mind to a teachable frame, which was more hardened in such matters than might have been expected from one at my early period of life. Having thus received some taste and knowledge of true godliness, I was immediately inflamed with so intense a desire to make progress therein, that although I did not altogether leave off other studies, yet I pursued them with less ardor."[34]

Calvin soon joined the reform movement in Paris, where his associations eventually forced him into exile. But in 1536, Calvin's life took yet another turn. As he was fleeing France to Strasbourg on the French-German border, the military maneuvers of French and Imperial forces forced him to take a detour south to Geneva, Switzerland. Calvin had planned to stay only the night, but William Farel, the tall fiery redheaded French reformer, begged him to stay and help him reform the church there. Calvin refused at first, explaining that he preferred to pursue his studies in peace and seclusion, but Farel persisted: "Farel, who was working with incredible zeal to promote the gospel, bent all his efforts to keep me in the city. And when he realized that I was determined to study in privacy in some obscure place, and saw that he gained nothing by entreaty, he descended to cursing, and said that God would surely curse my peace if I held back from giving help at a time of such great need. Terrified by his words, and conscience of my

---

34   John Calvin, preface to *Commentary on the Book of Psalms*, Geneva, July 22, 1557, trans. James Anderson, vol. 1 (Grand Rapids, Mich.: Eerdmans, 1948) p. xl–xli as quoted in Cottret 2000, 67. The translation by Anderson is available at "The Author's Preface," *Commentary on Psalms*, vol. 1, Christian Classics Ethereal Library: *www.ccel.org/ccel/calvin/calcom08.vi.html* (Accessed 17 December 2012).

own timidity and cowardice, I gave up my journey and attempted to apply whatever gift I had in defense of my faith."[35]

Feeling "thrust into the game," Calvin would spend the rest of his life in Geneva instituting his reforms until his death at age fifty-four.[36] He did finally make it to Strasbourg, but only after being expelled from Geneva for his radical ideas. Three years later, however, the political climate in Geneva changed, and with church attendance dwindling, Calvin was invited to return.

CALVINISM

If Luther's foundation was "justification by faith," Calvin's was "the sovereignty of God." If Luther's creed was "the just shall live by faith," Calvin's was "thy will be done." Having attended an Augustinian school and studying Augustine's writings extensively, Calvin was greatly influenced by the early Christian theologian. In fact, when the Catholic Church accused him of inventing his own doctrine, Calvin attributed all his work to Augustine, saying, "Augustine is so completely of our persuasion, that if I should have to make written profession, it would be quite enough to present a composition made up entirely of excerpts from his writings."[37]

Calvin preached over 2,000 sermons in Geneva—twice on Sunday initially and three times during the week until this proved to be too

---

35   *Autobiographical Sketch from the Dedication of the Commentary on the Psalms,* in *Calvin: Commentaries* (Library of Christian Classics), Joseph Haroutunian, ed., (Westminster: John Knox, 1979), 53: "John Calvin," *Wikipedia: en.wikipedia.org/wiki/John_Calvin* (Accessed 19 December 2012).

36   John Calvin, *Commentary on the Psalms,* preface: CH 256–57.

37   *Christian History Magazine* 19, no. 3 (Christian History Institute): 31: GGRR 250.

heavy a burden. Then he was allowed to preach only once on Sunday until attendance forced him again to preach twice on Sundays and weekdays on alternate weeks. Since Calvin's sermons lasted more than an hour and he did not use notes, a scribe eventually had to be hired to record his sermons. As Calvin preached, he often noticed how different people responded in different ways. While some embraced his teachings and grew, others just laughed or became bored. This greatly disturbed him. But after searching the Scriptures, Calvin believed the doctrine of predestination to be the proper explanation. Evidently, some had been created for eternal life and others for eternal damnation. Basing his beliefs on scriptures like Romans 9:18—"Therefore He has mercy on whom He wills, and whom He wills He hardens"—Calvin construed that God "does not indiscriminately adopt all into the hope of salvation, but gives to some what he denies to others."[38] Thus, since no one could know for sure whether they were God's elect or chosen, Calvin believed evangelism to be extremely important. He also believed there were three good tests for knowing whether one might be saved: 1) make a public profession of faith, 2) participate in the two sacraments (water baptism and the Lord's Supper), and 3) live an upright moral life, without which no one could be a true Christian. Consequently, social activism plays an important role in Calvinist churches to this day. Calvin also taught that everything belonged to God—our employment, possessions, our very lives—and to be slothful in one's employment was to be disrespectful toward God.

---

38 "John Calvin," *Christian History* Magazine 5, no. 4 (Christian History Institute): 24: GGRR 250.

A NEW CHURCH MODEL

Since Calvin's name is forever linked to the doctrines of election and predestination, many recognize Calvin as a great theologian. However, these doctrines played only a minor role in Calvin's theology. What relatively few seem to know about Calvin is that he was also a great organizer. Indeed, as a second-generation reformer, Calvin believed his primary mission was to restore the church—particularly its governmental organization—back to its original purity. Calvin simply believed the Word mixed with the Spirit is what shaped the true church. Using God's Word as his pattern, Calvin outlined four permanent orders of ministry: pastors, teachers, elders, and deacons. These four encompassed all church life: worship, education, holy living, and acts of service. Pastors were to give themselves to prayer and to the preaching of the Word, not wearing themselves out with everyday church maintenance or trying to visit and care for all the needs of the people. They were, however, to pray for the sick in the community as they felt led by God to do so. Teachers were charged with teaching theology and guarding the purity of the gospel. Lectures for adults were to be given Monday, Wednesday, and Friday to educate the congregation on the meaning of the Scriptures and to equip prospective pastors. Elders were chosen for their conduct, appointed by the lead pastor, and given the responsibility of overseeing the spiritual life of the church. Deacons were chosen to serve, oversee, and manage the church's financial and social affairs.

Calvin also called for the creation of a local governing body of elders called a Consistory (presbytery) to judge in ecclesiastical matters. And finally, Calvin reintroduced the biblical practices of personal counseling, corporate worship, congregational singing, and elders caring and praying for the sick. Calvin's model would soon become a pattern for churches around the world for centuries to come. Meanwhile, Geneva soon became known as "the city of the true Gospel," boasting there were no beggars, sick, or afflicted in the city who had not received the utmost care and attention. In 1559, Calvin also organized a college consisting of both a private preparatory school and a first-of-its-kind advanced academy for training and sending missionaries throughout the world. Within five years, there were 1,200 students in the grammar school and 300 in the advanced school. John Knox, the great Scottish reformer, who attended the school, wrote, "not since the days of the apostles was there a finer school for Christ."[39]

An anonymous sixteenth-century portrait of John Calvin formerly attributed to Hans Holbein the Younger. Calvin's teachings on the gifts and workings of the Holy Spirit were so complete he has been dubbed "the theologian of the Holy Spirit." Source: www.rvc.cc.il.us. Photo: Wikimedia/Paris16.

CALVIN ON SPIRITUAL GIFTS

Calvin believed the entire universe, like the church, had been created by a collaborative effort of the Word and the Spirit. In effect, Calvin believed the Spirit played such a vital and pivotal role in shaping the universe and creating order out of chaos that, if suddenly withdrawn,

---

39   Dr. William Lindner, *John Calvin* (Minneapolis: Bethany House, 1998), 132: GGRR 241.

the entire cosmic structure would collapse. Within this order, the Spirit was both the source and the sustainer of life-giving power. He "sustains, quickens and vivifies all things in heaven and on earth . . . in all things transfusing his vigor, and inspiring them with being, life, and motion."[40]

The Holy Spirit is also the source of particular gifts and fruit poured out on God's people. At the fall, the natural gifts present in humans were corrupted and the supernatural gifts were removed. Without these gifts and fruit, and without the Spirit's guidance, humans became subject to Satan's activity and prone to evil. Just as the world was first formed by the Spirit, so the church was also created by the Spirit working through fallen humans. Thus, the church represents the restoration of order in the world, the sphere of the regenerating work of the Spirit. Re-creation began at the incarnation when God took on human form through the Spirit's operation. The resurrection marked the beginning of Christ's reign over the church, making possible the outpouring of the Holy Spirit through whom God created a new people for himself.

Spiritual gifts were restored to the church as "benefits" on condition they would be applied to the common good of the church. Believers are enriched with spiritual gifts for the building up of the entire Christian community, and Christ is intimately associated with and in touch with his body, the church, through the presence of the Spirit. The enjoyment of Christ and all his benefits are due in part to the Spirit energizing believers to exercise their gifts on each other's behalf.

40 John Calvin, *Institutes of the Christian Religion*, 1.13.14–15 (trans. Ford Lewis Battles; LCC 20–21; Philadelphia: Westminster, 1960) and (trans. John Allen; 3 vols., 8th rev. ed., Grand Rapids, Eerdmans, 1949): MCRT 163.

Using one's gifts in the Christian community is the responsibility of the elect, for "There is no one so void of gifts in the church of Christ who is not able to contribute something to our benefit."[41]

Calvin believed Paul's spiritual gifts list in 1 Corinthians 12 was for his own generation, stating, "The Spirit of God . . . distributes them among us . . ." and "does not confer them upon us in vain." Though he believed they were only a partial listing of a much larger variety of divine gifts, he greatly diminished their supernatural character. Though the word of wisdom included "revelations that are of a more secret and sublime order," the word of knowledge was seen as merely grasping "ordinary information."[42] The gift of faith was also viewed as a special sort—not in merely apprehending Christ but in so far as miracles were performed in his name—while the gift of healing was seen as a temporary gift that quickly perished. Although Calvin admitted if anyone did receive a healing, he could affirm that "the Lord is indeed present with his people in every age; and [that] he heals their weaknesses as often as necessary, no less than of old," he then retracted and reaffirmed his position that God no longer did this.[43] Calvin also suggested the gift of miracles might refer to the restraining or putting to flight of demons and that, in any event, both healing and miracles manifested God's goodness and concern for the destruction of Satan. The gift of prophecy was seen as mere inspired preaching that required special illumination, while the discerning of spirits served just to distinguish between true and false ministers or to see past masks and false pretenses.

---

41 John Calvin, *Commentary on Romans* 1:12 in *Joannis Calvini Opera quae supersunt omnia* (Corpus reformatorum 29–87 Braunschweig: Schwetschke, 1863–1900): MCRT 166.

42 John Calvin, *Commentary on 1 Corinthians* 12:8: MCRT 167.

43 Ibid.

Calvin viewed the gift of tongues, like healing, as a temporary gift given to early Christian missionaries that enabled them to speak in foreign languages unfamiliar to them (xenoglossy), but he did admit they were also "to be an ornament to the gospel," perhaps inferring glossolalia.[44] Interpretation of tongues was seen simply as the supernatural ability to interpret foreign tongues in a native language. Like Luther, Calvin then contrasted what he deemed to be exaggerated reports of miracles in the Catholic Church, declaring them to be false, foolish, and delusional as compared with those of his own movement, which he said were not entirely lacking but "very certain and not subject to mockery."[45] So complete were Calvin's teachings on the gifts and workings of the Holy Spirit that twentieth-century scholar Benjamin Warfield dubbed him "the theologian of the Holy Spirit."[46]

Though Calvin was only interested in reforming the existing church, many of his followers would soon embrace the establishment of new churches. These included French Calvinists, Scottish Presbyterians, English Puritans, German and Dutch Reformed, as well as many Baptists and Congregationalists.

THE PRESBYTERIANS

Among the early Calvinists were the Scottish Covenanters, who were part of the Presbyterian movement in Scotland. George Wishart

---

44 John Calvin, *Commentary on Acts* 2:4 and *Commentary on 1 Corinthians* 12:8: MCRT 168.

45 John Calvin, *Institutes of the Christian Religion* preface to King Francis 3: MCRT 167.

46 Benjamin Breckinridge Warfield, "John Calvin the Theologian," in *Calvin and Augustine* (ed., Samuel G. Craig; Philadelphia: Presbyterian and Reformed, 1956), 484–85: MCRT 168.

(1513–1546), one of their early reformers, had a disciple and bodyguard named John Knox. When Wishart was arrested by Catholic authorities in 1545 for preaching against the veneration of the Virgin Mary, Knox was prepared to follow him to prison. But Wishart persuaded him to continue tutoring his students in the ways of reform and be blessed, saying, "One is sufficient for a sacrifice."[47] After Wishart was burned at the stake, Knox described him as "a man of such graces as before him were never heard with this realm, yea, and are rare to be found yet in any man, notwithstanding this great light of God that since his days has shined unto us. He was not only singularly learned, as well in godly knowledge, as in all honest humane science; but also he was so clearly illuminated with the spirit of prophecy that he saw not only things pertaining to himself, but also such things as some towns and the whole realm afterward felt, which he forespoke, not in secret, but in the audience of many, as in their own places shall be declared."[48]

John Knox (1514–1572) would soon become a fiery reformer in his own right. After preaching against the pope, Mass, and purgatory, Knox was arrested and sent to the French galleys (slave ships) by Mary of Guise, acting Regent of Scotland for her young daughter, Mary, Queen of Scots, who was living in France. After surviving nineteen months in the galleys, Knox went into exile in England, where he worked for the king and had a strong influence on the *Book of Common Prayer*—the founding documents of the Church of England.

---

47   Jasper Ridley, *John Knox* (Oxford: Clarendon, 1968), 43: "John Knox," *Wikipedia: en.wikipedia.org/wiki/John_Knox* (Accessed 21 December 2012).

48   David Laing, ed., *The Works of John Knox* (Edinburgh: The Woodrow Society, 1895), vol. 1, 125: MM 156.

THE CHURCH OF SCOTLAND

Later Knox spent time with Calvin in Geneva, but Calvin did not share his views regarding the use of force to resist rulers who tried to prevent their worship and mission. Many Scottish nobles, however, agreed with Knox, and when civil war broke out in Scotland in 1559, Knox rushed home. Soon the Calvinists controlled Edinburgh and formally deposed Mary of Guise as Knox's oft-repeated prayer, "Give me Scotland, or I die," was gloriously answered. In 1560, Knox drafted a Confession of Faith and Book of Discipline for the newly reformed Church of Scotland. In 1561, Mary, Queen of Scots, returned to Scotland, only to find it in the hands of "heretics," and for the next few years, it was Knox, the passionate preacher, versus Mary, the young Queen of Scots. However, events continued in Knox's favor as Scotland soon became the first devoutly Calvinist nation in the world. Knox, who was described as an "eminent wrestler with God in prayer," prevailed like a prince. As the Queen Regent herself once stated, she was "more afraid of his prayers than of an army of ten thousand men."[49]

John Knox preaching. Detail from a Victorian stained glass window in St. Giles' Catherdral, Edinburgh, Scotland. Source: Wikimedia/ Kim Traynor.

As with most other faith movements, the early Presbyterians were known as men of the Spirit. It is said of Robert Bruce, Moderator of

---

49   John Howie, *Biographia, Scotiana*, 2nd edition (1781), 82–83: MM 156.

the General Assembly of the Church of Scotland in 1588, that while he was a minister at Edinburgh, "he shone as a great light through all these parts of the land; the power and efficacious energy of the Spirit accompanied the word preached by him in a most sensible manner, so that he was a terror to evil doers, the authority of God appearing with him, insomuch that he forced fear and respect even from the greatest in the land. Robert Bruce was also a man who had somewhat of the spirit of discerning future events, and did prophetically speak of several things that afterwards came to pass; yea . . . and those who were past all recovery with epileptic disease, or falling sickness, were brought to Mr. Bruce, and were, after prayer by him in their behalf, fully restored from that malady."[50] It was also said that once when he prayed among a meeting of godly ministers about a very sad church matter, "there came an extraordinary motion on all present, and such sensible down-pouring of the Spirit, that they could hardly contain themselves."[51]

Many other such stories are told of the early Presbyterians, including John Scrimgeour of Myres Castle, Master of Work for the royal buildings and facilitator of worship at the Scottish Chapel Royal. It is said that while he was a minister in the coastal town of Kinghorn, a certain godly woman under his charge fell sick with a lingering disease. Though he often visited her, her trouble and terrors remained until one day "he went with two of his elders to her, and began first, in their presence, to comfort and pray with her; but she still grew worse. He ordered his elders to pray, and afterwards prayed himself, but no relief came. Then sitting and pondering for a

---

50 Ibid., 155, 159–160: MM 158.
51 Ibid: MM 158–159.

little space, he thus broke silence: 'What is this! Our laying grounds of comfort before her will not do; prayer will not do; we must try another remedy. Sure I am, this is a daughter of Abraham; sure I am, she hath sent for me; and, therefore, in the name of God, the Father of our Lord Jesus Christ, who sent Him to redeem sinners; in the name of Jesus Christ, who obeyed the Father, and came to save us; and in the name of the Holy and blessed Spirit, our Quickener and Sanctifier, I, the elder, command thee, a daughter of Abraham, to be loosed from these bonds.' Immediately peace and joy ensued."[52]

THE CHURCH OF ENGLAND

Unlike other Reformation Era churches, the Church of England came about, not as a theological disagreement, but as a purely political matter involving a king's need for a male heir. In 1528, King Henry VIII was in a quandary. His wife, Catherine of Aragon, had given birth to six children, but only one, Mary, had survived beyond infancy, and England was in no mood for a female heir (the last one had led to a succession of wars). To make matters worse, Catherine was now past the age of childbearing, leading many—including the pope and the king—to wonder if the king was under a curse. Consequently, the king asked the pope for a special annulment of his eighteen-year marriage to Catherine so he could marry Anne Boleyn, a lady-in-waiting in the king's court. The pope may have allowed this had Catherine not been the aunt of Charles V, Holy Roman Emperor and King of Spain. Thus, taking matters in his own hands, Henry secretly married Anne Boleyn while having an English court declare his

---

52   Ibid., 131–132: MM 160.

marriage to Catherine annulled. However, later that year when Anne gave birth to a daughter, Elizabeth, the pope excommunicated the king. Then, knowing that antipapal sympathies were running high in England at the time, the king simply declared an Act of Supremacy: "The king's majesty justly and rightly is, and ought to be, and shall be presumed the only supreme head on earth of the Church of England." England now had a national church with a monarchy as its head and an archbishop as its priest. Nonetheless, Henry had no intention of breaking with Catholicism. He simply wanted an English church that was independent of Rome. In fact, his only two major departures from Catholicism were the suppression of monasteries and the publishing of Tyndale's English Bible, completed by Myles Coverdale in 1535.

Portrait of Henry VIII by the workshop of Hans Holbein the Younger (1537-47), Walker Art Gallery, Liverpool, U.K. Besides his six marriages, Henry VIII is perhaps best known for his role in separating the Church of England from the pope and Rome and establishing himself as supreme head of the Church of England though he remained a believer of core Catholic teachings. Source: Google Cultural Institute. Photo: Wikimedia/Soerfm.

THE BOOK OF COMMON PRAYER

After Henry's death in 1547, a frail ten-year-old Edward VI ascended the throne. Edward was the son of Jane Seymour, whom Henry had married after executing Anne Boleyn on charges of adultery. Under Edward's brief reign, his advisers pushed for reforms—priests were allowed to marry, and Latin services were replaced by the Book of Common Prayer. This series of books included a distinct recognition of miraculous gifts and represented the Holy Spirit as still working miraculously and conferring miraculous gifts: "Now let us consider what the Holy Ghost is, and how consequently he worketh miraculous works toward mankind. The Holy Ghost doth always declare himself by his fruitful and gracious gifts; namely, by the word of wisdom, by the word of knowledge, which is the understanding of the Scriptures by faith, in doing of miracles, by healing them that are diseased, by prophecy, which is the declaration of God's mysteries, by discerning of spirits, diversities of tongues, interpretation of tongues, and so forth. All which gifts, as they proceed from one Spirit, and are severally given to men according to the measurable distribution of the Holy Ghost; even so do they bring men, and not without good cause, into a wonderful admiration of God's divine power."[53]

Five years later, Edward died, and Mary, a devout Catholic, ascended her father's throne. During her brief reign, Mary sent some 300 Protestants—including the archbishop—to be burned at the stake, earning her the title "Bloody Mary." After Mary died, Anne Boleyn's fiery red-haired daughter, Elizabeth, came to power. Though Elizabeth was Protestant, she tried her best to heal the rift between Catholics and Protestants by walking down the middle of the road, as the Church of England became a forerunner for a host of English-speaking churches throughout the world, including the Episcopal Church and some Baptists and Congregationalists.

THE CATHOLIC REFORMATION

When Montanus and his followers began working signs and wonders, the church ordered their bishops to "tame" the gifts by themselves

---

53 Boys, *Suppressed Evidence*, 316–331: MM 150.

assuming the prophetic gifts. A thousand years later, when the Cathars rejected the sacraments, replacing them with their *consolamentum* and pure lifestyles, the church called on the Dominicans to again outstrip the heretics in both piety and zeal. Likewise, when the University of Paris challenged the teachings of the church by reintroducing classical Greek and Eastern philosophies, the church dispatched Thomas Aquinas, one of the greatest Christian rationalists of all time. So how did the Roman Church respond to these reformers? By countering with a reformation of its own that included personal renewal, a revival of mysticism, and a new army of spiritual soldiers.

IGNATIUS OF LOYOLA

Ignatius of Loyola (1491–1556) was a Spanish knight of noble birth who, after being seriously wounded in battle by a cannonball, experienced a profound spiritual conversion in which he decided to lay down his sword and take up soldiering for Jesus instead. Ignatius founded the Society of Jesus, later known as the "Jesuits" for their incessant use of the name of Jesus. Approved by the pope in 1540, the Jesuits' purpose was to restore the Roman Church to its former position of spiritual power and influence. This was a zealous, versatile, and mobilized group of spiritual soldiers ready to go anywhere and perform any task the pope assigned "whether to the Turks, or to the New World, or to the Lutherans, or to others—be they infidel or faithful."[54]

Ignatius called his followers "the apostles of the possible." Their mission was to live energetically in the world without becoming a part of it. While Protestants stressed salvation by grace alone, Ignatius

---

54   CH 274.

emphasized a combination of grace and human cooperation. His mantra was "Pray as though everything depended on God alone, but act as though it depended on you alone whether you will be saved."[55] Ignatius believed that one had to choose between God and Satan and that, through the disciplined use of one's imagination, one could strengthen his will to choose God and his ways. His *Spiritual Exercises* included four weeks of meditation beginning with sin, death, judgment, and hell before moving on to Christ's life, death, and resurrection into an ever-growing obedience to the Holy Spirit. Ignatius believed the path to spiritual perfection included an examination of one's conscience, penance, and a resolute amnesia of guilt once a believer had been confronted with God's forgiveness. He also believed sickness, poverty, and pain were evils to be remedied with every means at our disposal. He taught that God gave us a mission to possess this world and make it our own, and that meant mastering the evils of this world. Those who worked in research, public health, justice, or for prosperity were all part of that mission.

Ignatius of Loyola by Peter Paul Rubens (1600s). Ignatius was a Spanish knight and son of a nobleman from northern Spain. After his right leg was shattered by cannonball fire in a battle with the French, boredom during his long period of convalescence led him to read a text on the *Life of Jesus* as well as books on the lives of the saints, which led to the beginning of a deep spiritual and mystical life and ultimately, the Society of Jesus (Jesuits). Source: Wikimedia/Heneral.

In his personal life, Ignatius enjoyed a level of spiritual intimacy with God that often resulted in a host of accompanying mystical

---

55   Francis Thompson, *Saint Ignatius Loyola* (Westminster, Md.: Newman, 1950): CH 277.

experiences, including inexpressible tears, joy, peace, and consolations. He also received frequent divine communications in the form of visions, illuminations, visitations, and mystical touches that often confirmed his decisions concerning the Society of Jesus. Ignatius prayed to the Spirit and pleaded with the Father to mediate with the Spirit and place the Spirit within him. He told of a time when he experienced the divine Third Person in a dense brightness the color of a burning flame. Ignatius also frequently experienced "the gift of tears," which he said he could not control. Actually, if he did not shed tears at least three times during Mass, he felt deprived. To Ignatius, tears represented the presence of the Holy Spirit.

But of all Ignatius's mystical experiences, perhaps the most interesting and novel was the gift of *loquela* (language), which he said sometimes came from exterior sources like a heavenly choir and other times from his own lips. Many scholars believe this to be similar to today's sung glossolalia or singing in tongues. Ignatius said an unexplainable peace would often overcome him when he experienced the interior *loquela*. He believed both were divine gifts for which he had prayed and asked God, and both brought great devotion and delight. But regardless of the source, Ignatius was often enraptured by music, which he said nourished both his spirit and soul.

In Ignatius's early days of ministry before founding the Society of Jesus, he and his companions were often jailed and interrogated by the Dominicans for their zealous and "suspicious activities" such as "street-corner" preaching and inciting others to "enthusiasm." They were accused of carrying on the activities of the *Alumbrados* or "enlightened ones," referring to various mystical sects that claimed the direct and constant inspiration of the Holy Spirit. Three of their female followers—Doña Leo, Doña Maria, and Doña Beatriz—were accused of becoming so hysterically zealous that when Ignatius and his companions preached in public, "one fell senseless, another sometimes rolled about on the ground, another had been seen in the grip of convulsions or shuddering and sweating in anguish."[56] Ignatius, who was singled out as the visionary leader of the movement, had to appear before the Spanish Inquisition but was later released. Consequently, Ignatius reserved any future discussions of spiritual matters to his private manuscripts. His *Spiritual Diary* illustrates how he often received instructions from the Lord through the gift of *loquela*: "Thursday, May 22. Before Mass in my room and in the chapel there were many tears. During much of the greater part of the Mass itself I was without tears but experienced much *loquela*. . . . As I proceeded a bit farther, I thought I might be taking too much pleasure in the tone of the sound of the *loquela* and was not paying enough attention to the meaning of its words. Immediately many tears flowed and I thought I was being taught about the procedure I ought to follow, meanwhile hoping always for further instruction for the future."[57]

By the time Ignatius died in 1556, he had dispatched nearly a thousand of his apostles on four continents, not only preventing Protestantism from sweeping across Europe but also limiting it to the northern part of the continent, where it remains to this day.

---

56   Jean Lacouture, *Jesuits, A Multibiography* (Washington, D.C.: Counterpoint, 1995), 27–29: "Ignatius of Loyola," *Wikipedia: en.wikipedia.org/wiki/Ignatius_of_Loyola* (Accessed 28 August 2014).

57   *Ignatius of Loyola: Spiritual Exercises and Selected Work*, ed., George E. Ganss (New York: Paulist, 1991), 263, 267–68: Stanley M. Burgess, ed., *Christian Peoples of the Spirit* (New York Univ. NY, 2011), 149 [hereafter CP].

JOHN OF ÁVILA

Another Spanish mystic who had an early encounter with the Inquisition and was later exonerated was John of Ávila (1499–1569). As a descendant of converts from Judaism, John was considered a "New Christian" and studied law at the University of Salamanca. Later, however, he was persuaded by a Franciscan to study philosophy and theology instead, which inspired him to eventually sell his inheritance and prepare for missionary work in the New World. However, as he was preparing for his voyage to Mexico, John was again persuaded— this time by a priest and archbishop—to become a missionary to his homeland of Spain instead. There he became a tireless reformer, a scholastic author, and founder of several universities and seminaries, earning him the title "Apostle of Andalusia" for his extensive ministry in that region of Spain. John's strong pleas for reform and accusations of vice and corruption in high places eventually got him in trouble with the Dominicans as they charged him with teaching extreme rigorism, exaggerating the dangers of wealth, and closing the gates of heaven to the rich. Though declared innocent in 1533, John would continue to have brushes with the Inquisition the rest of his life.

Despite this, many of John's mystical teachings and literary works were preserved, including his masterpiece on Christian perfection and his homilies on Pentecost, devoted to *The Holy Ghost*. For John of Ávila, the Spirit's activity in the human heart was beyond description: "No tongue can describe," he said, "no ear can hear, no heart can feel what the kiss, the embrace of the Holy Spirit means."[58] John spoke

---

58   Blessed John of Ávila, *The Holy Ghost* (Chicago/Dublin/London: Scepter, 1959), 151: MCRT 185.

continually on the importance of knowing, touching, and surrendering to the Holy Spirit, saying God wanted to send his Holy Spirit to all but the Spirit would not come to those who were unprepared. To prepare, one must recognize the Spirit's power to accomplish marvels, be willing to receive him as a guest, long for his presence, ardently petition him, subject himself to fasts and seclusions, free himself from earthly cares and desires, and finally, be alert and vigilant, expecting his arrival. It was not enough to ask or desire the Spirit's presence; one had to merit the Spirit's coming.

"The things of heaven are so lofty and so profound, so far above human understanding that to be able to speak of them, the speaker himself must have come down from heaven." John of Ávila, *The Holy Ghost* (Dublin: Sceptor, 1959), 55. Source: "Portraits of illustrious Spaniards," Royal printing press, Madrid, Spain (1791). Photo: Diócesis de Córdoba.

John also suggested several "signs" by which we could know the Spirit had come. We would feel a burning fire of charity. An unwavering love for God would leap in our heart, and we would be filled with a joy so wonderful and all pervading that we would be transported. We would not be allowed to fall into temptation, and all fear would be gone and all straw consumed.[59] A young woman would no longer be concerned about her clothes, how to make herself attractive, or what cosmetics to use on her face. Instead, she would choose tears to beautify her face, she would be humble, and she would no longer be interested in the swaggering young man. Likewise, a man would not lose his head over every pretty woman he saw, and he

---

59   1 Cor. 3:11–14

would not spend all his time eating, enjoying himself, and attending to his business. Instead, he would be disciplined not to dwell on carnal or sensual concerns.

The Spirit's coming would have the same effects as the apostles experienced waiting in the upper room on the day of Pentecost. Before Pentecost, the apostles were lifeless—like the dead bones described in Ezekiel. But when the Spirit descended, they came to life, full of strength and love, preached Christ with fiery eloquence, performed many miracles, cured the sick, and brought the dead back to life. Finally, the Holy Spirit would not remain with those who did not continuously submit themselves to divine grace. They had to constantly guard their hearts and raise their thoughts and desires to God, like eagles soaring upward, until they reached the Holy Spirit. Though they were free, they made themselves slaves. John's advice to all who sought the Holy Spirit was this: "Do not cease to ask for Him and to desire Him ardently!"[60]

TERESA OF ÁVILA

Teresa of Ávila (1515–1582) fell ill at a young age. During that time, she was first exposed to the writings of the great mystics. In her illness, she said she arose from the lowest stage of "recollection" to "devotions of ecstasy," a state of perfect union with God in which she received the rich "blessing of tears." In 1535, she entered a Carmelite Monastery in Ávila where she increasingly found herself at odds with the relaxed spiritual atmosphere of the Carmelites. Consequently, she was soon inspired to pursue a series of reforms. Teresa wanted to restore the

---

60   John of Ávila, *Holy Ghost*, 90: MCRT 187.

purity of the Carmelite Order to its "primitive rule" among the Desert Fathers. The primitive rule contained strict guidelines regarding contemplative prayer, devotional studies, abstinence, and poverty and fasts. It also included the singing of psalms, jubilation, and dance. Teresa's newfound Order of Discalced ("shoeless") Carmelites quickly spread through all of Spain.

Teresa's mystical teachings included four stages of experiential prayer: 1) "mental prayer," 2) a supernatural state called the "prayer of quiet," 3) an ecstatic state called the "devotion of union," and 4) a state of spiritual inebriation called the "devotion of ecstasy or rapture" in which the body itself was sometimes lifted up in space. Teresa herself was seen levitating during Mass on a number of occasions. In 1559, she also began receiving a series of visions that lasted almost uninterrupted for more than two years, including an appearance of Jesus in bodily form, though invisible.

Copy of an original portrait of Teresa of Ávila at age 61, by Fray Juan de la Miseria (1576). Teresa of Ávila is considered one of the great masters of the spiritual life in the history of the church. Source: www.umilta.net. Photo: Wikimedia/Spartanbu.

Teresa herself was a happy person, and she wanted everyone around her to be happy. "I won't have nuns who are ninnies," she said. Gloomy saints were not to her liking. When fervor took possession of her, she could not resist the urge of the Spirit and would begin to dance and twirl around, clapping her hands like King David before the ark. Other nuns would accompany her "in a perfect transport of spiritual joy."[61]

Teresa wrote, "Our Lord sometimes bestows upon the soul a jubilation and a strange kind of prayer, the nature of which it cannot ascertain. I set this down here, so that, if he grants you this favor, you may give him hearty praise and know that such a thing really happens. . . . Many words are spoken during this state, in praise of God, but, unless the Lord himself puts order into them, they have no orderly form. The understanding, at any rate, counts for nothing here; the soul would like to shout praises aloud, for it is in such a state that it cannot contain itself—a state of delectable disquiet. . . . O God, what must that soul be like when it is in this state! It would gladly be all tongue, so that it might praise the Lord. It utters a thousand holy follies, striving ever to please Him who thus possesses it."[62]

JOHN OF THE CROSS

Recognized as "the doctor par excellence of modern Western mysticism," John of the Cross (1542–1591) greatly aided Teresa of Ávila in her reforms as a cofounder of the Discalced Carmelites.[63] Though tortured and imprisoned for nine months by those who opposed his reforms, John

---

61 Marcelle Auclair, *St. Teresa of Ávila* (New York: Pantheon, 1953), 221: Eddie Ensley, *Sounds of Wonder: A Popular History of Speaking in Tongues in the Catholic Tradition* (New York: Paulist, 1977), 91 [hereafter SOW].

62 St. Teresa of Ávila, *Interior Castle*, translated and edited by E. Allison Peers (Garden City, New York: Doubleday, 1961), 167: SOW 92–93; St. Teresa of Ávila, *The Autobiography of St. Teresa of Ávila*, translated and edited by E. Allison Peers (Garden City, N.Y.: Doubleday, 1960), 163–164: SOW 95.

63 Louis Bouyer, "Some Charismatic Movements in the History of the Church," Edward D. O'Connor, C.S.C. ed., *Perspectives on Charismatic Renewal* (Notre Dame/ London: University of Notre Dame, 1975), 126.

eventually escaped from prison only to rejoin the movement, found fifteen new Carmelite houses, and spend the rest of his life in the service of reform. John is also considered one of the foremost poets of the Spanish language. Two of his poems—the "Spiritual Canticle" and "Dark Night of the Soul"—are considered masterpieces. The first thirty-one stanzas of the former, written during his imprisonment, were later read by the nuns who nursed him back to health, copied by them, and passed on to others. Both his theological works and poems reflect the mystical teachings of Teresa of Ávila: "In this state of life so perfect, the soul always walks in festivity, inwardly and outwardly, and it frequently bears on its spiritual tongue a new song of great jubilation in God, a song always new, enfolded in a gladness and love arising from the knowledge the soul has of its happy state. . . . There is no need to be amazed that the soul frequently walks amid this joy, jubilance, fruition, and praise of God."[64]

John of the Cross, by Francisco de Zubarán (1656). John of the Cross was a reformer and cofounder of the Discalced Carmelites, along with Teresa of Ávila. Also known as the "Mystical Doctor," his poetry is considered the summit of mystical Spanish literature and among the best of all Spanish literature. Source: Archdiocesan Museum in Katowice, Poland. Photo: Wikimedia/BurgererSF.

PHILIP NERI

Philip Neri's (1515–1595) Congregation of the Oratory in Rome was incredibly relaxed compared with the Jesuits or the Discalced Carmelites. Philip believed a joyful heart was more easily made perfect

---

64 *The Collected Works of St. John of the Cross*, translated by Kieran Kavanaugh, O.C.D. (Washington: ICS, 1973), 609: SOW 96.

than a downcast one and, like Teresa of Ávila, he strove to make all those around him cheerful and happy, training them in his "school of merriment." Even before entering the priesthood, Philip spent much of his life ministering to the poor and sick in Rome. Many miracles were attributed to Philip as he developed an amazing ability to empathize with people's pain and sorrow, which had a great healing effect. Philip's expressive style toward others was matched only by his expressive form of worship and peculiar manner of prayer. Philip's biographer wrote about how he would often roll on the ground in a state of ecstasy even while outdoors in public places: "In those places Philip often was surprised by such an abundance of spiritual consolations, that, unable any longer to endure so great a fire of love, he was forced to cry out, 'No more, Lord! No more!' Then, throwing himself down, he used to roll upon the ground, not having strength to endure the vehement affection which he felt in his heart."[65]

In addition to being the consummate "holy roller," Philip was often seen in public with his friends fervently singing hymns and calling tenderly on the name of Jesus. Once while at the deathbed of a young man, he burst into joy and began to sing the hymns sung at the Oratory, particularly the one that began, "Jesus! Jesus! Jesus! Let everyone call on Jesus!"[66] Even in his old age, Philip was often seen walking through the streets of Rome, conversing or playing ball with a train of young men following him. The Oratory mainly spread throughout Italy and France, where at least fifty-eight houses were built by 1760.

---

65 Pietro Giacomo Bacci, *The Life of St. Philip Neri* (London: Kegan Paul, Trench Trubner, 1902), vol. I. 21: SOW 98.
66 Ibid., 202: SOW 99–100.

Ecstasy of St. Philip Neri, by Gaetano Lapis (1754), Church of San Filippo Neri, Genoa, Italy. Known as "the Apostle of Rome," Philip was venerated by popes, cardinals, rulers, and ordinary people. He was consulted by rich and poor, powerful and helpless, for his spiritual wisdom and ability to look into people's minds. He often experienced visions and ecstasies such as rolling on the ground at the mention of Jesus' name and was accredited with many miracles and the gift of prophecy. Source: catholictradition.org.

THE COUNCIL OF TRENT

The Council of Trent (1545–1563) became the most important church council between Nicaea (325) and Vatican II (1962–1965) because it proved to the world that the unity of Western Christianity had been permanently shattered. It was dubbed an "Ecumenical Council," so Protestants were invited but given no voting rights. Calvinists and Jesuits led the charge, each calling for loyalty beyond national or political ties and each claiming to represent the true church. However, after twenty-five sessions and eighteen years, all it managed to do was condemn the doctrines of Protestantism, clarify the doctrines of Catholicism, and implement a few minor reforms surrounding the sale of indulgences. No other concessions were made—the seven sacraments, Mass, saints, confessions, indulgences all remained—stalemate. Catholicism could not crush the new heresy, and Protestantism could not reform Rome. When the Reformation first began, some thought Luther so right that the Catholic Church would soon adopt his ideas; others thought him so wrong that the movement would eventually wither away—neither happened at Trent. Who could have imagined that the truth could one day lie on both sides or that both could peacefully coexist as denominations within the same church?

THE NEW WORLD

When Constantinople fell to the Muslim Ottoman Turks in 1453, effectively destroying the Eastern Roman Empire and bringing an end to the Middle Ages, all land routes between Europe and Asia were severed, which gave rise to European nation states, the Renaissance, and the Age of Exploration. Then as Europeans turned to the sea in search of alternate trade routes, they inadvertently discovered the New World, which ultimately led to the church's global expansion. During this time, many Jesuits, Franciscans, Dominicans, and Augustinians carried the gospel to native lands while establishing Spanish and Portuguese colonies along the coasts of Asia, Africa, and America. Some, like Christopher Columbus, were able to convert the indigenous peoples through gestures of friendship and love. Others, like Francis Xavier, were able to convert the indigenous tribes through miraculous signs such as speaking and being heard in their native languages. Still others, like Miguel López de Legazpi's, were petitioned to use "force of arms," if necessary, to baptize Filipinos. Nevertheless, in every trading settlement, little Catholic missions began springing up, and within fifty years, the Spaniards had successfully conquered the New World from California to Cape Horn, South America.

Christopher Columbus landing on Hispianola, Dec. 6, 1492; greeted by Arawak Indians, engraving by Theodor de Bry (c. 1594). After Constantinople fell to the Muslim Turks in 1453, Christopher Columbus proposed an alternate trade route to Asia by going west by sea instead of east. Expecting to arrive in Japan, he accidentally discovered the New World. His voyages led to the first lasting European contact with the Americas, inaugurating a new period of European exploration, conquest, and colonization that lasted for centuries. Source: Library of Congress Prints and Photographs Division. Photo: Wikimedia/ПростоУчастник.

FRANCIS XAVIER

Once again, mass conversion had proven successful, and again, miracles had played a key role. In just seven years, the Franciscans baptized more than a million Mexicans. Jesuit Francis Xavier met with similar success in Goa, West India, where he rang a bell to call villagers to recite the Apostle's Creed, the Lord's Prayer, the Ten Commandments, and the Rosary. As soon as the villagers had learned the words and professed their belief in the creed, Xavier baptized them by the hundreds until his hands dropped in exhaustion. Xavier would go on to become one of the greatest Christian missionaries in history, leading more than 700,000 to Christ. He had the supernatural ability to speak and be heard in native languages. There were numerous reports of people being raised from the dead, others being healed by cloths that had touched his body. Thousands of reported healings and miracles accompanied the preaching of Francis Xavier.[67]

The Miracles of St. Francis Xavier (detail) by Peter Paul Rubens (1617-1618), Kunsthistorisches Museum, Vienna, Austria. Known as the "Apostle of the Indies," Francis Xavier became one of the most famous missionaries of all time, traveling to India, Indonesia, Malaysia, Timor, Japan, China, and beyond. It is said that he drew the hardened hearts of men to the true faith through innumerable miracles. By the power of God, he healed the sick, raised the dead, spoke in tongues, and predicted the future. Source: Google Cultural Institute/Wikimedia.

---

67 *Monumenta Xaveriana et autographis vel ex antiquioribus exemplis collecta . . .* (Madrid: Typis Gabreilis Lopez del Hormo, 1912), II, 143f., 224, 455, 512, 546f., 555, 625f., 689, 694, 698, 710; Benedictus XIV (1675–1758), *Opera Omnia in unum corpus collecta et nuncprimum in quindecim tomos distribute* (Venice: sumptibus J. Remondini, 1787–88), III, 250: Russell P. Spittler, ed., *Perspectives on the New Pentecostalism* (Grand Rapids, MI: Baker, 1976), 20-25 [hereafter PNP]; CP 151.

CONVERTING THE INDIGENOUS POPULATIONS

Not all Spanish explorers were in search of new converts. Some, like Hernán Cortés, were *conquistadors* (conquerors) in search of gold, treasure, and other valuable resources. Armed with horses, weapons, and gunpowder, many of these explorers literally raped and pillaged the New World. Nearly single-handedly, Cortés destroyed the great Mexican Aztec Empire and murdered the monarch of the Peruvian Incas. Even more were destroyed by European diseases to which the indigenous tribes had no immunity. Spain's long and passionate struggle in their *Reconquista* of their motherland against the Muslim Moors made them equally fierce and violent warriors overseas. Indeed, the same *encomienda* system used to enslave reconquered Muslims in Spain was used to enslave indigenous peoples throughout the world. But after the conversion of Bartholomew de Las Casas (1484–1566), the first priest to be ordained in the New World, Casas immediately began lobbying the king of Spain about "the remedies that seem necessary in order that the evil and harm that exists in the Indies cease."[68] Casas feared that Spain would come under divine punishment for their mistreatment of the indigenous peoples, and though the *encomienda* system was not formally abolished until 1720, after Casas, it lost much of its effectiveness.

Meanwhile, as news of Columbus's discovery quickly spread through Europe, French, Dutch, and English explorers—both Catholic and Protestant—soon followed. The moment Western Christianity

---

68 Victor N. Baptiste, *Bartolomé de las Casas and Thomas More's Utopia: Connections and Similarities* (Labyrinthos, 1990), 14: "Bartolomé de las Casas," *Wikipedia:* en.wikipedia.org/wiki/Bartolom%C3%A9_de_las_Casas (Accessed 2 January 2013).

became divided was the moment it began spreading into the New World. When Columbus discovered land in the Bahamas, he called it *San Salvador*, meaning "Holy Savior," before further exploring the coastlines of Hispaniola (Haiti) and Cuba. Thinking he had landed somewhere in the West Indies, he mistakenly called the Native Americans "Indians."

THE PURITANS

England's reformation came in two stages: constitutional reform came through Henry VIII; theological reform came almost a century later at the hand of the Puritans. Initially, Queen Elizabeth I considered the Puritans to be just an obnoxious group of complainers within the Church of England whom she tolerated. She once described them as "geese which only gaggle and cannot hurt" unlike others who were "dogs which both can bark and bite."[69] The term "Puritan" was ascribed to them for their incessant complaining and faultfinding with the queen's compromises. Much like the Anabaptists before them, the Puritans were not happy with the pace of progress and reform. As Calvinists (though they also found fault with Calvin), their primary goal was to purify the Church of England by introducing various reforms and thus make it less like the Church of Rome.

THE KING JAMES BIBLE

When Elizabeth's long reign finally ended in 1603, the Puritans grew hopeful. Since Elizabeth had never married and died without an heir,

---

69 Samuel Hopkins, *The Puritans and Queen Elizabeth* (New York: Anson D.F. Randolph, 1875), 331; CH 293.

King James VI of Scotland, son of Mary, Queen of Scots, became King James I of England, for the first time uniting the two kingdoms. All hopes that James would bring Protestant Presbyterianism to England soon faded, however, when James embraced the Anglican bishops. Evidently, working with the Presbyterians in Scotland did not bode well for him. He said, "Presbyterians agree with the monarchy about as well as God and the devil."[70] Undeterred, the Puritans continued pushing for reform, but the only request granted them was the creation of a new English translation of the Bible—the Authorized King James Version, completed in 1611.

THE PILGRIMS

By 1608, some Separatists within the movement, growing impatient for change, decided they would become free to worship—with or without their king—by moving to Holland. In 1609, one such group came under the influence of Anabaptist Mennonites, forming the first English Baptist church, ironically, in Holland. Though their leader, John Smyth, soon joined the Mennonites, most eventually returned to England. But a second group, after living in Holland for ten years, realized their children were growing up out of touch with their homeland—even forgetting their native language. Unwilling to return to England and give up their newfound freedoms, they began considering a third option. They had heard about an English colony in Jamestown, Virginia, in the New World. Perhaps America held the answer. Though daring for sure, they were willing to try. Thus, after returning to England and meeting up with some like-minded

---

70 Haller, William, *The Rise of Puritanism* (New York: Harper, 1938): CH 295.

adventurers, about one hundred brave souls departed from Plymouth aboard the *Mayflower* on a pilgrimage to the New World. Two months later, on November 11, 1620, they stepped ashore on the rocky coast of New England near what is now Plymouth, Massachusetts.

Landing of the Pilgrims by Michele Felice Cornè (c. 1803-1807). The Plymouth Colony, established in 1620, became the second successful English settlement after Jamestown, Virginia, in 1607, and the oldest continuously inhabited English settlement in what would become the United States of America. The Pilgrims' story of seeking religious freedom would become a central theme of the history and culture of the United States. Source: The White House Historical Association. Photo: Wikimedia/Scewing.

THE ENGLISH CIVIL WAR

For most Puritans, separating from the Church of England or moving to America was far too risky, so they continued to wait for reform. All hope was lost, however, in 1625 when King James's son, Charles I, ascended the throne. Not only was he unwilling to make concessions, but he also reversed many of the hard-fought reforms gained over the last century—like reintroducing stained-glass windows and crucifixes. The Puritans were appalled! Many more joined the Separatist movement and moved to America in protest—some 21,000 between 1620 and 1640—and soon, Puritans towns and churches were springing up all over the Massachusetts Bay Colony. The final straw came when King Charles tried to force the Scottish Presbyterians to worship the Anglican way. The Scots refused, even daring to take up arms against their king. But to put an army in the field, Charles would need the support of Parliament, and the Puritan majority-ruled Parliament was divided. As the English Civil War erupted in 1642, most of the king's loyal Parliamentary members went off to defend their king, leaving Parliament nearly entirely in Puritan hands. At last, their long-awaited opportunity had arrived. That same year, the *Westminster Confession of Faith and Catechism* was produced, which, though never officially sanctioned, many Presbyterian and Congregational churches use to this day.

A KING IS BEHEADED

Meanwhile, the war was being won by Scottish and Parliamentary forces led by the military genius of one self-styled Puritan, General Oliver Cromwell. Cromwell, known to his men as "Old Ironsides" because he never faced defeat, believed their role in history was a call from God. It was the Puritan Crusaders against the enemies of righteousness. Often they would pray and sing hymns as they plunged into battle. By 1646, the king's armies had surrendered, but the king did not. Instead, he conspired to further split Parliament and form a secret alliance with the Scots, and a second civil war ensued. In 1649, seven years of fighting finally ended as King Charles, who would have been entitled to limited constitutional powers after the first civil war, was now on trial for high treason for provoking a second war and putting his own interests above the good of the people. Charles was soon found guilty by a Puritan-controlled Parliament and beheaded. The Puritans had overplayed their hand. Though other English monarchs had been murdered before, none had ever been tried and executed by their own people. Centuries of English royal tradition could not be ignored. After the execution, a portrait was widely distributed allegedly depicting the king's last hours. In the portrait, the king knelt beside a table where a Bible rested. With his royal crown on the floor and a crown of thorns in his right hand, his eyes were lifted to a crown of glory above. The Puritans had unwittingly created a martyr, and public sentiment soon turned against them. Oliver Cromwell's theocracy lasted only four years, and when Cromwell died in 1658, the Puritan spirit died with him. Two years later, the English monarchy was restored as an exiled King Charles II, son of the beheaded king, took the throne.

Cover illustration by William Marshall, *Eikon Basilike: The Pourtrature of His Sacred Majestie in His Solitudes and Sufferings*, by King Charles I (likely ghostwritten by Bishop John Gauden). The book appeared immediately after Charles' execution in January 1649, portrayed Charles as a Christian saint who had been martyred for defending the Church of England against Puritan fanatics, and effectively turned public opinion against them. Source: Beinecke Rare Book & Manuscript Library, Yale University. Photo: Wikimedia/MarmadukePercy.

THE NEW ENGLAND PURITANS

Life did not bode much better for the New England Puritans. Though they were instrumental in establishing religious freedom and democracy in America, their unbridled freedom would soon become their own undoing. The American Puritans believed their new society to be a "shining city on a hill." Since children who could not read would become "barbarous" and rebellious against capital laws without an understanding of the Bible, every child was required to have a schoolmaster and to be taught literacy. One such school, founded in 1636, became known as Harvard College. New England Puritans were also more radical than their English counterparts, especially in social matters, including the banning of sexual relations outside marriage, gambling, toasting, drunkenness, music, drama, dancing, entertainment, toys, dolls, festivities—even Christmas and Easter celebrations were forbidden. If a wife failed to perform her marital duties to her husband, she could be disciplined. But perhaps most disturbing of all, for a people bent on religious freedom, was their intolerance toward other religious groups like the Quakers, Baptists, and Anglicans—basically, anyone who did not share their beliefs could be persecuted and executed. Apparently, their "shining city" did not include others.

THE SALEM WITCH TRIALS

One popular seventeenth century idea left over from the Middle Ages was that all misfortunes were the work of the Devil. If an infant died, crops failed, or there was friction in a church, the Devil was to be blamed. Consequently, when New England Puritan ministers like Cotton Mather began preaching that demons were alive and well among them, mass panic and hysteria ensued. In all, over 150 men, women, and children were accused or tried on charges of witchcraft near Salem, Massachusetts, between 1692 and 1693. Reasons ranged from family feuds and infighting, homelessness and begging, not attending church meetings regularly, getting remarried, telling enchanted stories or fortunes, or possessing horoscopes, cultic books, or pots of ointment to having an ugly wart somewhere on their body. Before sentencing, the advice of several local influential ministers was sought. Though the ministers described the situation as deplorable, urged caution, and warned of miserable consequences should presumptively innocent people be executed, the court proceeded. Of the 150 arrested and imprisoned, 29 were convicted, 14 women and 5 men were hung, while another man was crushed to death with heavy stones. Five more died while in prison. As with the beheading of King Charles, public sentiment quickly turned against the New England Puritans after their witch trials. One historian put it this way: "The Salem witchcraft was the rock on which theocracy shattered."[71] Having already lost their Massachusetts Bay Charter in 1684, many New England Puritans scattered, while those who remained eventually joined up with Congregational or Presbyterian churches. In the years following the trials, many family members filed petitions as public justice demanded that many of the convictions be reversed.

Mary Warren (forefront) testifies at the Salem witch trials, pointing across the room where she claims to see the ghost of a man she believes Giles Corey killed. Though Corey, an 80-year-old farmer (on stand), was previously accused of murdering his servant, Jacob Goodale, who suddenly died, he refuses to enter a plea and is later acquitted. Nevertheless, Giles Corey was pressed to death by stones being piled on his chest. Source: Henry Wadsworth Longfellow, "Giles Corey of Salem Farms," (Boston, Mass.: Houghton Mifflin, 1902), p. 752. Artist: John W. Ehninger (1880). Photo: Wikimedia/Ogram.

71 George Lincoln Burr, *Narratives of the Witchcraft Cases*, 1648–1706 (1914), 197: "Salem witch trials," *Wikipedia: en.wikipedia.org/wiki/Salem_witch_trials* (Accessed 5 January 2013).

THE END OF AN ERA

Despite the legalistic Puritans, one sign of the church's coming of age in the seventeenth century was its growing tolerance and acceptance of religious differences. The denominational idea that truth can be found on both sides of an argument only appeared after both sides— Catholics and Protestants—collapsed in exhaustion. In the mid-1500s, Lutheran princes fought Catholic Imperial forces to a stalemate in Germany. Both sides agreed to stop fighting, but only after a territorial settlement had been reached at the Peace of Augsburg. In the late 1500s, France experienced another series of civil wars between French Calvinists and Roman Catholics until another territorial compromise was reached—the Edict of Nantes. Dutch Reformers fought a similar battle for independence from Catholic Spain. However, none were as devastating as the Thirty Years' War. Essentially, what began as a struggle between Catholics and Protestants in Germany ended in a continental conflict much like the two world wars of the twentieth century. It took thirty years of war for Catholics to realize they could not subdue the Protestants in the North and for Protestants to realize they could not control the Catholics in the South. The 1648 Peace of Westphalia represented the end of an era. Christianity's alliance with civil authorities dating back to Constantine's reign was crumbling, and a new Modern Age that separated faith from force and theologies from territories was fast approaching.

What eventually became English colonies in North America began primarily as commercial ventures designed to contribute to the developing prosperity of the British Crown. The unprecedented promise of religious toleration and freedom in those colonies provided a powerful incentive for Christian believers and colonial settlers alike. Quakers and Anabaptists settled in Pennsylvania, Catholics in Maryland, and the Dutch Reformed in New York. They were later joined by Swedish Lutherans, French Calvinists, English Baptists, and Scottish Presbyterians. Religious diversity in the American colonies was calling for a new understanding of the church. Though the term "denomination" would not be used until the 1740s, the concept was being hammered out a century earlier.

Sects were exclusive; denominations were inclusive because they implied that one group called by a certain name was but one member of a larger group called the "church." Denominationalism taught that the true church could not be defined by any one group and that no denomination, theological persuasion, or ecclesiastical system could claim to represent the whole body of Christ. Each simply constituted a different form of worship within the larger life of the church. In the seventeenth century, however, few could have imagined the thousands of independent groups and churches represented under that one umbrella called the "church" today.

Though the term *Protestant* was first used in 1529 concerning the "protestation" of Lutheran princes, it was not used in any broader sense until the seventeenth century, and not officially until the formation of the Protestant Episcopal Church in 1783. The term simply means "one who publicly protests." Perhaps then, the greatest accomplishment of the Reformation Era was not so much the reforms instituted but the foundations for freedom and diversity that those reforms laid for future generations. Certainly the invention of Gutenberg's Press in 1439 also greatly contributed to the development of the Modern Age, simply by making the Bible more accessible to a variety of groups, thus subjecting it to a broader range of interpretation.

STUDY QUESTIONS

1. What eventually led John Wycliffe to believe that the pope was "Antichrist"?

2. On the day Jan Hus was executed on July 6, 1415, he prophesied, "This day you roast a goose, but a hundred years hence you shall hear a swan sing, that you shall not roast." How accurate was his prophecy? Explain.

3. What were the implications of Martin Luther's "justification by faith" doctrine?

4. How would you describe Martin Luther's beliefs concerning miracles?

5. What did Swiss Reformer Hyuldrych Zwingli do that was considered extremely radical in his day?

6. How were the early Anabaptists much like modern Pentecostals and charismatics?

7. John Calvin's teachings on the gifts and workings of the Holy Spirit were so extensive he has been dubbed "the theologian of the Holy Spirit." How would you characterize Calvin's beliefs on spiritual gifts? How prevalent do you think Calvin's teachings on spiritual gifts are today?

8. How would you compare the Scottish Covenanters and early Presbyterian reformers of the sixteenth century with the Presbyterian Church of the twenty-first century? Could the same be said of other faiths? Why do you think that is?

9. Ignatius of Loyola, founder of the Jesuits, had many mystical experiences including the gift of *loquela* (language), which he said sometimes came from exterior sources like a heavenly choir and other times from interior sources like his own lips. How is this similar to modern-day singing in tongues?

10. Name some peculiar mannerisms that Philip Neri, "the Apostle of Rome," had in common with early Pentecostals.

11. Catholic missionary Francis Xavier, like many others, reportedly spoke (xenoglossy) and was heard (heteroglossolalia) in languages unknown to him, in addition to speaking in angelic, heavenly, or ecstatic languages (glossolalia). Which of these do you think was in operation on the day of Pentecost?

12. Despite the fact that the Puritans are accredited with the King James Bible and the second successful English settlement in North America, they did not survive as a people or a religion in England or in New England. What reasons do you see for that?

2

GREAT AWAKENINGS

(c. 1651 – 1800)

Jesus once spoke of a time when men would sleep and an enemy would come and sow tares among the wheat.[1] As Catholics and Protestants alike were preoccupied with infighting and reform, another revolution was taking place inside the Western church that would ultimately become its greatest enemy. When Constantinople fell to the Muslim Ottoman Turks in 1453, many Greek and Roman scholars fled west to Florence, Italy, and an intellectual and cultural revolution was underway that would eventually spread throughout Europe and the world. The Renaissance was a literal "rebirth" of classical Greek, Roman, and Eastern literature, philosophy, and culture. Perhaps best known for its impact on the arts and socio-political world, the Renaissance was primarily a revolution in education and learning.

---

1   Matt. 13:25

RENAISSANCE HUMANISM

Though *humanism* was conceived during the Renaissance Era in response to the perceived "narrow-mindedness" of medieval scholasticism, the term would not be coined until much later in the nineteenth century. While scholasticism focused primarily on preparing men to become doctors, lawyers, and priests by teaching from approved textbooks, humanism sought to create an entire society of men and women who could speak and write clearly and eloquently, and thus be capable of engaging in civil and community life while persuading others to become "virtuous" and "prudent." This could be accomplished by teaching the humanities of grammar, rhetoric, history, poetry, and moral philosophy. *The Cambridge Dictionary of Philosophy* describes the ensuing impact of humanism on the West: "Here, one felt no weight of the supernatural pressing on the human mind, demanding homage and allegiance. Humanity—with all its distinct capabilities, talents, worries, problems, possibilities—was the center of interest. It has been said that medieval thinkers philosophized on their knees, but, bolstered by the new studies, they dared to stand up and to rise to full stature."[2]

Though initially little more than a body of literary knowledge and linguistic skills based on late antiquity and used by church scholars, humanism increasingly took on its modern secular usage as it sought to elevate humanity through the sciences and intellect. What's more, many early reformers like Calvin and Zwingli studied the teachings of Erasmus of Rotterdam—a Catholic humanist. Martin Luther also had

---

2   "Humanism," *The Cambridge Dictionary of Philosophy*, Second Edition (Cambridge University, 1999): "Humanism," *Wikipedia: en.wikipedia.org/wiki/Humanism* (Accessed 12 January 2013).

great respect and admiration for Erasmus, and in turn, Erasmus was once accused by Catholic monks of preparing the way for Luther. But while reformers were busy challenging Catholic doctrine and practices, humanism would ultimately challenge the notion that a supernatural God even existed. Although humanism claimed to promote freedom and toleration for all, in the end, it could do so only by failing to recognize any absolute truth—including the God of Christianity.

The *Vitruvian Man* by Leonardo da Vinci (c. 1490) with notes based on the work of ancient Roman architect Vitruvius, who believed the human body was the ideal and principal source of symmetry and proportion for all classical architecture. It has since come to symbolize the relationship between man and nature, the blending of art and science during the Renaissance, and more generally, Renaissance humanism—including its elevation and worship of man above God. Source: eldritch00.wikidot.com.

If the Middle Ages were all about experiencing a supernatural God through a tenderhearted faith in Jesus, the Reformation or Renaissance Era was all about an intellectual pursuit of God. However, while the Reformation highlighted the denial of certain supernatural aspects of the faith, the Renaissance would set out to replace faith with science and reason and make them the new cornerstones of civilization. While some Christians tried to counter this intellectual revolution with more intellectualism, others countered with a cultural revival of faith in the supernatural. One such group emerged in England about 1650.

GEORGE FOX

George Fox (1624–1691) was born in the Puritan village of Drayton-in-the-Clay (now Fenny Drayton), Leicestershire, England. A bit of a loner and oddity in his younger years, he sensed the call of God from his youth: "When I came to eleven years of age, I knew pureness and righteousness; for, while I was a child, I was taught how to walk to be kept pure. The Lord taught me to be faithful, in all things, and to act faithfully two ways; inwardly to God, and outwardly to man."[3] Not surprisingly, everyone expected Fox to become a priest, but he never showed any interest in higher learning. At nineteen, Fox had seen much of the behavior of so-called Christians. One night after leaving a couple of acquaintances at a local pub, he heard an inner voice say to him, "You see how young people go together into vanity, and old people into the earth; you must forsake all, young and old, keep out of all, and be as a stranger to all."[4] So Fox began traveling the countryside in search of answers to the burning questions in his heart. He sought the help of priests, Puritans, and Dissenters alike, but none seemed to have the answers he was looking for.

> For I saw there was none among them all that could speak to my condition. And when all my hopes in them and in all men were gone, so that I had nothing outwardly to help me, nor could tell what to do, then, oh, then, I heard a voice which said, 'There is one, even Christ Jesus, who can speak to your condition;' and when I heard it my heart did leap for joy. Then the Lord let me see why there was none upon the earth that could speak to my condition, namely, that I might give Him all the glory; for all are concluded under sin, and shut up in unbelief as I had been, that Jesus Christ might have the pre-eminence

---

3   John L. Nickalls, ed., *The Journal of George Fox* (Cambridge University: Reprinted by the Philadelphia Yearly Meeting, 1952), 1–2; Rufus M. Jones, ed., *George Fox—An Autobiography*, (Richmond, Indiana: Friends United Press, 2006), chap. 1: "George Fox," *Wikipedia: en.wikipedia.org/ wiki/ George_Fox* (Accessed 15 January 2013).

4   Nickalls, *The Journal of George Fox*, 3.

who enlightens, and gives grace, and faith, and power. Thus when
God does work, who shall prevent it? And this I knew experimentally.[5]

As a young mystic, Fox formed his entire belief system on what he called the "inner light" of Christ. He believed salvation was not something that could be obtained by natural birth, baptism, church attendance, or good works, but by simply knowing Christ personally and daily relying on the help of the Holy Spirit. Fox also believed formal training did not make one a minister, nor could education or intellect determine one's calling. A true minister of God would simply sense the call of God in his heart by the Holy Spirit and then search the Scriptures for illumination, edification, and advice. The Holy Spirit was the only qualification for ministry, and anyone—including women and children—had the right to minister as long as the Spirit was guiding them. He also believed worship should not be confined to church buildings, which he called "steeple-houses," but could be held in a field, orchard, or anywhere God's presence could be felt. Most of all, Fox resented the letter-of-the-law mentality of the churches of his day that left out the quickening, illuminating presence of the Holy Spirit, who made the Scriptures come to life. Fox believed in mixing the Spirit and Word together and that anyone could be led by the Spirit, as long as his actions were validated by the Word.

Fox tells of his early days of preaching in fields, pubs, marketplaces, and steeple-houses:

A report went abroad of me that I was a young man that had a
discerning spirit; whereupon many came to me, from far and near,
professors, priests, and people. The Lord's power broke forth, and

---

5   Ibid., 11.

I had great openings and prophecies, and spoke unto them of the things of God, which they heard with attention and silence, and went away and spread the fame thereof . . . Many great and wonderful things were wrought by the heavenly power in those days; for the Lord made bare His omnipotent arm, and manifested His power, to the astonishment of many, by the healing virtue whereby many have been delivered from great infirmities. And the devils were made subject through His name; of which particular instances might be given, beyond what this unbelieving age is able to receive or bear.[6]

George Fox, English missionary and founder of the Society of Friends, engraving by S. Allen (1838) based on a painting by S. Chinn (n.d.). Followers of the movement later became known as "Quakers" because of their agitated movements when they felt God's presence or received revelations. Source: Wikimedia/Magnus Manske.

THE QUAKERS

At first, Fox's followers called themselves "Children of the Light" or "Friends of the Truth," then simply "Friends" based on Jesus' words: "I have called you friends."[7] Fox, who often preached against the practices of the state-run churches, was frequently arrested and imprisoned. Once when arrested at Derby on charges of blasphemy, Fox rebuked a local magistrate, telling him he ought "to tremble at the Word of the Lord." The judge snarled and snapped back, calling Fox and his followers "quakers" for their much trembling. Robert Barclay, a fellow

6   *The Journal of George Fox*, Cambridge: 1911 Vol. 1 Chap. 1, 3: MM 187-188.
7   John 15:15

traveler with Fox, wrote, "And from this the name of Quakers, i.e. Tremblers, was first reproachfully crafted upon us; which though it be none of our choosing, yet in this respect we are not ashamed of it, but have reason to rejoice therefore, even that we are sensible of this power that has oftentimes laid hold of our adversaries, and made them yield unto us, and join with us, and confess to the truth."[8]

Fox rebuked not only judges and magistrates but also lawyers for putting personal gain above people, doctors for not crediting God for healing, merchants for not dealing fairly with their prices, and entertainers for causing men to fall into sin with their crude jokes and humor. In turn, Fox was often imprisoned for trivial matters such as refusing to swear by oath, refusing to take up arms, causing a disturbance, or traveling without a pass. Truth be told, most early Quakers were imprisoned at one time or another—sometimes by the hundreds or even thousands.

EARLY QUAKER MEETINGS

A typical early Quaker meeting was described by Fox:

While waiting upon the Lord in silence, as we often did for many hours together, with our hearts toward Him, being stayed in the light of Christ from all fleshy motions and desires, we often received the pouring down of His Spirit upon us, and our hearts were made glad, and our tongues loosened, and our mouths opened, and we spoke with new tongues, as the Lord gave us utterance, and His Spirit led

---

8   Robert Barclay, *An Apology for the True Christian Divinity: Being an Explanation and Vindication of the Principles and Doctrines of the People Called Quakers* (1678; reprint, Phila.: Joseph James, 1789), 359: CC 89.

us, which was poured upon sons and daughters. Thereby things unutterable were made manifest, and the glory of the Father was revealed. Then we began to sing praises to the Lord God Almighty, and to the Lamb, who had redeemed us to God, and brought us out of bondage of the world, and put an end to sin and death . . . and mighty and wonderful things hath the Lord wrought for us, and by us, by His own out-stretched arm . . . Being prepared of the Lord, and having received power from on high, we went forth as commanded of the Lord . . . We sounded the word of the Lord, and did not spare; and caused the deaf to hear, the blind to see, and the heart that was hardened to be awakened; and the dread of the Lord went before us and behind us, and took hold of our enemies.[9]

A distinct characteristic of early Quakers was their ability to be quiet before the Lord while listening and waiting for him. Quakers often assembled and sat in silence waiting for the Spirit to move on someone to witness, pray, speak, or sing. If the Spirit did not move, they would disassemble, reflecting quietly on the Lord. They were taught never to be hasty but to try to prove all things before the Spirit; then and only then could they be confident in the Lord's leading in order to act. Fox believed the leading and guiding of the Holy Spirit to be first and foremost, often quoting Romans 8:14, "For as many as are led by the Spirit of God, they are the sons of God," which he referred to as Christ's "inner light" and to which he adhered in his own life and ministry.

---

9   Epistle to the Reader by Edward Burrough, prefixed to *The Great Mistery of the Great Whore Unfolded, and Anti-Christ's Kingdom Revealed unto Destruction* by George Fox: published in Edmund Goerke's essay (Plainfield, N.J.: Full Gospel Business Men's Fellowship International, 1964), Part 1 of 3, "The Gift of Healing in the Life of George Fox," *QuakerInfo.com: www.quakerinfo.com/healing1.shtml* (Accessed 17 January 2013).

Prayer, being filled with the Spirit, and speaking in tongues were a vital part of early Quaker meetings. One historian wrote, "Frequently, the people in the meetings would shake with 'groans, sighs, and tears' much like a 'woman in labor.' Some would swoon as 'with epilepsy,' and while lips quivered and hands shook, the worshipers might lie on the ground in this condition for hours at a time."[10] About one such occasion, Fox wrote, "The Lord's power was so great that the house seemed to be shaken. When I had finished, some of the professors said it was now as in the days of the apostles, when the house was shaken where they were."[11] Divine healing and casting out demons were also trademarks of Fox's ministry. Often people were healed simply by standing in his presence. Occasionally, he concocted herbs to aid in healing, depending on the ailment. Both Fox's *Journal* and *Book of Miracles* are filled with miraculous accounts of healings and other supernatural occurrences.

Quaker Meeting in London: A female Quaker preaches (c.1723) engraving by Bernard Picard. The Quakers were known for their equal treatment of women and strongly held belief in the universal priesthood of all believers. A female preacher was unheard of in other eighteenth-century western churches. Source: www.virtualmuseum.ca. Photo: Wikimedia/Matanya.

10 H. Larry Ingle, *First Among Friends, George Fox and the Creation of Quakerism* (New York: Oxford University, 1994), 59: GGRR 357.

11 Rufus M. Jones, ed., *George Fox; An Autobiography* (Phila.: Ferris and Leach, 1919), 90: CC 91.

FOX IN AMERICA

By the 1660s, the Quakers had more than 20,000 converts and missionaries in Ireland, Scotland, Wales, and the American colonies. In 1671, Fox felt led to visit the Quaker settlements of America and the West Indies. After a seven-week journey, he landed first in Barbados and Jamaica, where he noticed that many of the Quakers owned slaves. Adamantly opposed to slavery, Fox promptly urged them to train up their slaves and arrange for their soon release. American Quakers were among the first to formally protest slavery at their Philadelphia Yearly Meeting in 1688—nearly two centuries before the Emancipation Proclamation.

Fox then sailed north to Maryland where, though tired, he joined a four-day Quaker meeting already in session. Fox's favorite audience in America, though, was the indigenous peoples. He often made a point of traveling through the backwoods and isolated areas just so he could visit their villages. Fox spent the next two years traveling by horseback through Maryland and parts of New England, guided through the dense wilderness by two Indians, while also attempting to avoid the Puritans in Massachusetts, who forbade the Quakers to even land on their shores. Once while on a boat to Long Island, Fox held a meeting with some Quakers and Indians and learned how some of their tribesmen had joined the Puritans and allegedly made a turn for the worse. Those same Indians told Fox they believed his brand of Christianity to be the true way and wanted to join him but could not for fear of being hung by the Puritans.[12]

---

12   H. Larry Ingle, *First among Friends, George Fox and the Creation of Quakerism* (New York: Oxford University, 1994), 239: GGRR 76.

While on their way from Rhode Island to hold meetings in New Jersey in 1672, Fox wrote about one of his colleagues, John Jay, who was suddenly thrown from a horse, killed, and raised back to life.

> *A friend that was with me went to try a horse and got on his back and the horse ran and cast him on his head and broke his neck as they call it, and the people took him up dead and carried him a good way and laid him on a tree, and I came to him and felt . . . him and saw that he was dead, and as I was pitying his family and him . . . and I took him by the hair of the head, and his head turned like a cloth it was so loose, and I threw away my stick and gloves and took his head in both my hands, and set my knees against the tree; and raised his head and I did perceive it was not broken out that ways, and I put my hand under his chin, and behind his head, and raised his head two or three times with all my strength and brought it in, and I did perceive his neck began to be stiff, and then he began to rattle, and after to breathe, and the people were amazed, and I bid them have a good heart, and carry him into the house, and then they set him by the fire, and I bid them get him some warm thing and get him to bed; and after he had been in the house awhile he began to speak and did not know where he had been: and the next day we passed and he with us pretty well, about sixteen miles to a meeting at Middletown.*[13]

Fox then traveled to Carolina and portions of Virginia before returning to England in 1673, where he remained strong in ministry, experiencing as many miracles in his later years as in his former years.

---

13   *The Journal of George Fox*, Cambridge: 1911, page 227, vol. II: Edmund Goerke, Part 1 of 3, "The Gift of Healing in the Life of George Fox," *QuakerInfo.com: www. quakerinfo.com/healing1.shtml* (Accessed 17 January 2013).

PENNSYLVANIA

Meanwhile in 1681, William Penn, a Quaker and personal friend and traveler with Fox, persuaded King Charles II to issue a land grant for the express purpose of granting a safe haven for Quakers in America. Because of a debt the king owed Penn's father, an admiral in his fleet, the king agreed, and one of the largest land grants ever bestowed upon an individual was granted. The king called the grant "Pennsylvania." Penn, fearing people may think he had named it after himself, preferred simply "Sylvania" or "New Wales," but the king refused to rename it. When Fox died in 1691, it was William Penn who broke the news to his wife, stating, "He died as he lived, a lamb, minding the things of God and His church to the last in a universal spirit."[14]

THE SOCIETY OF FRIENDS

By the eighteenth century, the Quakers had become less evangelistic and more legalistic, formalizing under their current title: the Religious Society of Friends. Marrying outside the Society eventually became outlawed as their numbers dwindled to less than 20,000 in England by 1800. Today, the total number of Quakers worldwide is about 360,000, with their greatest concentration in Kenya, East Africa, because of a successful nineteenth-century missionary effort there. American Presidents Herbert Hoover and Richard Nixon were both Quakers. Sadly, most Americans know the Quakers today only by their fictional caricature on the *Quaker Oats* label dating back to 1877.

---

14   George Fox, *The Journal of George Fox* (London: Temple: JM Dent, 1948), 347: GGRR 394.

THE FRENCH HUGUENOTS

Another group experiencing a revival of the supernatural during this time was French Calvinists or "Huguenots." After fighting between French Catholics and Calvinists ceased in 1598, the Calvinists were granted religious freedom. However, in 1685, King Louis XIV revoked their charter and persecution resumed. Some 400,000 fled to England, Prussia, Holland, South Africa, the American colonies, and other parts of the world. Most of those who remained lived in the Cévennes mountainous region of Dauphin in southern France.

Huguenots was a derogatory name assigned to these French Calvinists by the Catholic Church. The word means "little Hugo's." According to Catholic legend, Hugh (Hugo) Capet (938–996), King of the Franks, did not go to purgatory when he died. Instead, his ghost returned each night to terrify the living by roaming the streets of Tours, France. Also living in Tours at the time were French Calvinists, who were so closely watched during the day, they were forced to assemble at night to pray, preach, and sing psalms. Though they frightened no one, because they frequently came out at night, Catholic priests mocked them, likening them to the notorious spirit.

THE CAMISARDS

Those who concentrated in the mountainous regions of southern France were called "Camisards" because of the black *camise* or peasant smocks they wore over their clothing to disguise themselves during their night raids against their Catholic persecutors. Those who took refuge in England were called "French Prophets" for their belief in the supernatural power of God. After praying and diligently studying the Scriptures, French Calvinists affirmed, "God has no where in the Scriptures concluded himself from dispensing again the extraordinary Gifts of His Spirit unto Men." Indeed, a "more full Accomplishment" of Joel's prophecy than that of Acts could be awaited.[15] Speaking in tongues, visions, prophetic utterances, and other supernatural occurrences were common among them. But perhaps most outstanding and peculiar was the prophetic anointing that frequented their young children in fulfillment of Joel's prophecy "your sons and your daughters shall prophesy." Church leaders gathered the young of both sexes from among the peasantry and breathed into their mouths the breath of Pentecost, and children as young as three years old were often heard prophesying and delivering discourses in perfect fluent French (though French was not their native tongue).

One eyewitness recorded this:

When I came to the assembly, there was a girl preaching with an eloquence and fluency to me most admirable. This girl, after the Spirit of God had honored her with His gifts, learned a little to read. When her sermon was over, there came in many more, who showed a great desire to hear her. She said she was in no ways able of herself to gratify them, but presently fell upon her knees, and earnestly besought God, of His good pleasure, to unloose her tongue, that she might again declare His word, for the consolation of His people. She was immediately answered; the Spirit fell upon her, and she made a long prayer. Me thought I heard an angel, so charming were the

---

15   John Lacy, *A Cry from the Desert* (London: n.p., 1708), 5–6: Michael P. Hamilton, ed. *The Charismatic Movement* (Grand Rapids, Mich.: Eerdmans, 1975), 75 [hereafter CM].

words that came from her mouth. After prayer she set a psalm, and tuned it melodiously; then she gave us a discourse, so excellent, so touching, so captivating, with that holy gracefulness and ardent zeal, that we could not help but believe it was more than human that spoke in her. A poor simple girl, as she was, could certainly never be capable of speaking at that rate. I went away, pierced to the very heart and soul, and full of the impression of those wonderful things that faithful servant of God had pronounced, and I wrote down a good part of them, as well as I could remember. She quoted many texts from the Old and New Testament, as if she had the whole Bible by heart and she applied them so aptly, that it affected us strangely. She expressed a sad lamentation for the deplorable condition of the churches of France; for those that were in the dungeons or in the galleys, in the convents or in banishment; adding, that our sins were the sole cause thereof: but she uttered, at the same time, the noblest and sweetest consolations possible, promises of mercy, peace, grace, delight, and joy everlasting. She declared these things in the name of God, all-sufficient, and abounding in goodness, to those who obstinately reject not the paternal solicitations of His kindness. She promised also, on the same part, after a manner very powerful, exact, and pressing, that religion, in its purity, should be re-established in the kingdom.[16]

Another testified, "I am very sure I have seen sixty other children between three and twelve years of age, in the same condition; the

---

16   *Testimony of Matthew Boissier, of Dauphiny.* Maximilian Misson, *Le Theatre Sacre Des Cévennes, 1707: A Cry From the Desert and Testimonials of the Miraculous Things Lately Come to Pass in the Cévennes,* translated from the originals, Preface by John Lacy, Esq. London 1707, 2nd Edition: MM 192.

discourses of all which tended constantly to press with fervor an amendment of life, and foretold also several things." Sometimes they also spoke in languages that were unknown to them and then interpreted. "Several persons of both sexes I have heard in their ecstasies pronounce certain words which seemed to the bystanders to be some foreign language, and in effect, he that spoke declared sometimes what his preceding word signified."[17]

Others testified, "I saw three or four small children, between three and six years of age, in particular that of James Bousiege, aged about three, who was taken with the Spirit. . . . He said that we were in the last times, that we ought to fight bravely the fight of faith, exhorting at the same time to repentance in general. Another of those little infants was Susan Joncquet, between four and five years old. . . . She spoke louder, in good French, as she could not out of that fit."[18] "Most of the inspired were young people, and very ignorant, and those spoke ordinarily their best in their revelations; some of them told me they could remember nothing said by them in that time, others could somewhat, but very little."[19] "Even one who was astoundingly no more than fourteen-months-old, who had never previously spoken before, suddenly began exhorting on 'the works of repentance' in a loud, childish voice."[20]

Another testified of a young man: "The boldness of this youth astonished me, and the method wherein he took cognizance of my inward workings and related them to the congregation; and, in short,

---

17 Ibid., *Testimony of James du Bois, of Montpelier:* MM 193.
18 Ibid., *Testimony of William Bruguier, of Aubissargues:* MM 193.
19 Ibid., *Testimony of De Caladon:* MM 195.
20 John Lacy, *A Cry From the Desert,* 15: CC 87.

how marvelous a thing was it, that a child so bashful and ignorant should take upon him to instruct an assembly, for him to preach in a language he knew not how to speak at another time, to express himself in lofty style, to pour out excellent instructions in abundance."[21]

But children were not the only ones seized by the Holy Spirit. One lady had a reputation for acting so drunk and erratic under the power of the Spirit that after she uttered a prophecy fluent and wonderful in character, one bystander shouted, "This ass of Balaam has a gold mouth!"[22] Other testimonies described scenes in which many fell on their backs, shut their eyes, heaved their breasts, remained in trances, and then came out of them twitching and uttering all that came into their mouths.[23] One eyewitness said this:

I saw. . .[an] abundance of people of every age and sex, that fell into violent agitations of body in an extraordinary manner; during which they uttered large discourses very pious, and strongly exhorting of repentance. . . . They were forewarned and directed in a multitude of things, relating either to their own particular conduct, or to the religious assemblies for their safety. They always spoke good French in the inspiration, though they never could at other times; and during their discourses then, they spoke in them, saying, 'I tell thee,' 'I declare to thee, my child,' etc. One John Heraut, of our neighborhood, and four or five of his children, had all of them the gift of inspiration. The two youngest were, one of five and a half, and the other seven

---

21 Ibid., *Testimony of John Cavalier, of Sauve*: MM 194.

22 Morton Kelsey, *Tongue Speaking* (Garden City: Doubleday, 1964), 53: CC 87.

23 De Brueys, *Histoire du fanatisme de notre temps* (Paris, 1692), 137: CM 75–76.

years old, when they first had it. I have seen these many a time in their ecstasies.[24]

The same evidence was found among the French Huguenot refugees scattered throughout the world. One who escaped to England recalled hearing his mother speak in fluent French while under the power of the Holy Spirit, saying she was unable to do so at any other time. Another English nobleman reported hearing one of the French Prophets "repeat long sentences in Latin, and another speak in Hebrew, neither of whom could speak a single word in these languages when not in spiritual ecstasy."[25]

Once when a Dr. Middleton in England contended that since apostolic times, not a single example could be found of anyone having exercised or even pretending to exercise the gift of tongues, John Wesley replied, "Sir, your memory fails you again. . . . It has been heard of more than once, no further off than the days of Dauphin."[26] Sadly, by 1711, the French Calvinist resistance was crushed and the movement dispersed.

An etching of a group of ex-Camisards, known as the "French Prophets," who, under the guidance of Elie Marion, immigrated to London in 1706. Published by Longman & Co. (1810.) Source: Own stock.

---

24 John Lacy, *A Cry From the Desert, Testimony of Isabel Charras, of les Roches*: MM 193.

25 Cutten, *Speaking with Tongues: Historically and Psychologically Considered*, 55: CC 87.

26 John Wesley, vol. 10 of *The Works of John Wesley*, (Grand Rapids, Mich.: Zondervan, n.d.), 56: CC 88.

John Lacey, one of the French Prophets in England, in his *Spirit of Prophecy Defended* linked the Camisards to the church's ancient prophetic traditions and warned the church not to make the same mistakes it had made with the Montanists. Besides having committed adultery, Lacey was known for his prophecies, divine healings, supernatural ability to speak in French, Greek, and Latin, laughing in the Spirit, and divine levitation. More than a hundred years later, Lacey's work would be edited and reprinted by Edward Irving—a leader of a similar nineteenth-century prophetic movement in England that would also link itself to the Montanists and French Prophets.

MADAME GUYON

French Protestants were not the only ones experiencing revival in those days. Madame Jeanne Guyon (1648–1717), a French Catholic mystic, was also making waves in the church at the time. At sixteen, Madame Guyon was arranged to marry Jacques Guyon, a wealthy man who was twenty-two years her senior and who fell into ill health. Though Madame Guyon had been led to the Lord by a godly Franciscan at age twenty, she still attended society parties with her husband and found herself easily influenced by the world. Two years later, Guyon was walking across a bridge with her servant near Notre Dame when a poor monk, who seemed to know everything about her, began talking to her. She wrote, "He gave me to understand that God required not merely a heart of which it could only be said it is forgiven, but a heart which could properly, and in some real sense, be designated as holy, that it was not sufficient to escape hell, but that He demanded also the subjection of the evils of our nature, and the utmost purity and height of Christian attainment."[27]

Immediately Guyon's spirit bore witness with the man's words as she resolved, "From this day, this hour, if it be possible, I will be wholly the Lord's. The world shall have no portion of me."[28]

By age twenty-eight, Madame Guyon had become widowed and soon began her public ministry. As people felt drawn to her teachings on cleansing, purity, and power, she quickly found herself counseling and ministering from morning until night. Sometimes God would give her discernment into peoples' lives and she would speak words of encouragement. Other times, she would command sicknesses to leave their bodies, often with instant results. According to one author, "Her soul was all ablaze with the unction and power of the Holy Spirit, and everywhere she went she was besieged by multitudes of hungry, thirsty souls, who flocked to her for the spiritual meat that they failed to get from their regular pastors. Revivals of religion began in almost every place visited by her, and all over France earnest Christians began to seek this deeper experience taught by her. Father La Combe began to spread the doctrine with great unction and power. Then the great Archbishop Fénelon was led into a deeper experience through the prayers of Madame Guyon as he too began to spread the teachings all over France."[29]

---

27 J. Gilchrist Lawson, *Deeper Experiences of Famous Christians* (Anderson, Ind.: Warner, 1911), 97: Wesley L. Duewel, *Heroes of the Holy Life* (Grand Rapids, Mich.: Zondervan, 2002), 69 [hereafter HHL].

28 Lawson, *Deeper Experiences*, 98: HHL 69.

29 Ibid., 103: HHL 71.

Steel engraving of Madame Jeanne Guyon, France (c. 1845). Source: www. antique-prints.de. Photo: Wikimedia/Adam sk.

In 1695, Madame Guyon was accused of teaching Quietism—the belief that holiness could be achieved simply through quiet contemplation. She rejected this notion with horror, stating that it was absolutely necessary to offer positive resistance in the face of temptation. Even so, she was imprisoned for seven years, spending her last four at the infamous Bastille and her last two in solitary confinement. Despite her harsh treatment in prison—even being poisoned at one point—Madame Guyon continued to display an indomitable spirit in her writings. While in prison, she produced a twenty-volume commentary on the Bible, an autobiography, and many shorter works—poems, songs, and essays. Friends and enemies alike said she had a "prodigious capacity" for ministry. She wrote, "I was astonished at myself. There was nothing which I was not fit for, or in which I did not succeed. . . . I know I had but meager capabilities, but that in God my spirit had received a quality it never had before. I experienced something of the state the apostles were in after they received the Holy Spirit."[30]

Wesley once said of her, "How few such instances do we find of exalted love to God, and our neighbor; of genuine humility; of

---

30   Abbie C. Morrow, ed., *Sweet-Smelling Myrrh* (Cincinnati: God's Revivalist Office, n.d.), 109: HHL 76.

invincible meekness and unbounded resignation."[31] In one of her shorter works entitled *Short and Easy Method of Prayer*, Guyon taught that the highest form of prayer was when you let God speak and act through you, filling you with his divine influences. Believing that one should pray all the time and that, in whatever one does, one should spend time with God, she wrote, "Prayer is the key of perfection and of sovereign happiness; it is the efficacious means of getting rid of all vices and of acquiring all virtues; for the way to become perfect is to live in the presence of God. He tells us this Himself: 'walk before me, and be thou perfect.' Prayer alone can bring you into His presence, and keep you there continually."[32]

Madame Guyon's writings were first published by Protestants in the Netherlands in 1704 and quickly gained popularity among English and German-speaking peoples alike. Guyon had a profound effect on the Quakers and the Wesleys as she helped lay the foundation for Methodism and the modern Holiness and Pentecostal movements. Though her teachings were almost entirely Protestant, Madame Guyon clung to her Catholic faith until her death in 1717.

SECULARISM AND THE ENLIGHTENMENT

By the turn of the eighteenth century, the Renaissance was being replaced by yet another cultural revolution called the "Age of Enlightenment," "Age of Reason," or simply "the Enlightenment." As

---

31   "Who Is Jeanne Guyon?" *The Last Days.net: www.thelastdays.net/whoguyon.htm* (Accessed 23 January 2013).

32   De La Motte Guyon, Jeanne Marie Bouvier, *Le Moyen Court Et Autres Écrits Spirituels* (*The Short and Easy Method of Prayer*) (1685): "Jeanne Guyon," *Wikipedia: en.wikipedia.org/wiki/Jeanne_Guyon* (Accessed 23 January 2013).

the Renaissance would give birth to humanism, so the Enlightenment would ultimately give birth to secularism. Having faith or hope in the next life no longer mattered. What mattered was having happiness and fulfillment in this life, and the best way to achieve that was through mind and reason—not faith or superstition. Secularism, which was not defined until the nineteenth century, was not an argument against Christianity but independent of it. George Jacob Holyoake wrote, "It does not question the pretensions of Christianity; it advances others. Secularism does not say there is no light or guidance elsewhere, but maintains that there is light and guidance in secular truth, whose conditions and sanctions exist independently, and act forever. Secular knowledge is manifestly that kind of knowledge which is founded in this life, which relates to the conduct of this life, conduces to the welfare of this life, and is capable of being tested by the experience of this life."[33] And, much like its predecessor, secularism sought to develop the physical, moral, and intellectual nature of humanity to its highest possible point as the immediate duty of life. A secularist then was one who believed that every human need could be met by material means, that science alone was the providence of man, and that doing good simply for the sake of doing good was sufficient. In time, however, secularism took on its modern meaning—strict separation of the state from religious institutions and dignitaries, the right to be free from religious rules and teachings, and belief that public and political activities and decisions should not be influenced by religious beliefs or practices. As humanism elevated the individual above God,

---

33   George Jacob Holyoake, *The Principles of Secularism* (London, 1860): Dubray, Charles (1912), "Secularism," *The Catholic Encyclopedia* (New York: Robert Appleton Company): "Secularism," *New Advent: www.newadvent.org/cathen/13676a.htm* (Accessed 27 January 2013).

secularism sought to elevate an entire culture and society above God, and Paris was its new cosmopolitan capital.

DEISM

As logic, reason, and rational proof became the new vogue god, deism—belief that God's existence could be proven by reason alone—became the new vogue religion. The Bible was dismissed as superstitious and obsolete as science alone could reveal the mysteries of the universe. Faith in the supernatural was no longer necessary. God was like the great watchmaker in the sky who created the universe, wound it up, and then let it run on its own. Many of America's founders, including Thomas Paine, Thomas Jefferson, and Benjamin Franklin, were deists. Thomas Jefferson literally used a razor blade to cut out New Testament Scriptures omitting the supernatural and the resurrection to create what he called *The Life and Morals of Jesus of Nazareth*, also referred to as "The Jefferson Bible." Deists, like Jefferson, sought to reduce the Bible to a book of morals and Christ to a good moral teacher because that was "reasonable." Christians, on the other hand, fought over doctrine, practiced bigotry, hatred, and intolerance, and taught absolute truth—all of which were completely "unreasonable." However, deism did not last beyond the eighteenth century because it eventually proved to be itself "unreasonable" and unable to satisfactorily explain the evils of this world. It was a religion based on false hopes and false optimisms. Most deists eventually drifted into Unitarianism—disbelief in the divinity of Christ—or to its next natural progression, atheism—disbelief in God altogether.

The Life and Morals of Jesus of Nazareth, commonly referred to as the *Jefferson Bible*, was a book constructed by Thomas Jefferson in the later years of his life (c.1820). The Third President of the United States painstakingly cut passages out of the Bible, including sections about the resurrection and Holy Spirit that he felt could not be supported by reason to produce what he considered a more accurate history of Jesus and his teachings. Source: theparagraph.com.

PIETISM

The God of the deists was a cold, impersonal God who did not supernaturally intervene in the course of humanity and who could only be understood, not felt. In contrast, Pietism developed as a movement within Protestant Lutheranism that emphasized warm, experiential faith as opposed to cold liturgy, deeper, closer relationships with God as opposed to cold, institutional membership in state-run churches, and practical Christianity as opposed to theological disputation.

German mystic Johann Arndt (1555–1621), a forerunner of Pietism, was once removed from his church for refusing to stop casting out demons during baptism. He wrote an influential book on the mystical union between Christ and the believer called "True Christianity." But the "father of Pietism" was Philipp Jakob Spener (1635–1705) who, after being influenced by a number of professors at Strasbourg, including a Waldensian and former Jesuit, became convinced that another reformation was needed in the Lutheran Church to develop more devoted followers of Christ. Spener began holding meetings in his home twice a week where he expounded on excerpts from his sermons and passages from the New Testament before asking those present to join him in conversation. These first-of-its-kind small group home Bible studies eventually became known as "gatherings of the pious." Spener stressed the necessity of deep repentance prior to a new birth experience followed by a separation from the world. Pietism taught that Christianity consisted chiefly of a change of heart and subsequent life of holiness that included shunning common worldly amusements such as dancing, the theatre, and public games.

Of course, the movement was met with great opposition from church leaders who viewed it as a social danger that "seemed either to generate an excess of evangelical fervor and so disturb the public tranquility or to promote a mysticism so nebulous as to obscure the imperatives of morality. A movement which cultivated religious feeling almost as an end itself." Even the term "Pietist" was originally used as a form of ridicule. Spener died in 1705. Nevertheless, the movement continued to spread through August Francke (1663-1727) who became professor of theology at the University of Halle where Spener's godson, Count Zinzendorf, was a pupil. Pietism would not only greatly influence Zinzendorf, but also the Moravian revival of 1727, the establishment of worldwide Protestant missionaries, John Wesley and the Methodist movement, and evangelicalism in North America, indirectly through Methodism and directly through German immigrants.[34]

JANSENISTS

Meanwhile, Dutch Catholic theologian Cornelius Otto Jansen (1585–1638) and his protégé Jean du Vergier (1581–1643) wanted to

---

34 "Pietism," *Wikipedia: en.wikipedia.org/wiki/Pietism* (Accessed 18 May 2016)

establish a more rigorous moral code for Catholic clergy to combat what they perceived was extreme leniency or the "relaxed moral" code of the Jesuits. Similarly, they felt the best way for Catholicism to defeat Calvinism was to go straight to their source by reviving a truer and more accurate interpretation of Augustine's teachings on original sin, human depravity, the necessity of divine grace, and predestination— doctrines the church had never repudiated but had somehow let fall through the cracks. So without mentioning the Jesuits by name, Jansen argued that good works never saved anyone because the human will was not free and human nature was corrupt. Only by God's grace could humanity be saved. Though Jansen died in an epidemic in 1638, his teachings lived on through his partner, du Vergier, who was made abbot of the Abbey of Saint-Cyran in France in 1620, and through his posthumous work entitled *Augustinus*, published in 1643. After both died, the two abbeys at Port-Royal near Paris became major strongholds for the movement, as Antoine Arnauld, Blaise Pascal (inventor of the mechanical calculator), and Jean Racine (the famous playwright) and many others joined the movement.

Though Catholic authorities initially tolerated the movement, the Jesuits branded them "Jansenists" in hopes of identifying them as Calvinists in Catholic garb. It worked. The Jansenists were eventually condemned by two papal bulls in 1653 and 1713. The latter marked the end to Catholic toleration of Jansenism as their main convent was dissolved and Port-Royal destroyed. Nevertheless, elements of the movement continued. By 1727, having failed to win the theological argument, some Jansenists turned directly to the testimony of God— namely, miracles—to validate their doctrine. To the Jansenists, miracles represented God's grace manifested in human history, separated the "pure of heart" from the hard-hearted church hierarchy, and served as divine proof that God was on their side.

THE CONVULSIONNAIRES

Between 1727 and 1731, numerous miraculous cures were being reported for everything ranging from paralysis and cancer to blindness at the tomb of one of their deacons and saints, François de Pāris, in the tiny cemetery of Saint-Médard. In 1728, Cardinal Noailles, Archbishop of Paris, who took issue with the pope and believed some elements of Jansenism to be orthodox, declared the miracles at Médard to be genuine. In 1731 alone, no less than eight hundred miracles were reported as rumors began spreading throughout Paris that people were being healed, experiencing strange agitations, nervous commotions, and "violent transports of the Spirit," barking like dogs, stomping on Bibles, or dancing until they collapsed. Some, when seized by compulsions, spoke in unknown tongues and could understand any language in which they were addressed, but much of it was not understood.[35] Normally, a quiet and tranquil place, the cemetery was bustling with people praying, singing, and convulsing. Pilgrims ranging from the sick and curious to those just wanting to be entertained began flocking to the cemetery. Some even brought chairs to sit and watch. Countesses, duchesses, dignitaries, members of the Parisian Parlement—even the president of France—came to observe the miracles at Saint-Médard.

---

35 Robert Dale Owen (February–March 1864), "The Convulsionists of Saint-Medard," *The Atlantic Monthly*, featured at Romancatholicism.org (Retrieved 15 March 2012): *Wikipedia: en.wikipedia.org/wiki/Fran%C3%A7ois_de_P%C3%A2ris* (Accessed 24 August 2016); P.F. Mathieu, *Histoire des miraculés et des convulsionnaires de Saint Médard* (Paris, 1864): CM 76.

One contemporary wrote, "There surely never was a greater number of miracles ascribed to one person, than those, which were lately said to have been wrought in France upon the tomb of Abbé Paris, the famous Jansenist, with whose sanctity the people were so long deluded. . . . Many of the miracles were immediately proved upon the spot, before judges of unquestioned integrity, attested by witnesses of credit and distinction, in a learned age, and on the most eminent theatre that is now in the world."[36] Another eyewitness wrote, "We have cases of fire having no power to burn the convulsionaries; of their being dragged in different directions by terrifying mechanical apparatus, which cause neither dislocation nor pain; of violent blows being dealt them with extremely heavy objects, without producing bruises, and sometimes with the effect of curing inveterate ankylosis; of swords and spits being pressed forcibly against their cheeks and throats, yet failing to pierce them. On other occasions these instruments have penetrated into the breast, the intestines, the hands, the feet of people who underwent crucifixion, without leaving the slightest trace of a wound; people have rolled about in barrels that were armed with steel points, with knives and razors, and have come out full of life. They have spoken Arabic and other languages they had never learnt."[37]

The "convulsionnaires," as they became called, viewed their bodies with contempt and disgust as a source of sinfulness, disease,

---

36   David Hume, "An Essay Concerning Human Understanding" (1777), 84: "Convulsionnaires of Saint Médard,"
       Wikipedia: en.wikipedia.org/wiki/Convulsionnaires_of_Saint-M%C3%A9dard
       (Accessed 4 September 2014).

37   R.A. Knox, *Enthusiasm: A Chapter in the History of Religion* (Oxford: Clarendon, 1950) 372, 384: CP 171.

and corruption. The convulsions were believed to be bodily manifestations of such, which needed to be driven or released from the body through violent cuttings or beatings or various other forms of self-torture. Flogging themselves with a whip or hanging from a cross simply helped them identify with the sufferings of Christ and the early martyrs. Such extremes were recurrent among persecuted Christians throughout the ages.

Portrait of French Catholic deacon and saint, François de Pâris (1690–1727). Though born into wealth, de Pâris died in extreme poverty at the age of thirty-six, having given all his earnings to the poor. In the four years that followed his death, his tomb became the site of religious pilgrimages and great miracles that often left people in a state of ecstasy. These people became known as the "Convulsionnaires of Saint-Médard" for the violent convulsive movements that overtook them when touching or coming within the vicinity of the tomb. At least 800 were reportedly healed in 1731 alone, including a magistrate, a member of parlement, and several prominent citizens. Source: Google Books: *La vie de monsieur de Paris, diacre*, by Pierre Boyer (1731). Photo: Wikimedia/Charles Matthews.

Finally, in 1732, the cemetery was closed by order of King Louis XV, drawing much public sympathy to their cause. One writer protested, "All powerful though he was, the king had no right to suppress the news of the marvels of God."[38] Another posted a sign in the cemetery that read, "By order of the King, it is forbidden to the Divinity to perform any more miracles in this vicinity."[39] Undaunted, the convulsionnaires continued their practices outside the cemetery gate but were eventually forced to meet in private homes throughout

---

38 Dale Van Kley, *The Religious Origins of the French Revolution* (New Haven: Yale, 1996), 130; David Garrioch, *The Making of Revolutionary Paris* (Berkeley: Univ. of Calif., 2002), 145–6: "Convulsionnaires of Saint Medard," *Wikipedia:* en.wikipedia.org/wiki/Convulsionnaires_of_Saint-M%C3%A9dard (Accessed 4 September 2014).

39 Ibid.

Paris and other French cities. Social classes were ignored in these meetings as nobility, commoners, and clergy alike met together, often with women hosting and men preaching. Those who attended began living ascetic lifestyles in communal homes called "cooperatives" and calling each other "brother" or "sister" or some Bible name. Prophetic dreams and visions were also common among them, and their preaching often included themes of persecution, martyrdom, divine judgment, and the imminent return of Christ.

But eventually the convulsion phenomena began to rival and eclipse even the miracle phenomena, and by the mid-1730s, public opinion had turned against them as more scandalous stories of torture and violence came to light. One convulsionary leader claimed to be "Elijah." He was eventually arrested and imprisoned. Many Jansenists sought to distance themselves from the convulsionnaires during this time. By the 1740s, the movement had further descended into increasingly brutal self-torturing, while spiritual content decreased. The Jansenists were eventually forced to flee France altogether, many of them taking refuge in Holland or England, where they were more or less tolerated.

THE SHAKERS

Under the influence of the French Prophets in England, Quakers Jane and James Wardley decided to break away from the Quakers at a time when the Quakers were trying to wean themselves from more ecstatic forms of worship. Forming the Wardley Society in Manchester in 1747, they eventually became known as the "Shaking Quakers." Future leader Ann Lee (1736–1784) and her parents joined the charismatic group in 1758. Lee, the daughter of a blacksmith, was uncomfortable with her sexuality and planned to remain celibate—until her father forced her to marry. She became pregnant eight times, experiencing four stillbirths and giving birth to four children, none of whom survived past age six. After all that, one could understand her growing conviction toward abandonment of sexual relations in favor of celibacy and ascetic perfection. Lee claimed to receive several visions and revelations from God affirming that celibacy and confession of sin were the only true road to salvation.

Much like the Quakers, the early Shakers believed strongly in the "Divine light" of God's Spirit to guide them through prophecy, visions, and revelations and that men and women could lead equally in spiritual matters. Much like the convulsionnaires, Shakers believed shaking or trembling were manifestations of sin being purged from the body, but with one difference—Shakers believed this was the power and work of the Holy Spirit. Another doctrine unique to Shakers was the belief that since God made man in his image, male and female, God must also be male and female. This, coupled with the strong conviction that the second coming of Christ was near, would soon lay the groundwork for this sect of restorationist believers. The Shakers clearly believed in the mystical experience of personal union with Christ that led to a life in the Spirit with a number of spiritual gifts. They also believed the primitive church had all but lost its gifts but that the restoration of all things was at hand. To them, life in the Spirit meant both a personal equipping for perfection and a preparation for the end times.

In 1770, "Mother Ann," as she was called, was revealed by "Divine light" in revelation to be the second coming or female version of Christ. Christ, the male version, had given birth to the first Christian

Church, and now Ann Lee, the female version of Christ, had come to give birth to the second Christian Church. In 1771, Lee organized the group under the name the United Society of Believers in Christ's Second Appearing (USBCSA) or "Shakers" for short. Early Shaker meetings were notoriously fervent, often producing extraordinary bodily shakings, tongues, interpretations, as well as all other spiritual gifts. Men and women shared equally in leadership and women often preached and received revelations as the Spirit fell on them. Unfortunately, as their meetings began to grow throughout the Manchester area, many members were persecuted, mobbed, or stoned. Lee herself was also frequently imprisoned during this time for her displays of "blasphemy" such as dancing and shouting on the Sabbath. Also during this time, numerous miracles, healings, and miraculous escapes from death were accredited to Mother Ann. Once she even spoke in tongues for four hours to a group of clergyman who had been called in to examine her.

THE SHAKERS IN AMERICA

After receiving another revelation in 1774, Mother Ann felt led to bring a select group of family members and followers to America. Settling in Watervliet, near Albany, New York, Mother Ann embarked on a series of missionary journeys that soon resulted in the establishment of a string of Shaker communities throughout New York and New England. By 1779, the Shakers were in full revival mode, which drew considerable attention both for and against. While many were drawn by the reports of all the gifts of the Spirit being in operation like at Pentecost, others came with violent mobs to oppose the young movement. Nevertheless, an increasing number were convinced "there must be something of God there, else Satan would not bark so."[40] Samuel Johnson, a Presbyterian minister and graduate of Yale who participated in the revival, became convinced the gifts of the Spirit were genuine and a sure sign of the restoration of the church long promised in Scripture. Another first-time visitor recalled witnessing "several young people present who had already confessed their sins, and had received the power of God, which was manifested in various and marvellous operations, in signs and visions, in speaking with tongues and prophesyings."[41] Though many converts experienced tongues as part of the initial sign of the operation of the Spirit, they soon became a part of their normal Christian experience. Around Christmas, the Shakers held special "Quick Meetings" called "Shaker Highs" in which the faithful professed to receive "all the divine gifts given to the apostles on the day of Pentecost."[42]

The Shakers' firm belief in the end times restoration of all spiritual gifts was well documented by this testimony of 64-year-old Noah Wheaten—a member of the first Shaker community of New Lebanon, New York, in 1780:

Being employed in clearing land, about forty or fifty rods from his own house, and being thirsty, he left his work to go to a spring on the opposite side of a fence, which was very high, in jumping off, by a mis-step, dislocated his ancle outwardly, and split or broke the outer

---

40   Abijah Worster, "Testimony of Abijah Worster," *Testimonies Concerning the Character and Ministry of Mother Ann Lee*, ed. S.Y. Wells (Albany, N.Y., 1827), 138: CM 82.

41   Jethro Turner, "Testimony of Jethro Turner," Ibid., 80: Ibid.

42   William Haskett, *Shakerism Unmasked* (Pittsfield, Mass., 1828), 189: CM 83.

bone of his leg, just above the ancle joint. . . . That his ancle began to swell, and the pain increased, yet there he continued, tumbling and rolling about, for the space of two or three hours, in great distress of mind as well as pain of body. That at length he crawled home on his hands and knees, and although under extreme mortification of spirit for his misfortune, yet he was full of faith and confidence in the gift of miracles, which he had before strongly testified to his unbelieving neighbors . . . At length, as his family, consisting of ten in number, were assembled at their evening worship, in the room where he was then sitting upon a chest, the power of God came suddenly upon him, and he was instantly hurled from his seat, and set upon his feet, and whirled swiftly round, like a top, for the space of two hours, without the least pain or inconvenience. That he then retired to rest, well and comfortable, and the next morning arose in health, took his team and went plowing.[43]

Unfortunately, Mother Ann grew increasingly frail from her many persecutions and hardships and died in 1784 at the age of forty-eight. In one of Lee's visions for America, she said, "I saw a large tree, every leaf of which shone with such brightness as made it appear like a burning torch, representing the Church of Christ, which will yet be established in this land."[44]

---

43   Benjamin S. Youngs, *Testimony of Christ's Second Appearing, Exemplified by the Principles and Practices of the True Church of Christ*, 4th ed. (Albany, NY: Van Benthuysen, 1856) 415–417: CP 175–76.

44   Frederick William Evans, *Shakers: Compendium of the Origin, History, Principles, Rules and Regulations, Government, and Doctrines of the United Society of Believers in Christ's Second Appearing : with Biographies of Ann Lee, William Lee, Jas. Whittaker, J. Hocknell, J. Meacham, and Lucy Wright* (Appleton; 1859) 23–24, 138–44; William J. Haskett, *Shakerism Unmasked, Or The History of the Shakers . . .* (author, E.H. Walkley, printer; 1828) 25–34: "Shakers," *Wikipedia: en.wikipedia.org/wiki/Shakers* (Accessed 12 September 2014).

NINETEENTH-CENTURY SHAKERS

After Mother Ann died and much of the movement's initial enthusiasm waned, Joseph Meachan (1742–1796) and later Mother Lucy Wright (1760–1821) became the new Shaker leaders. Meacham introduced a more stringent code, asking members to sign written covenants pledging themselves to the four highest Shaker virtues of virgin purity, communalism, confession of sin, and separation from the world. Though Shakers never actually forbade marriage, Shaker sympathizers who preferred to remain with their families were forced to live in "non-communal orders" as less-committed believers living less-than-perfect lives. Many children were also added to the community through conversion, adoption, or the occasional child being left on a doorstep. All were welcomed, well cared for, and well educated. Once children reached the age of twenty-one, they were given the option to remain Shakers. Less than 25 percent chose to remain. Thus, one of the greatest living legacies of Shakers is the thousands of descendants of Shaker-raised seceders. Introduced during this time was a more orderly form of worship that included new hymns and choreographed marches and dances complete with symbolic gestures. Nineteenth-century Shakers often marched, danced, jerked, twitched, and shouted to "shake off sin," "trample evil underfoot," or rid themselves of sexual desires.

Following Mother Ann's missionary tradition during America's First Great Awakening, Mother Lucy Wright extended Shaker influence westward into Kentucky, Ohio, and Indiana by participating in the frontier camp meetings of America's Second Great Awakening in the early 1800s. Shaker revival meetings during this time were described as "trembling, weeping and swooning away, till every appearance of life was gone, and . . . more than a thousand persons fell to the ground apparently without sense or motion. . . . Towards the close of this commotion, about the year 1803, convulsions became prevalent. Men and women fell in such numbers that it became impossible for the multitude to move about without trampling them, and they were hurried to the meeting house. At no time was the floor less than half covered."[45]

THE ERA OF MANIFESTATIONS

The Shaker's "golden age," also known as the "Era of Manifestations" or "Mother Ann's work," did not occur until later in the century. Beginning in Watervliet in 1837, this age of revivalism was marked by visions and ecstatic utterances expressed through song, dance, and drawings and spread rapidly through Shaker society, lasting until the mid-1850s. According to Shaker tradition, angels or heavenly spirits were believed to have come to earth during this time, bringing with them visions that were often given to younger Shaker women who danced, whirled, spoke in tongues, and then interpreted these visions through their drawings and dances. Children often told of visits to other cities in the spirit realm or brought back messages from Mother Ann to the community. Others simply spoke in tongues. In fact, many of the lyrics used in Shaker tunes produced during this time contained words and syllables from unknown tongues.[46] At one point,

45 Ronald Knox, *Enthusiasm* (New York, NY: Oxford University, 1961), 535: Lee A. Howard *Manifestations Throughout Church History: Examining the Physical Evidence of Revival* (April 15, 2012), Kindle Edition. Kindle Locations 311–314 [hereafter MCH].

46 "The Shakers," Shaker Historic Trail, *National Park Service: www.nps.gov/ nr/ travel/ shaker/ shakers.htm*: "Shakers," *Wikipedia: en.wikipedia.org/ wiki/ Shakers* (Accessed 12 September 2014).

they even had to bar the public from the meetings because of the unprecedented spiritual messages being received. Sacred places were also set aside in each community for special "mountain meetings" or feasts to be held in the spring and fall. Also during this time, Shaker furniture, architecture, arts, crafts, music, dance, and inventions were recognized as "spirit gifts" and popularized for their simplistic design. To this day, many Shaker folk traditions are considered an important part of America's cultural heritage.

Shaker dance and worship at the meeting hall in New Lebanon, New York, during the Era of Manifestations, engraving (c. 1830). Shakers believed in marching and dancing to "shake off sin," "trample evil underfoot," and rid themselves of sexual desires. Source: Library of Congress Prints and Photographs Division.

Though the Era of Manifestations was embraced by many younger Shakers, in time many of the older members grew increasingly disenchanted, and the Era of Manifestations ended. Later some Shaker communities even expressed embarrassment over what they considered to be the "emotional excesses and mystical expressions" of the period. Though the movement grew to about 6,000 members at its peak, turnover after the Civil War was high as handmade Shaker products could no longer compete with the mass-produced products of an industrialized economy and the temptations of the world became too great, forcing many Shakers to leave and move to the larger cities and suburbs. In the twentieth century, the Shaker communities continued to lose members, mostly through attrition (believers had no offspring). By 2017, the last remaining active community—the Sabbathday Lake Shaker Village of Maine—had two members, while most of the other settlements had been converted into village museums.

THE MORAVIANS

One expression of eighteenth-century Pietism came in the form of a revival among the Bohemian Brethren or *Unitas Fratrum* (United Brethren), also known as the Moravian Church, founded by Jan Hus in the fifteenth century. Though the Moravian Church flourished during the Reformation, severe persecution resumed during the Thirty Years' War, and by 1722, one battered group of Moravian refugees decided to flee Bohemia in search of safe haven. They found such a place in Saxony, Germany, on the estate of Pietist Count Nicolaus Ludwig von Zinzendorf (1700–1760). Zinzendorf had come from a long line of Austrian nobles. His grandfather was a Lutheran Pietist who had relocated to Germany to avoid forced conversion to Catholicism in Austria. Zinzendorf's grandmother helped raise him after his father died and his mother remarried. Both were influential in his life. Zinzendorf's own spiritual and social reform ideas were far ahead of his time. He believed strongly in "religion of the heart"—the idea that one's religion should include one's emotions as well as one's intellect. Indeed, he and a childhood friend had once set out to create their own revival of "True Christianity" by printing large quantities of inexpensive Bibles, books, catechisms, hymnals, and gospel tracts. Zinzendorf felt that true Christianity could best be promoted by free associations of Christians with no connections to the state and that churches should reach out to all peoples of all classes while working ecumenically in unity with one another. Being personally committed to helping the poor and needy, and having no idea that this would become his grand opportunity to put his reform ideas into practice, Zinzendorf agreed to let the Moravians settle on his lands.

The Moravians named their new home Herrnhut, meaning "under the Lord's watchful care," but almost immediately, the village became known as a place of refuge and freedom for *all* persecuted groups. By 1727, major disagreements had emerged among the various factions, dividing the community. Zinzendorf was now forced to take indefinite leave from his court commission in Dresden to move back to his estate and devote himself full time to resolving the conflict. He called the men of the village together for intense prayer and study of the Scriptures to determine the proper and biblical model for living together in Christian community. The result was the *Brüderlicher Vertrag* (*Brotherly Agreement*) signed by all members of the community on May 12, 1727.

Now acting as their new charismatic leader and realizing that people had different spiritual needs and different relationships with their Savior at different stages of life, Zinzendorf organized the village into a church body made up of small communal groups called *banden* or "choirs," based on age, marital status, and gender. He called the body of believers the "Church of God in the Spirit." A radical equality of spiritual and social life was achieved in which nobles and commoners—men, women, and children of all ages—could equally serve Christ. Zinzendorf had studied the history of the Bohemians and was amazed to find many similarities between their early practices and their newly established order at Herrnhut. However, instead of a new or separate denomination, he envisioned Herrnhut to be the spark that would ignite a renewal among all denominations. Using only the Word of God as his foundation, he appointed elders and pastors who encouraged each member to begin seeking God for a gracious outpouring of his Holy Spirit. Zinzendorf himself often led the meetings with fervent supplications and prayers that lasted well into the night, and a spirit of prayer that touched adults and children alike soon prevailed over the community. One group of young girls stayed up until 1:00 a.m. praying, singing, and weeping.

THE MORAVIAN REVIVAL

On August 13, 1727, the Moravians' prayers were answered as one of the pastors leading a meeting suddenly felt the presence of the Lord and fell to the floor. Then the entire congregation, overwhelmed by the Spirit and presence of the Lord, sank to the floor with him. The service continued until midnight with prayer, singing, weeping, and supplication.[47] One Moravian historian wrote, "They hardly knew whether they belonged to heaven or earth."[48] Zinzendorf said it was "a day of the outpourings of the Holy Spirit . . . ; it was our Pentecost."[49] He wrote, "A sense of the nearness of Christ bestowed in a single moment upon all the members that were present and it was so unanimous that

---

47 John Greenfield, *When the Spirit Came* (Minneapolis: Bethany House, 1967), 24: CC 95.

48 Ibid., 11.

49 Dr. A.K. Curtis, *A Golden Summer*, Zinzendorf Jubilee, Comenius Foundation. This article first appeared in *Glimpses of Christian History*, "Glimpses 37: Zinzendorf," from the Christian History Institute: Roberts Liardon, *God's Generals: The Revivalists* (New Kensington, Pa.: Whitaker, 2008), 17 [hereafter GGR].

two members, at work twenty miles away, unaware that the meeting was being held, became at the same time deeply conscious of the same blessing."[50] As word continued to spread throughout the region, many flocked to Herrnhut to join the new movement. It was also during this time that miraculous healings and other spiritual gifts began to manifest in their midst. Women and children were also being filled with the Spirit, speaking in tongues, and prophesying. One critic accused the Moravians in England of reviving the Montanist practice of "strange convulsive heavings, and unnatural postures," saying "they commonly broke into some disconnected jargon, which they often passed upon the vulgar 'as the exuberant and resistless evacuations of the Spirit.'"[51]

Another observer wrote, "At this juncture, various supernatural gifts were manifested in the church, and miraculous cures were wrought. The Brethren and the Sisters believed, in childlike spirit, what the Savior had said respecting the efficacy of prayer; and when any object strongly interested them, they used to speak to Him about it, and to trust in Him as capable of all good: then it was done unto them according to their faith."[52] Another wrote, "The miraculous aids and manifestations related in the records of the Brethren are so numerous, that, in coming to detail them, one might hesitate where to begin."[53] Zinzendorf confirmed, "To believe against hope is the root of

50 Greenfield, *When the Spirit Came*, 12: CC 95–96.

51 J. Roche, *Moravian Heresy* . . . (Dublin: printed by the author, 1751), 44, Stanley Burgess, "Medieval and Modern Western Churches," Gary B. McGee, ed., *Initial Evidence: Historical and Biblical Perspectives on the Pentecostal Doctrine of Spirit Baptism* (Eugene, Oregon: Wipf & Stock, 1991), 32 [hereafter IE].

52 Rev. A. Bost, *History of the Church of the Brethren*; Boys, *Suppressed Evidence*, 258–303: MM 173.

53 Ibid.

the gift of miracles; and I owe this testimony to our beloved Church, that Apostolic powers are there manifested. We have had undeniable proofs thereof in the unequivocal discovery of things, persons and circumstances which could not humanly have been discovered, in the healing of maladies in themselves incurable, such as cancers, consumptions [tuberculosis], when the patient was in the agonies of death, all by means of prayer, or of a single word."[54]

THE MORAVIAN MISSIONARIES

As part of the revival, a group of twenty-four men and twenty-four women agreed to take turns praying for one hour round-the-clock. Others soon joined in as the group grew to seventy-seven intercessors. The children organized a similar plan. This continued for a decade, and the first large-scale Protestant missionary force in history ensued. Through intercessory prayer, the Moravians developed a burning desire to make Christ known among the poorest and most despised people groups of the world. Zinzendorf's own interest was sparked after encountering two children converted by a missionary in Greenland and a Danish freed slave who told of the oppression among the slaves in the West Indies. In 1732, the first Moravian missionaries left Herrnhut en route to St. Thomas in the Caribbean. Another soon followed to Greenland. Others went among the indigenous peoples of North and South America, coastal Africa, Asia, and other parts of Europe. On one such journey, bound for the English colony of Georgia, a group of Moravian missionaries met a young minister by the name of John Wesley.

---

54   Gordon, *The Ministry of Healing*, 67: CC 96.

Moravians kneeling prostrate on the floor; men below; women atop; Lamb of God above all. The banner speaks of the bloody wounds Christ felt for us all. The Moravians' 24-hour/100-year prayer-watch ignited worldwide missions, the Wesleyan-Methodist revivals in England, and America's First Great Awakening. Source: Christliches Gesangbuch der evangelischen Brüder Gemeinen 1735, ed. 4 (1741). Photo: Wikimedia/Wst.

So widespread and profound was this Moravian missionary force that one historian declared, "This small church in twenty years called into being more missions than the whole evangelical church has done in two centuries."[55] In all, they launched 232 missions, establishing more than 30 international settlements based on the Herrnhut model of prayer, worship, and simplistic communal living. Two notable American settlements still in existence today are Bethlehem, Pennsylvania, cofounded by Zinzendorf on Christmas Eve, 1741, and Old Salem in Winston-Salem, North Carolina. Zinzendorf, who had no qualms about mixing with other classes, races, or religions, became one of the first European nobles to set foot on American soil, often meeting with Native Americans, settlers, colonists, commoners, and leaders alike. Indeed, in 1742, in respect for other religious groups that held that Saturday was the Sabbath as well as those who believed Sunday was the Lord's Day, Zinzendorf advocated the first practice of a two-day weekend in America.

---

55   John Greenfield, *When the Spirit Came* (Minneapolis, MN: Bethany, 1967), 15: CC 97.

Eighteenth-century painting of Count Zinzendorf preaching to people from many nations. In addition to being the oldest Protestant denomination, the Moravian Church was the first Protestant church body to begin missionary work, first to send lay missionaries, first to minister to slaves, and first Protestant presence in many countries as they sent hundreds of missionaries to the Caribbean, the Americas, the Arctic, Africa, and the Far East. Source: Wikimedia/Paul Barlow.

Today nearly a million Moravians survive worldwide, and nearly half of them live in East Africa. The Moravian revival became a model and fountainhead for all modern revivals. After researching, one historian was led to write, "We are, indeed, well aware, that, so far from its being possible to prove by Scriptures, or by experience, that visions and dreams, the gift of miracles, healings, and other extraordinary gifts, have absolutely ceased in Christendom since the Apostolic times, it is on the contrary proved, both by facts and by Scripture, that there may always be these gifts where there is faith, and that they will never be entirely detached from it. We need only take care to discern the true from the false, and to distinguish from miracles proceeding from the Holy Ghost, lying miracles, or those which, without being so decidedly of the devil, do not so decidedly indicate the presence of this Spirit of the Lord."[56]

JOHN WESLEY

The England in which John Wesley (1703–1791) was born was fully in need of revival. Living conditions were harsh. Humanism and secularism were taking their toll. Infidelity and moral decay were on the rise. The infant mortality rate was high because of killer diseases

---

56   Bost, *Church of the Brethren*: MM 172.

such as smallpox, dysentery, consumption, and typhus. Adding to that a shortage of food, inadequate housing conditions, a general disregard for hygiene, and the excessive drinking of cheap gin created a recipe for societal ruin. Parents often abandoned or sold their children just to feed their addictions, and, despite the high mortality rate, many lived in crowded, cramped living quarters. Seventy-five percent of children never made it past their fifth birthday. John Wesley was one of nineteen born to Samuel and Susanna Wesley of Epworth, England. Wesley's mother, Susanna, was twenty-fifth out of twenty-five. John was fifteenth with only six surviving siblings at the time of his birth. Actually, he was named "John Benjamin" after two previously deceased brothers. John was born into a long line of Anglican ministers. His father had been a Puritan Dissenter who eventually made peace with the Anglican Church, becoming rector of its Epworth parish in 1697. Susanna, also from a family of nonconformists, was brilliant and well versed in Hebrew, Greek, and Latin. She taught her children history, language, literature, music, and the Scriptures. In typical Puritan fashion, every moment from dawn to dusk was structured in prayer, Bible reading, and other personal disciplines.

A FIREBRAND FOR GOD

One night as the Wesley household slept, the Epworth parsonage was mysteriously set on fire. Samuel and Susanna quickly gathered the children and hurried outside. Once outside, everyone was accounted for except five-year-old John, who was still sleeping upstairs. As his father made several failed attempts to reenter the house, the rest of the family prayed outside when John suddenly awoke to a flickering light. Leaping from his bed, John ran to a second-story window where a neighbor spotted him. The neighbor hastily climbed up on another man's shoulders and pulled John from the inferno—moments before the roof collapsed. After being reunited with his family, Samuel looked at his son and quoting from Zechariah 3:2 said, "Is this not a brand plucked from the fire?"[57] From that moment, Susanna knew John had a special call on his life, but no one knew just how prophetic those words would become.

"The Rescue of the young John Wesley from the burning parsonage at Epworth, Lincolnshire" by Henry Perlee Parker (1840). Mezzotint by S.W. Reynolds. After the rescue, his father Samuel spoke these prophetic words over his life from Zechariah 3:2: "Is this not a brand plucked from the fire?" Source: wellcomeimages.org. Photo: Wikimedia/Hazhk.

THE HOLY CLUB

Graduating from Oxford University in 1727 with the highest degree possible, John was ordained an Anglican minister at twenty-five. While at Oxford, he was exposed to the writings of some of Christianity's greatest theologians, past and present. Though John would begin preaching during this time, the fact that he saw no fruit from his labors would lead to a time of intense inner turmoil. After returning to Oxford in 1729, he found that his brother Charles and George Whitefield had started a new club to combat the spread of deism at the university. John soon joined the club, becoming its leader. The "Holy Club," as they were called, met every evening from six to

---

57   Robert Southey, *The Life of Wesley and the Rise and Progress of Methodism* (London: Frederick Warne, n.d., c. 1820), 11: GGR 29.

nine for prayer and Bible study, fasted every Wednesday and Friday, received Communion weekly, took food to the poor, and visited prisoners and orphans. This attracted both attention and derision as many other titles were soon assigned to their little club, including Sacramentarians, Bible Moths, Reforming Club, Enthusiasts, and Methodists. The latter stuck. However, it seemed no matter how hard John worked, studied, and prayed, he still lacked the inner peace his heart longed for.

WESLEY IN AMERICA

In 1735, the Wesley brothers were invited to Savannah, Georgia, to become ministers of a newly formed Anglican parish there. Perhaps his answers lay overseas. The Wesleys boarded the good ship *Simmonds* bound for Savannah and sailed right into a series of violent storms. As the waves came crashing up over the bow of the ship, even breaking the main mast at one point, John feared for his life. He had preached salvation to others, but he himself was afraid to die—and he was ashamed. But after hearing the testimonies of some of the Moravian missionaries on board and seeing the faith of their women and children who calmly sang psalms without fear, he became greatly encouraged in his own faith and began ministering to his fellow Englishmen, many of whom were still crying and trembling. He recorded in his *Journal*, "This was the most glorious day which I have hitherto seen."[58]

---

58 John Wesley, *Journal of John Wesley*, Sunday, January 25, 1736: "The Moravians and John Wesley," Posted 01/01/1982, *Christianity Today/Christian History Magazine: www.christianitytoday.com/ch/1982/issue1/128.html* (Accessed 15 September 2014).

When they finally landed in Savannah in 1736, John sought the advice of a Moravian pastor who, in turn, inquired about his own faith: "Does the Spirit of God witness with your spirit that you are a child of God?" John did not know how to answer him. "Do you know Jesus Christ?" the man persisted. "I know he is the Savior of the world," John replied. "True, but do you know he has saved you?" the man directed. John finally answered, "I do," but later recorded in his *Journal*, "I fear they were vain words."[59] One Wesley biographer wrote, "The conversation was worth the journey across the ocean."[60] Wesley did not last long in America, however—barely two years. In his view, the indigenous peoples were "liars, drunkards, gluttons, thieves, adulterers, and murderers"—and the colonists were not much better![61] The feeling was mutual. The colonists resented Wesley's rigid high church ways. To make matters worse, John had fallen in love with the eighteen-year-old niece of Savannah's chief magistrate, but when he tried to break off the relationship, accusations followed by a series of mistrials ensued. Now, spiritually and emotionally drained, John was ready to return home. He wrote, "I went to America to convert the Indians, but, oh, who shall convert me?"

ALDERSGATE

Upon returning to England in 1738, John's brother Charles had an assurance experience on Pentecost Sunday. Three days later, John was

---

59 Ibid., 87.

60 Ibid.

61 *The Works of the Rev. John Wesley, Vol. 8: With the Last Corrections of the Author* (London: Wesleyan Conference Office, 1872), 190, *Google Books: books.google.com/books/about/Works.html?id=F4QrAAAAYAAJ*.

attending a Moravian Society meeting on Aldersgate Street in London where Luther's *Preface to the Epistle to the Romans* was being read. John journaled, "About a quarter before nine, while he was describing the change which God works in the heart through faith in Christ, I felt my heart strangely warmed. I felt I did trust in Christ, Christ alone for my salvation and an assurance was given me that He had taken away my sin, even mine, and saved me from the law of sin and death."[62]

From that moment on, John would never stop preaching on the importance of having faith for salvation and the witness of God's Spirit. At last, the answer he had been seeking all his life would become the basis for both his personal life and public ministry. But it seemed the more he preached on salvation by faith alone, the less he was welcomed in the Anglican churches, so instead, John began speaking to the growing group of Oxford "Methodists" who were now meeting in capacity-filled rooms.

WESLEY AT HERRNHUT

Since John was no longer welcomed in his own church, he began frequenting the Moravian Society on Fetter Lane in London. The Moravians had made an enormous impression on him in America. Perhaps it was time to take a closer look at them, and what better place to look than at Herrnhut where it all began? John arrived at Herrnhut in 1738 amid the Moravian's decade-long prayer service but stayed only a couple of weeks. He found many of their customs to be a bit strange for his tastes and expressed concern over Zinzendorf's

---

62 Wesley, *Journal of John Wesley*, May 24, 1738, *Christian Classics Ethereal Library:* *www.ccel.org/ccel/wesley/journal.vi.ii.xvi.html*: GGR 53.

almost cult-like followership. "Is not the Count all in all?" he quipped.[63] Though he greatly admired the Moravians and, indeed, owed his very faith and message to them, he felt God was calling him on to something else. John wrote, "I would gladly have spent my life here; but my Master calling me to labor in another part of His vineyard, I was constrained to take my leave of this happy place."[64]

THE METHODIST REVIVAL

When John returned from Herrnhut, he was stricken by the news of the recent mass conversions at Jonathan Edwards' church in Northampton, Massachusetts, but had no idea he would soon be caught up in a similar movement of God in England. On New Year's Eve 1738, the Wesley brothers, once again joined by George Whitefield, who had recently returned from his own missionary work in Savannah, and others, held a love feast at the Moravian Society on Fetter Lane. As midnight struck, they began to pray and worship, continuing into the wee hours of the morning. John recorded, "At about three in the morning, as we were continuing instant in prayer, the power of God came mightily upon us, insomuch that many cried out for exceeding joy, and many fell to the ground. As soon as we were recovered a little from that awe and amazement at the presence of his Majesty, we broke out with one voice: 'We praise thee, O God, we acknowledge thee to be the Lord.'"[65] Suddenly, the same events that had taken place among the Moravians in Germany, and more recently among the

---

63 Tomkins, Stephen *John Wesley: A Biography*, (Grand Rapids, Mich.: Eerdmans, 2003): CH 336

64 Southey, *Life of Wesley*, 113: GGR 58.

65 Curnack, ed., *The Journal of the Rev. John Wesley A.M., vol. 2*, 122–125: CC 102.

colonists in New England, were taking place in London. Whitefield confirmed, "It was a Pentecost season indeed; sometimes whole nights were spent in prayer. Often have we been filled as with new wine; and often have I seen them overwhelmed with the Divine Presence."[66] Their critics, however, believed they had fallen prey to a wrong spirit, and more and more churches closed their doors. But Whitefield had a better idea. Once when a crowd was being turned away because the building was too full, he stood outside on a tombstone and addressed the hundreds who had gathered outside.

Whitefield immediately took to the open fields, preaching to the coal miners and shipyard workers of Bristol who seldom ever went to church. The result was so intense, Wesley said, you could see the "white gutters" of tears streaming down the blackened cheeks of the coal miners. Thoroughly inspired, Wesley preached his first open-air meeting the next day. He preached from Luke 4: "The Spirit of the Lord God is upon me." After the meeting, John was so ecstatic he decided he would spend the rest of his life preaching from anywhere he could—barns, fields, churches, town squares, or tombstones. Before Bristol, he had considered "the saving of souls almost a sin if it had not been done in a church."[67] After Bristol, he wrote, "I look upon all the world as my parish."[68] Suddenly John found himself preaching to crowds of several thousands, and the conversions were as real as those he had read about in New England. The Wesleyan Methodist revival

---

66 Southey, *Life of Wesley*:123: GGR 59.

67 Stephen Tomkins, *John Wesley: A Biography* (Grand Rapids, Mich.: Eerdmans, 2003), 69: CH 337.

68 Wesley, *Journal of John Wesley*: *Christian Classics Ethereal Library*: *www.ccel.org/ccel/wesley/journal.vi.iii.v.html* (Accessed 5 February 2013).

had begun. One historian wrote, "The effects on Wesley were equally remarkable. Up to this point he was filled with anxiety, insecurity, and futility. After Bristol he was a firebrand for God."[69] Wesley himself wrote, "So many living witnesses hath God given that his hand is still 'stretched out to heal,' and that signs and wonders are even now wrought by his holy child Jesus."[70]

John Wesley preaching outside a church. Wherever Wesley and his circuit preachers went, multitudes gathered and were converted as the Spirit confirmed the Word with signs following. Reports of healings, miracles, people falling, trembling, roaring, crying, shouting and laughing often accompanied their preaching. Source: Shawn Harrison/six11.wordpress.com.

Believing they were not all from God, Whitefield took issue with some of the manifestations such as people falling and going into "convulsions." He personally confronted Wesley one day for encouraging such. The next day, however, four people dropped to the floor while Whitefield was preaching. Wesley recorded, "One of them lay without sense or motion. A second trembled exceedingly. The third had strong convulsions all over his body, but made no noise, unless by groans. The fourth, equally convulsed, called upon God, with strong cries and tears. From this time, I trust we shall all suffer God to carry on his own work in the way that pleaseth him."[71]

---

69 CH 337.

70 Wesley, *Journal of John Wesley*, April 17, 1739: MM 201.

71 Ibid., July 7, 1739: MCH 276–280.

PARTING WAYS

Now that the Wesleys were experiencing a revival of their own, both John and the Moravians felt it was time to part ways. Though his brother Charles would maintain relations with the Moravians throughout his life, the Moravians felt John was falling into heresy by teaching that, in addition to faith, one had to pray, study, and do good works. On the other hand, John believed the Moravians were falling into heresy by teaching Quietism—belief that one could quietly wait for salvation while the intellect remained passive and still. Therefore, John officially parted with the Moravian Society in 1740, forming his own separate society. He wrote, "Thus, without any previous plan or design, began the Methodist Society in England."[72]

Meanwhile, another rift continued to develop between Wesley and Whitefield. John had recently delivered a message stating that the grace of God was "free for all"—an Arminian theology originating with Protestant theologian Jacobus Arminius (1560–1609) that stood in stark contrast with the Calvinist predestination teachings to which Whitefield ascribed. So they agreed to disagree. Whitefield returned to America, and then there were three revivals—the Wesleys in England, Whitefield in America, and the Moravians around the globe—all due in part to a decade-long prayer meeting.

METHODIST MIRACLES

John continued traveling throughout England on horseback, preaching in open-air meetings, as Charles composed hymns based

---

72 John Emory, *The Works of the Reverend John Wesley*, Vol. 3 (New York: 1831), 493: *Google Books: books.google.com/books?id=c3k9AAAAYAAJ* (Accessed 6 February 2013).

on John's sermons. John's gift touched people through his sermons, and Charles's gift touched people through his hymns. Wherever they went, people gathered by the thousands, multitudes were converted, and the Spirit confirmed the Word with healings, deliverances, and unusual manifestations such as falling, trembling, roaring, crying, and laughing. John wrote about one such meeting at Newgate when "immediately one, and another, and another sank to the earth. They dropped on every side as if thunderstruck. All Newgate rang with the cries of those whom the word of God cut to the heart."[73]

He wrote of another occasion when he and Charles were taking a walk in a meadow intending to sing psalms of praise to God, but as soon as they started singing, they broke out into holy laughter. Before long, the two were laughing uncontrollably. He also recorded miracles that he himself experienced: "In the evening, beside the pain in my back and head, and the fever which still continued upon me, just as I began to pray I was seized with such a cough that I could hardly speak. At the same time came strongly to my mind, 'These signs shall follow them that believe.' I called aloud on Jesus to increase my faith and to confirm the word of His grace. While I was speaking, my pain vanished away, the fever left me, my bodily strength returned and for many weeks I felt neither weakness nor pain. Unto thee, O Lord, do I give thanks."[74]

Wesley was labeled an "enthusiast" by his contemporaries, who often accused him of stirring religious excitement and claiming extraordinary spiritual powers or revelations. But Wesley simply

---

73 Curnack, *Journal*, 184–185: CC 102.
74 Wesley, *The Works of John Wesley*, vol. 8, 458–459: CC 103.

countered that he was following Scripture and the early church concerning spiritual gifts, which he believed was normative for all ages. Once, when accused of practicing miraculous cures, John replied, "As it can be proved by abundance of witnesses that these cures were frequently (indeed almost always) the instantaneous consequences of prayer, your inference is just. I cannot, dare not, affirm that they were purely natural. I believe they were not. I believe many of them were wrought by the supernatural power of God. . . . Yet I do not know that God hath anyway precluded himself from thus exerting his sovereign power, from working miracles in any kind or degree, in any age, to the end of the world. I do not recollect any Scripture wherein we are taught that miracles were to be confined with the limits either of the apostolic age, or the Cyprian age, or of any period of time, longer or shorter, even till the restitution of all things."[75]

Such activities were not limited to Wesley's meetings, however. The early Methodists were accused of "laying claim to almost every apostolic gift, in a full and ample manner, as they were possessed of old."[76] Wesley wrote of other Methodist revivals, such as at the Anglican parish of John Berridge in Everton: "This occasioned a mixture of various sounds; some shrieking, some roaring aloud. The most general was a loud breathing, like that of people half strangled and gasping for life. Great numbers wept without any noise; others fell down dead; some sinking in silence; some with extreme noise and violent agitation."[77] He wrote of another woman who "fell trembling

---

75 Ibid., 457, 465: CC 103–104.

76 William Warburton, Bishop of Gloucester, *The doctrine of grace, or, the office and operations of the Holy Spirit vindicated from the insults of infidelity and the abuses of fanaticism* (1762): Richard Green, *The Works of John and Charles Wesley: A Bibliography* (London: C. H. Kelly, 1869), 123.

77 Ibid., vol. 2, 483: CC 104.

to the ground. She then cried aloud, though not articulately, her words being swallowed up."[78] A friend and colleague of Wesley told of his own experience: "The influence of His Spirit wrought so powerfully upon me that my joy was beyond expression. This morning the Lord gave me a language I knew not of, raising my soul to Him in a wonderful manner."[79] And to an objecting Dr. Middleton, Wesley wrote, "He who worketh as He will, may, with your good leave, give the gift of tongues where He gives no other; and may see abundant reasons to do so, whether you and I see them or not."[80]

The Methodists soon gained a reputation for being loud and boisterous, earning them the title "shouting Methodists." Often their cries would interrupt the preaching, making their meetings appear to outsiders to be chaotic and unruly. However, to insiders, such outbursts were considered acts of worship that displaced Satan from their camp. Some Methodists in Wales in the 1760s were called "Jumpers" because after the preaching of the Word, they would often break out into song and dance, rejoicing and jumping for joy for hours on end. According to one of Wesley's colleagues, Wesley himself encouraged such manifestations: "At first, no one knew what to say, but it was soon called the pangs of the new birth, the work of the Holy Ghost, casting out the old man, etc., but some were offended and left the Societies entirely when they saw Mr. Wesley encourage it. I often

---

78 Ibid., vol. 8, 213: CC 104.

79 William R. Davies, *Spirit Baptism and Spiritual Gifts in Early Methodism* (Jacksonville, Fla.: Cross Fire Ministries, 1974), 12: CC 104.

80 *Wesley's letter to Middleton,* in Robert G. Tuttle, Jr., "John Wesley and the Gifts of the Holy Spirit," *adapted from a series that first appeared in Catalyst published by A Foundation for Theological Education: The UnOfficial Confessing Movement: ucmpage.org/ articles/ rtuttle1.html* (Accessed 8 February 2013).

doubted it was not of the enemy when I saw it and disputed with Mr. Wesley for calling it the work of God. . . . Frequently when none were agitated in the meetings, he prayed, 'Lord! where are thy tokens and signs,' and I don't remember ever to have seen it otherwise than that on his so praying several were seized and screamed out."[81]

METHODIST SOCIETIES

The Wesleys eventually established hundreds of societies throughout England, and their converts became so plentiful John soon had to ordain lay preachers to help teach and minister to these new societies. These were ordinary, uneducated men who had knowledge of the Bible and had proven themselves fit for ministry. John wrote, "Give me one hundred preachers who fear nothing but sin and desire nothing but God, and I care not a straw whether they be clergy or laymen, such alone will shake the gates of hell and set up the Kingdom of Heaven upon earth."[82] John was able to organize these Methodist Societies into classes and bands (which he learned from the Moravians) as well as circuits and districts complete with class leaders, delegates, officers, teachers, and traveling "circuit preachers." Much like John Calvin, in addition to being a gifted preacher, John Wesley was a gifted organizer.

---

81   Arnold A. Dallimore, *George Whitefield: The Life and Times of the Great Evangelist of the Eighteenth-Century Revival*, vol. 1 (Westchester, IL: Crossway, 1980), 326: MCH 257–262.

82   John Wesley, *The Letters of the Rev. John Wesley*, A.M., vol. 6, ed. John Telford (London: Epworth, 1931) p. 271, quoted in Darius L. Salter, *America's Bishop: The Life of Francis Asbury* (Nappanee, IN: Francis Asbury Press, 2003), 23: GGR 180.

METHODISTS WORLDWIDE

By 1768, a Methodist chapel had opened in New York, and by 1771, Wesley had commissioned Francis Asbury to oversee the new work in America. Following in Wesley's footsteps, Asbury became a circuit-riding preacher. In 1775, when America was on the brink of war, Wesley sent a letter exhorting the colonists to remain loyal to England, but the colonists did not take too kindly to the letter. In 1791, John wrote another letter to William Wilberforce, a member of the British Parliament who had dedicated his life to ending slavery, saying, "Go on, in the name of God and in the power of His might, till even American slavery (the vilest that ever saw the sun) shall vanish away before it."[83] Wesley remained strong until his death at eighty-seven. At eighty-six, he was still able to preach a hundred sermons in a nine-week circuit. According to his *Journal*, he had clocked over 250,000 miles on horseback—ten times the circumference of the earth. One hundred fifty years after that initial New Year's Day outpouring, the number of Methodists worldwide equaled the entire population of England in Wesley's day. Today there are nearly a million Methodists in England and over 70 million worldwide. Though the Wesley brothers never left the Church of England and considered Methodism to be an extension of Anglicanism, after their deaths, English Methodists followed their American brethren in separating from the Church of England.

---

83 *John Wesley to William Wilberforce*, 24 February 1791, John Wesley: Holiness of Heart and Life, General Board of Global Ministries, United Methodist Church: GGR 88.

THE SECOND WORK OF GRACE

Perhaps Wesley's most enduring legacy was his doctrine on the "second work of grace," which he considered to be subsequent to the new birth—a concept taught by Jesus and the apostles, the early church fathers, Madame Guyon, and many others. Wesley's "second work" doctrine also reflected the teachings of many of the Eastern spirituals including Clement of Alexandria, Macarius of Egypt, and the Cappadocian Fathers, whose teachings he studied at Oxford, eventually planting the seeds for the modern Methodist, Holiness, Pentecostal, and charismatic movements worldwide. For this reason, some historians have called Wesley "the father of the modern Pentecostal movement."[84]

Portrait of John Wesley by John Faber (c. 1730-1756). Known as "the father of the modern Pentecostal movement," Wesley's "second work of grace" doctrine planted the seeds for Methodism and the modern Holiness, Pentecostal, and charismatic movements worldwide. Source: Library of Congress Prints and Photographs Division.

Though Wesley defined his second work as "Christian perfection" or "entire sanctification," John William Fletcher, a French Huguenot, early Methodist theologian, friend, and Wesley's designated successor, preferred "baptism in the Holy Spirit" to Wesley's "sanctification," citing a clear distinction between the two. In Fletcher's letter to Charles Wesley in 1763, he wrote, "What I

---

84 Vinson Synan, *The Holiness-Pentecostal Tradition: Charismatic Movements in the Twentieth Century* (Grand Rapids, Mich.: Eerdmans, 1971), 13 [hereafter HPT]; CC 105.

want is the light and mighty power of the Spirit of God. As to my parish, we are just where we were; we look for our Pentecost, but we do not pray sufficiently to obtain it."[85] Many of the early Methodists shared Fletcher's persistent and increasing longing, including one Elizabeth Johnson, whose diary Wesley published: "Friday in the morning I rose with these words strongly and sweetly impressed on my mind, 'Insatiate to the spring I fly, I drink and still am ever dry.' O my dear Lord what angel tongue can speak thy praise, [I] burn with desire to praise thee; words I find fail, there is no language known among mortals to express it; a glimmering expectation I have to be ere long, where I shall have new language."[86] Fletcher's own wife, Mary, prayed to be filled with the Spirit "that [her] tongue, being touched with the fire of heavenly love, might be able to plead the cause of truth." She wrote, "An outpouring of [God's] Spirit will soon be given, and 'times of refreshing shall come from the presence of the Lord.' . . . We must look for the baptism with the Holy Ghost, I've tasted, but I want the fulness."[87] As for her husband, John, one Methodist historian wrote, "[Fletcher] lived and died in the assurance that this prevalence of the Spirit was limited in the world only because the faith of the Church regarding it was feeble, and that the glorious wonder of a Pentecostal Church would yet be seen among men."[88]

---

85 John Fletcher, vol. 2 of The Works of Rev. John Fletcher, 2 vols. (London: Printed for Thomas Allman), 538: CC 106.

86 John Wesley, An Account of Mrs. Elizabeth Johnson (Bristol, 1799), 48, 69: CM 80.

87 Henry Moore, ed., The Life of Mary Fletcher (New York, 1840), 270–324: CM 81.

88 Abel Stevens, A Compendious History of American Methodism, vol. 2 (out of print), 271–272.5: CC 106.

GREAT STIRRINGS IN AMERICA

By the 1670s, New England Puritan leaders began calling for a new outpouring of the Holy Spirit to revive their languishing churches. Samuel Torrey, pastor at Weymouth, Massachusetts, began raising doubts as to whether the churches' reform efforts were even possible without an effusion of the Holy Spirit and proactive prayer for revival. In 1705, Samuel Danforth Jr. wrote, "We are much encouraged by an unusual and amazing Impression, made by God's Spirit on all Sorts among us, especially on the young Men and Women." Danforth said he had no time for his regular pastoral duties because of constant visits from young people seeking salvation and believed it to be a sign of greater things to come. He said, "I think sometimes that the Time of the pouring out of the Spirit upon all Flesh, may be at the Door."[89] In 1713, Solomon Stoddard of Northampton, Massachusetts, grandfather of Jonathan Edwards, wrote, "The Spirit of the Lord must be poured out upon the People, else Religion will not revive."[90] He believed seasons of revival characterized by special outpourings of the Spirit were necessary to quicken believers' faith, convert sinners, and make disinterested people interested in the things of God. In 1721, Samuel Whiting's church in Windham (now Maine) saw eighty new people join the church in six months. Observing this, another minister wrote, "Pray that the Spirit may be poured out from on High on every

---

89   Jon Butler, "Enthusiasm Described and Decried: The Great Awakening as Interpretative Fiction," *Journal of American History 69*, no. 2 (Sept. 1982): 309, Thomas S. Kidd, *The Great Awakening: The Roots of Evangelical Christianity in Colonial America* (Yale University, 2007), 5 [hereafter GA].

90   Solomon Stoddard, *The efficacy of the fear of Hell, to restrain men from sin* (Boston, 1713), 34: GA 7.

part of the land."[91] Then in 1727, an earthquake rocked New England. Suddenly churches everywhere were being filled with anxious people seeking salvation as church leaders began wondering if this was not the nature of all revivals to happen suddenly and unexpectedly. Revival did ensue but not for long.

THE GREAT AWAKENING

Finally, in 1733, a revival broke out at Jonathan Edwards' church in Northampton. During one six-month period in 1734, nearly 300 new converts had joined his church. In 1735, he wrote, "The town seemed to be full of the presence of God. . . . There was scarcely a single person in the town, old or young, left unconcerned about the great things of the eternal world."[92] The revival featured many miraculous and ecstatic manifestations of the Holy Spirit, which some critics used to try to denounce the revival. This included outbreaks of laughter during the services; some experienced visions or "impressions," and others fell into trances or "faintings," as Edwards called them. He said, "There were some instances of persons lying in a sort of trance, remaining perhaps for twenty-four hours motionless, and with their senses locked up; but in the mean time under strong imaginations, as though they went to heaven and had there visions of glorious and delightful objects."[93] Edwards also wrote about a remarkable season of healing in which prayer requests for sick relatives, which had

---

91 Eliphalet Adams, *A Sermon Preached at Windham, July 12th, 1721* (New London, 1721), ii-vi, 39–40: GA 9.

92 Jonathan Edwards, "A Narrative of Surprising Conversions," *Jonathan Edwards on Revival* (Carlisle, PA: Banner of Truth, 1984), 13: CC 108.

93 Ibid., 154: Jonathan Edwards, "Revival of Religion in Northampton in 1740–1741": CC 111.

previously been common, ceased coming in for many weeks on end. Edwards mentioned thirty-two other communities in Connecticut and Massachusetts that were experiencing similar awakenings, saying. "In every place, God brought saving blessings with him, and His Word attended with His Spirit . . . returned not void."[94] About that same time, William Tennent, a Presbyterian minister, and Theodorus Frelinghuysen, a Dutch Reformed minister, were experiencing similar revivals in New Jersey. But they remained regional revivals until the father of modern mass evangelism landed on America's shores.

GEORGE WHITEFIELD

George Whitefield (1714–1770) grew up in Gloucester, England, where his parents were innkeepers. Whitefield discovered his love for theater as a child, often playing lead roles in school plays. By day, he served patrons at the family tavern, and by night, he memorized his lines, perfected his delivery, and read other plays. Often he would attend church just so he could go home and mimic the preaching to his sisters. Eventually desiring to become a preacher himself, Whitefield was able to get into Oxford for free as a servant to other students. There, he would meet the Wesley brothers, who would forever change his life. The Wesleys were the first to invite Whitefield to America, but by the time he arrived, the Wesleys were on their way home. So after some brief work in Savannah, Whitefield returned to England to secure funds for his growing Savannah mission and orphanage he wanted to build. But when he returned to England, he found that

---

94 Jonathan Edwards, "A Faithful Narrative of the Surprising Work of God," (November 6, 1736): "The Writings of Jonathan Edwards," *International Outreach, Inc.: www.jonathan-edwards.org/Narrative.html* (Accessed 13 February 2013).

many of the church doors had closed to him and the Wesleys and he resorted to open-air preaching. Wesley and Whitefield made quite the contrast in preaching styles: Wesley was the scholarly gentleman who was often shouted down by the crowds. Whitefield was the gifted orator who often left his audiences speechless. Whitefield could make his audiences feel the anguishes of hell, and then, with tears in his voice, make them feel the love of God as they begged for mercy. One noted British actor and playwright wrote, "I would give a hundred guineas if I could only say 'Oh!' like Mr. Whitefield."[95]

Portrait of George Whitefield by Joseph Badger (c. 1745). Whitefield was renowned for his oratory, powerful voice, dramatizations, record crowds, and spellbound audiences, but most of all, the operations and manifestations of the Spirit that accompanied his preaching. Source: Harvard University Portrait Collection, H27. Photo: Wikimedia/Gamaliel.

WHITEFIELD IN AMERICA

After George Whitefield landed north of Philadelphia on October 30, 1739, America was taken by storm. Immediately, he traveled to Philadelphia, where he was warmly welcomed by record crowds—impressing even Benjamin Franklin. From all over the countryside, people came by horse-drawn carriage, barge, ferry, or on foot to hear the famous preacher from England deliver his dramatic sermons. Some came out of curiosity, others from sincere desire to hear the Word, while still others came merely to be entertained. Often the

95 Quotation by David Garrick, Wood, A. Skevington, *The Inextinguishable Blaze* (Grand Rapids, Mich.: Eerdmans, 1960): CH 336.

crowds who came to hear him outnumbered the population of the towns in which he spoke. Unlike in England, however, where he had to resort to open-air meetings because he was unwelcome in churches, in America, he often spoke in open fields or public squares because no church or building was large enough to hold the crowds.

America has always been awestruck by its celebrities, but how ironic that its first celebrity was a preacher. Whitefield eventually made his way through Georgia, the Carolinas, Virginia, Maryland, Pennsylvania, and New York, uniting the English colonies for the first time under the banner of revival. Whitefield went to all denominations and all denominations came to his revivals. Between 1740 and 1742, the Great Awakening swept 25,000 to 50,000 new members into New England churches alone, and between 1750 and 1760 no less than 150 new churches were planted.

JONATHAN EDWARDS

When Whitefield preached at Jonathan Edwards' church in Northampton, many in the church were reminded of the revival they had experienced just a few years earlier. Edwards (1703–1758) was so deeply touched, he wept through the entire service, as did much of his congregation. Shortly thereafter, Edwards preached what would become his most famous sermon: "Sinners in the Hands of an Angry God." Fire and brimstone was not at all indicative of Edward's preaching. Most of his sermons were focused on God's beauty and love. Personally, Edwards was a sensitive individual with a soft, tender voice, who meticulously read his sermons. Unlike Whitefield, Edwards was not a powerful preacher, but he was a powerful prayer who often spent days and weeks in prayer, sometimes devoting up to eighteen hours in prayer before delivering a single sermon.[96] The result was a revival that transformed not only a community but an entire nation.

Portrait of Jonathan Edwards. America's First Great Awakening began in Jonathan Edwards' church in Northampton, Massachusetts, in 1733 and featured many miraculous and ecstatic manifestations of the Spirit, including outbreaks of laughter, visions, trances, and "a remarkable season of healing." Source: Wikimedia/Themadchopper.

BENJAMIN FRANKLIN ON WHITEFIELD

Benjamin Franklin often wrote about the effects of Whitefield's preaching in America, noting the "wonderful . . . change soon made in the manners of our inhabitants. From being thoughtless or indifferent about religion, it seem'd as if all the world were growing religious, so that one could not walk thro' the town in an evening without hearing psalms sung in different families of every street."[97] Franklin became a lifelong friend of Whitefield's, though there is no record of his ever being converted. Franklin often printed Whitefield's sermons on the front page of his *Gazette*, devoting forty-five issues to Whitefield's activities and using the power of the press to spread Whitefield's fame by publishing many of his sermons and journals. Actually, most of Franklin's publications between 1739 and

96 *Change the World School of Prayer*, Word Literature Crusade, D-38: CC 109.

97 *The Autobiography of Benjamin Franklin*, (Bedford, Mass.: Applewood, 2002), 104–108; Samuel J. Rogal, "Toward a Mere Civil Friendship: Benjamin Franklin and George Whitefield," *Methodist History* 35(4) (1997): 233–243: "George Whitefield," *Wikipedia: en.wikipedia.org/wiki/George_Whitefield* (Accessed 15 February 2013).

1741 contained information about Whitefield's work as he helped promote America's Great Awakening.

Franklin was pessimistic of Whitefield's claims to have preached to tens of thousands in England and decided to test out his claims. Once while listening to Whitefield preach from the Philadelphia courthouse, Franklin walked away toward his shop on Market Street until he could no longer distinctly hear him. He then estimated the distance, calculated the area of a semicircle centered on Whitefield, allowing two square feet per person, and computed that Whitefield could be heard by over 30,000 people in the open air. Indeed, Whitefield's powerful farewell sermon on Boston Common in 1740 drew an estimated 23,000 people— the largest crowd ever to have gathered in America to date and larger than Boston's entire population at the time. Before Whitefield's death in 1770, no less than four out of five colonists had heard the "Great Orator," "Divine Dramatist," and "Heavenly Comet" preach at least once.

WHITEFIELD'S CRITICS

Of course, Whitefield's theatrics were not without controversy, especially regarding the operations of the Spirit. Whitefield believed that religion did not consist in outward things but in righteousness, peace, and joy in the Holy Ghost. Consequently, people often approached him inquiring about inward feelings or about receiving the Holy Ghost. Not surprisingly, one member of St. Anne's Parish vestry in Maryland criticized him for being exclusively concerned with the work of the Holy Spirit, stating, "The only 'divinity' Whitefield promoted was 'the particular of the Holy Spirit, whose Operations are so violent & powerful in those who are possessed with it, as, according to his Account of it, to enable them to do anything but work miracles.'" He concluded, "[Whitefield] has the best delivery with the Worst Divinity that I ever mett with."[98] The power of God often moved spontaneously as he spoke. Following his messages, further manifestations of the Spirit would occur. Whitefield observed, "Look where I would, most were drowned in tears. Some struck pale as death, others wringing their hands, others lying on the ground, others sinking into the arms of their friends and most lifting up their eyes to heaven and crying out to God."[99]

EARLY AMERICAN SIGNS AND WONDERS

By the 1740s, the Great Awakening was in full swing. The preface to Jonathan Edward's book *The Distinguishing Marks of a Work of the Spirit of God* described, "an extraordinary season wherein God is pleased to carry on a work of his grace in a more observable and glorious manner. . . . The apostolic times seem to have returned upon us." Particularly interesting seemed to be the general impact of the Spirit on "all ranks and degrees: some of the great and rich, but more on the low and poor," including "poor Negroes" who had "been vindicated into the glorious liberty of the children of God."[100] In York (now Maine), another testified

---

98   Richard Cox, ed., "Stephen Bordley, George Whitefield, and the Great Awakening in Maryland," *Historical Magazine of the Protestant Episcopal Church*, 46 (1977): 303–307: GA 51.

99   George Whitefield, *George Whitefield's Journals*, (London: The Banner of Truth Trust, 1965), 425: CC110.

100 William Cooper, "Preface," in Jonathan Edwards, *The Distinguishing Marks of a Work of the Spirit of God*, in Jonathan Edwards, *The Great Awakening*, ed., C.C. Goen, vol. 4 of *The Works of Jonathan Edwards* (New Haven, CT, 1972), 217–21; Anonymous Boston writer to George Whitefield, in the *Weekly History* (London), 17:4: GA 100

that the presence of God "came down . . . like a mighty rushing Wind" and that all manner of people had been touched "young & old, Rich and poor, White & black."[101] Jonathan Parsons in Lyme, Connecticut, wrote about a revival among his church's youth when many cried out, fell down, and had fits. "Those that could not restrain themselves were generally carried out of the Meeting-House," he wrote. But then he wondered if he had not made a mistake by restricting such outbursts because he found no scriptural justification knowing that even in apostolic times there were many noisy disruptions in response to gospel preaching. He concluded, "If the Lord is pleas'd to make this open Shew of the Victories of his Grace, his Will be done."[102]

Jonathan Edwards agreed that the apostles had established standards for testing whether religious excitement was legitimate, arguing that such manifestations might indeed signal the presence of the Spirit but that wisdom recommended waiting to see what kind of fruit the excitement bore. He considered "bodily effects" incidental to the real work of God, acknowledging that divine visitations often overpowered the body as supported by Scripture, but urged balance. Though Edwards firmly believed religion of the heart to be more important than religion of the head, he also believed that "the more you have a rational knowledge of divine things, the more opportunity will there be, when the Spirit shall be breathed into your heart, to see the excellency of these things, and to taste the sweetness of them."[103] Edwards also argued in favor of

---

101 Samuel P. Savage to Gilbert Tennent, Feb. 2, 1741/2; "Extract of a Letter from Piscatagua," in Samuel P. Savage Papers, Massachusetts Historical Society, Boston; Winiarski, ed., "Jornal," 58–59: GA 103.

102 Thomas Prince, ed., *Christian History*, June 23, 30, 1744, 2:136–39: GA 109.

103 Jonathan Edwards, "The Importance and Advantage of a Thorough Knowledge of Divine Truth," *The Works of Jonathan Edwards* (Worcester), Vol. IV, 1–15: *Christian Classics Ethereal Library: www.ccel.org/ccel/edwards/sermons.divineTruth. html* (Accessed by 17 February 2013).

spiritual gifts, stating, "The Holy Spirit is sovereign in his operation; and we know that he uses a great variety; and we cannot tell how great a variety he may use, within the compass of the rules he himself has fixed. We ought not to limit God where he has not limited himself." And again, "Let us all be hence warned, by no means to oppose, or do anything in the least to clog or hinder, the work; but, on the contrary, do our utmost to promote it. Now Christ is come down from heaven in a remarkable and wonderful work of his Spirit, it becomes all his professed disciples to acknowledge him, and give him honor."[104]

Another in Charlestown, New Hampshire, reported "strange things" happening there, much like Pentecostal scenes from Acts.[105] In Ipswich, Massachusetts, "a Woman was So filled with ye Spirit of God, that She fell on her Knees, and blessed & praised God—in Sermon another Spake out; the Power of ye Ld [Lord] was Present." Also, "a negroe man was wonderfully fill'd wth. ye Love of Xt [Christ]." Another wrote, "These meetings would continue till 10, 11, 12 o'clock at night; in the midst of them sometimes 10, 20, 30 and sometimes many more would scream and cry out, or send forth the most lamentable groans, whilst others made great manifestations of joy by clapping their hands, uttering ecstatic expressions, singing psalms and inviting and exhorting others."[106]

---

104 Jonathan Edwards, *The Distinguishing Marks of a Work of the Spirit of God, Applied to that Uncommon Operation that has lately Appeared on the Minds of Many of the People of This Land: With a Particular Consideration of the Extraordinary Circumstances with Which this Work Is Attended* (1741): MM 197–198

105 Parkman Journal, Mar. 11, 20, 29–30, in Tracy, *Great Awakening*, 205–6; Schmidt, "Second and Glorious Reformation," 220–221 Diary of Joseph Bean, Apr. 4, 1742: GA 135.

106 David S. Lovejoy, *Religious Enthusiasm and the Great Awakening* (Englewood Cliffs, N.J.: Prentice Hall, 1969), 77: CC 112.

Others, like Mercy Wheeler of Plainfield, Connecticut, in 1743, reported miraculous and instantaneous healings. Mrs. Wheeler had been unable to walk independently for sixteen years but could walk a little with her crutches. At her request, a special lecture by pastor Hezekiah Lord was arranged at her home. A few days before the meeting, Mrs. Wheeler meditated on John 11:40, where Jesus said, "Did I not say to you that if you would believe you would see the glory of God?" and other healing scriptures that built her faith in the power of God. While Mr. Hezekiah Lord was preaching, Mrs. Wheeler began to tremble and shake. When someone asked her how she felt, the only words that came out of her mouth were "gibberish." Thinking she needed to lie down and rest, they placed her on the bed when suddenly she heard again the words of Jesus: "Did I not say to you that if you would believe you would see the glory of God?" Immediately upon hearing these words, "she felt a strange irresistible Motion and Shaking, which began first with her Hands; and quickly spreading over her whole Frame. . . . And as she had this Sensation of new Strength and Freedom, she felt as if she was a raising up, and must rise; and immediately rose up and walked away among the People, with evident Sprightliness and Vigour, to the Astonishment of her self and those about her. She went this Time near 16 Feet, crying out, 'Bless the Lord Jesus, who has healed me!'"[107] The shocked Hezekiah Lord told her she was in a 'Frenzy' and forced her to sit down on the bed, but Wheeler would not remain there. She walked across the room several more times.

---

107 Benjamin Lord, *GOD Glorified in His Works, of Providence and Grace* (Boston, 1743), 29–36: GA 163.

AWAKENINGS NORTH AND SOUTH

Baptists in the South were also reporting signs, wonders, and divine communications. North Carolina Baptist minister James Read reported receiving "frequent teachings from God" and dreams calling him into Virginia. Read toured Virginia several times in the 1760s, baptizing hundreds of converts. Meetings typically ran late into the night and "sometimes the floor would be covered with persons struck down under conviction of sin."[108] Another Baptist preacher, John "Swearing Jack" Waller, was reported to have remarkable preaching gifts that included miraculous healings. The wife of one Baptist minister was healed of "deplorable violent spasms" by Waller's prayers and anointing oil.[109] John Williams wrote in 1771 about an all-day meeting of preaching and testimonies after which the congregation "proceeded to baptism, & oh, such a baptism I never saw, not only with water, but in a great measure by the Holy Ghost. The Christians [went] to shouting, sinners trembling & falling down convulsed, the Devil a raging & blaspheming."[110]

By 1775, the societies of sanctified Methodists of Brunswick County, Virginia, were experiencing a revival of their own, led by their pastor, Robert Williams, and Anglican minister Devereaux Jarratt. Jarratt said many were "panting and groaning for pardon" while others were "entreating God with strong cries and tears to save

---

108 Robert B. Semple, *A History of the Rise and Progress of the Baptists in Virginia* (Richmond, 1894), 21–24: GA 246.

109 Edwards, Materials, 2:54–55: Rhys Isaac, *The Transformation of Virginia*, 1740–1790 (Chapel Hill, N.C., 1982), 162–63: GA 246.

110 "John Williams' Journal," 803: Daniel Fristoe's Journal, 1771, in Little, *Imprisoned Preachers*, 242–43: Isaac, "Evangelical Revolt," 355–56: GA 251.

them from the remains of inbred sin, to sanctify them throughout." Others testified of being sanctified "instantaneously, and by simple faith."[111] Jarratt said that at times their emotions seemed to exceed the limits of control as "some would be seized with a trembling, and in a few moments drop on the floor as if they were dead; while others were embracing each other with streaming eyes, and all were lost in wonder, love and praise." Some wept for grief while others shouted for joy "so that it was hard to distinguish one from another." At other times, the congregations would "raise a great shout" that could be heard for miles around. But regrettably, Jarratt observed, when the emotional element abated, "the work of conviction and conversion abated too."[112] Francis Asbury's revivals were also often characterized by swooning, shouting, weeping, and a kind of wild behavior known as "the jerks" despite his insistence that all Methodist Society meetings be conducted with order.[113]

Samuel Buell reported similar occurrences at his Easthampton, Long Island, church in 1764. Thousands reportedly flocked to see an outpouring of the Spirit that one minister said "exceeds" what he ever saw, read, or heard of since the days of the apostles. Buell wrote, "From Time to Time, Day after Day, the Holy Ghost evidently came down as a mighty rushing Wind; sometimes almost as sudden as a Flash of Lightning; bowing our Assembly, and producing the most amazing

---

111 Devereaux Jarratt, *A Brief Narrative of the Revival of Religion in Virginia, in a Letter to a Friend* . . . (4th ed., London, 1779), 7–12; W.W. Sweet, *Religion in Colonial America* (New York, 1965), 306–11; John Leland Peters, *Christian Perfection and American Methodism* (New York, 1956), 84–85; Wesley M. Gewehr, *The Great Awakening in Virginia* (Durham, 1930), 143–48: HPT 9.

112 Gewehr, *The Great Awakening in Virginia*, 153–155: HPT 9.

113 Francis MacNutt, *Overcome by the Spirit* (Old Tappan, NJ: Chosen Books, 1990), 107: MCH 303–305.

Agonies of Soul, & Cries, that ever you heard."[114] Buell hoped the "Days are not very far off, when such Outpourings of the Spirit will become more frequent and general among the Lord's People: And in Process of Time the World over." Buell dreamed of a day when "an immence Plenty of the Lord's spiritual Waters, will be pour'd out upon thirsty Souls."[115] That same year, Jacob Johnson reported the same from his church in Groton, Connecticut, and defended his daughter's claim to have had a vision of Jesus, declaring that although God normally spoke through the Word, he also used extraordinary means like miracles, signs, prodigies, apparitions, and audible voices. Johnson believed that all great outpourings of the Holy Spirit, beginning with Pentecost, were accompanied by extraordinary communications by God. He also believed that miracles did not cease with the apostles because he had seen and heard them.

AWAKENINGS AMONG AFRICAN AMERICANS

The Great Awakening also brought salvation to many African-American slaves and freedmen. In the South, Baptist and Methodist preachers were converting both black and white, slave and free, as congregations welcomed black people into their active roles—even as preachers. In Virginia in the 1750s, Samuel Davies, a Presbyterian minister, was especially known for converting African slaves in large numbers. He described the Africans as particularly given to "music, and a kind of ecstatic delight in Psalmody." He said they were especially fond of Isaac Watts' hymns. Davies, who often invited

---

114 "More Light on a New Light: James Davenport's Religious Legacy, Eastern Long Island, 1740–1840," *New York History 73*, no.1 (1992), 10–11: GA 275–276.

115 Buell, *Faithful Narrative*, 22–23, 48, 77: GA 280.

them to his home, wrote, "Sundry of them have lodged all night in my kitchen; and sometimes, when I have awaked about two or three a clock in the morning, a torrent of sacred harmony poured into my chamber, and carried my mind away to Heaven. In this seraphic exercise, some of them spend almost the whole night."[116] John Wright, another Presbyterian minister in Virginia, described a revival among African Americans in 1761: "When ye revival began, it spread more powerfully among ye Black than ye Whites, in so much yt [yet] they crowded to me in great numbers . . . to know what they should do to be saved."[117] Thus, before the American Revolution began, black Baptist churches were being founded in South Carolina, Georgia, and Virginia. Freed Baptist preacher and Black Loyalist David George, together with a few other slaves, are believed to have founded the first continuously operating black church in America in Silver Bluff, South Carolina, sometime between 1773 and 1775—before the signing of the Declaration of Independence.

"Black People's Prayer Meeting" by John Lewis Krimmel (c. 1811). The message of spiritual equality and emotionality of America's First Great Awakening appealed to many African Americans, who converted to Christianity in large numbers. A number of African American pastors and leaders also emerged from the revival. Source: The Metropolitan Museum of Art, Rogers Fund, 1942 (194) Library of Congress. Photo: Wikiart.org.

---

116 Samuel Davies to Joseph Bellamy, Feb. 23, 1757, in *Evangelical and Literary Magazine* (Nov. 1823), 568–569: Sobel, *World They Made Together*, 183–187: GA 239–240.

117 John Wright to Joseph Bellamy, Nov. 7, 1761, Joseph Bellamy Papers, Presbyterian Historical Society, Phila.: GA 241.

John Marrant, another Black Loyalist and freedman from New York, moved his family to Charleston, South Carolina, in the 1760s. There he became a self-described musician and heavy drinker—until he heard George Whitefield. As the great preacher scanned his audience, he pointed directly at Marrant and announced his text with a thunderous voice: "Prepare to Meet Thy God, O Israel." As Whitefield spoke these words, the Spirit of God literally knocked Marrant to the ground, where he remained for half an hour. After the meeting, Whitefield came over to see him and said, "Jesus Christ has got thee at last."[118] Days later, still unable to move, Marrant said, "The Lord was pleased to set my soul at perfect liberty."[119] As family and friends began persecuting him for his newfound faith, Marrant often retreated to the woods to pray and read the Scriptures. There, he befriended a Cherokee hunter who took him to his fort. Instead of welcoming him, the tribal leaders tried and sentenced him to death. At his execution, Marrant cried out to God, first in English then, to everyone's shock and amazement (including Marrant's), in Cherokee! Immediately, he was released and eventually returned to his family, who received him as "one brought back from the dead." Soon he went to work at a local plantation as a free carpenter where he taught the Bible to African slaves. This new "society" grew to thirty slaves until the plantation owner raided one of their meetings and flogged several of the slaves to death, forcing Marrant to leave (though the slaves continued meeting in secret).

---

118 John Marrant, *A Narrative of the Lord's Wonderful Dealings with John Marrant, A Black*, 4th ed. (London 1785) in Joanna Brooks and John Saillant, eds. "Face Zion Forward": First Writers of the Black Atlantic, 1785–1798 (Boston, 2002), 50–52 "Afro-American Conversion as a Forgotten Chapter in Eighteenth Century Southern Intellectual History," *Bulletin of the Center for the Study of Southern Culture and Religion 3*, no. 3 (Nov 1979): GA 226.

119 Ibid., 52–67, quote 53: GA 226.

During the American Revolution, Marrant fought for the British navy. After the war, Marrant was ordained in London before traveling to Nova Scotia, where he preached to a black community. In one of his first meetings, he preached to a mixture of whites, blacks, and Indians. He wrote, "groans and sighings were heard through the congregation, and many were not able to contain." That night, Marrant tried to preach again, but the power of God was so strong it rendered him mute for five minutes. A month later, Marrant was preaching to another audience of mixed races, and again he was struck dumb by the Spirit. Determined to go on with the meeting, however, he baptized five people before "the rest were fallen to the ground." Still undeterred, he baptized by sprinkling the rest right where they were on the floor as the others cried out, "Lord, have mercy upon us."[120]

THE AMERICAN REVOLUTION

Many saw the hand of God move in the war and through the continued outpourings of the Spirit that occurred even as the battles raged on. Indeed, some of the more radical groups like the Freewill Baptists, Shakers, and Come-Outers blossomed during the Revolutionary War. Benjamin Randel, one of the key founders of the Freewill Baptists, said he was in a cornfield when God told him he must give up all tradition and rely on the leadings of the Spirit and the Word. Other independent groups like the "Come-Outers" in what is now Maine were known for their dancing, stomping, whirling around, and falling on the floor in a spiritual state or "trance."

---

120 Ibid., 104, 109: GA 227–228.

In truth, the Great Awakening may well have saved America from British tyranny. Colonial Christians believed the American Revolution was "design'd by the Lord to advance the cause of Christ in the world; or as one important step towards bringing in the glory of the latter day." They also thought it not "at all improbable, that America is reserved in the mind of Jehovah, to be the grand theatre on which the divine Redeemer will accomplish glorious things" and called on the churches to pray for "a more universal effusion of the Holy Ghost."[121] Jonathan Edwards believed these early revivals had a global eschatological significance: "'Tis not unlikely that this work of God's Spirit . . . is the dawning, or at least a prelude, of that glorious work of God, so often foretold in Scripture."[122]

The Great Awakening also played a key role in the development of democracy. Those who participated in the revivals believed that revival had come to America because God graciously poured out his Spirit and that the revivals were God's gift for the creation of a Christian America. These early revivals certainly aided in the creation of a new American culture. Whitefield was among the first to preach universal equality and liberty in Christ "claiming liberty of conscience to be an inalienable right of every rational creature."[123] Others saw hypocrisy in America's call for freedom, saying, "Can it be believed that a people

---

121 Mark A. Noll, *America's God: From Jonathan Edwards to Abraham Lincoln* (London/ New York: Oxford University Press, 2002), 166: GA 321.

122 Jonathan Edwards, *Some Thoughts Concerning the Present Revival of Religion in New-England* (Boston, 1743, in Jonathan Edwards, *The Great Awakening*, ed. C.C. Goen, vol. 4 of *The Works of Jonathan Edwards* (New Haven, Conn.: Yale, 1972), 345, 353, 358: GA 158.

123 Bernard Bailyn, *The Ideological Origins of the American Revolution*, (Harvard University Press, 1992), 249: *Wikipedia: en.wikipedia.org/wiki/Benjamin_Franklin* (Accessed 19 February 2013).

contending for liberty should, at the same time, be promoting and supporting slavery?"[124] Even George Washington, after having lunch with Francis Asbury one day, was urged to sign an emancipation document that Washington agreed was needed but felt it was not the time. God would not forget the hypocrisy of a Christian America. At the same time, America's independence meant that churches, for the first time since the fourth century, would be forced to shoulder the burden of evangelism alone without the support or protection of the state. Christianity would once again be on its own.

"Prayer at Valley Forge," by H. Brueckner, engraving by John C. McRae (c. 1866). "To my astonishment I saw the great George Washington on his knees alone, with his sword on one side and his cocked hat on the other. He was at Prayer to the God of the Armies, beseeching to interpose with his Divine aid, as it was ye Crisis, & the cause of the country, of humanity & of the world," Rev. Nathaniel Randolph Snowden as told by Isaac Potts (1777). The Great Awakening had a profound effect on the American Revolution. Many believed both the revivals and the revolution had a global eschatological significance. Source: Library of Congress Prints and Photographs Division.

THE NEW LIGHTS

The early colonists prayed for a revival of Puritanism to save their religion from extinction. However, when revival finally came, it was not a Puritan revival. Instead, the Great Awakening brought a new emphasis on seasons of revival, outpourings of the Holy Spirit, personal conversion, and experiential faith. These new revivalists believed converts would know exactly when their conversion

---

124 Jacob Green, *A Sermon Delivered at Hanover* (Chatham, N.J., 1779), 5, 12–13, 16
Mark A. Noll, *Christians in the American Revolution* (Regent College Publishing, 2006), 102: GA 302.

happened because the Spirit's witness would be perceived by their "outward Senses." Those who adopted this new style of preaching were called "New Lights," while those who continued with their intellectual discourses were considered "Old Lights." The Old Lights were the traditionalists who believed morality should be legislated and emotions had no place in the church. The New Lights were revivalists who believed Christians should be passionate about their faith and morality thrived in an atmosphere of spiritual freedom. Many of these New Lights began separating themselves from parish churches and organizing their own congregations. The Baptists, especially, believed all ties between church and state would have to be severed for America to be a truly free and Christian nation. The end of the war brought even more opportunities for spiritual innovation. Americans loved their newfound freedoms and were open to exploring new frontiers— whether geographical or spiritual.

In the end, the Great Awakening taught Americans that a Christian America could be achieved if a majority of its citizens could be persuaded to submit voluntarily to the laws of God. Christianity meant voluntary obedience to God, and revivals were God's means to that end. In this, the reasonable men of the Enlightenment, like Jefferson and Franklin, found common ground with the revivalists of the Great Awakening. This alliance won America's independence. Jefferson was repulsed by coercion but especially religious coercion, which he said managed "to make one half of the world fools, and the other half hypocrites."[125] This alliance gave birth to the United States

---

125 Martin Marty, *Religion, Awakening and Revolution* (Wilmington: McGrath, 1977): CH 349.

and became even more evident in 1791 in America's First Amendment to its Constitution: "Congress shall make no law respecting an establishment of religion, or prohibiting the free exercise thereof." Both were united in their fight for freedom but with different visions for the future—one envisioned freedom *of* religion, the other dreamed of freedom *from* religion.

STUDY QUESTIONS

1. What was the Renaissance and what influence did it have on the Reformation and on Christianity as a whole?

2. How would you characterize the life and ministry of George Fox?

3. Describe an early Quaker meeting. Why did they feel it necessary to be quiet before the Lord to listen and to wait?

4. What was scriptural (Acts 2:17–18) yet outstandingly peculiar about the prophetic anointing that frequented the Camisards or French Prophets?

5. In what way did Madame Jeanne Guyon's life and teachings influence the modern Methodist, Holiness, and Pentecostal movements?

6. How does secularism differ from humanism?

7. Why did Thomas Jefferson literally cut sections pertaining to the resurrection, the Holy Spirit, and the supernatural out of his Bible?

8. Who were the convulsionnaires and what ultimately led public opinion to turn against them?

9. How would you describe early Shaker meetings and worship? Why are the Shakers considered an important part of America's cultural heritage?

10. What three concurring international revivals could be attributed to the Moravian's 100-year 24-hour prayer watch?

11. What distinguishing marks do the Moravian missionaries have in history?

12. In what ways did the Moravians influence the life and ministry of John Wesley?

13. Why was John Wesley accused of being an "enthusiast"? What was his respond to such accusations?

14. Besides founding Methodism, what might be considered John Wesley's most enduring legacy? How did he develop this doctrine, and how did John Fletcher's views differ from Wesley's views on the subject?

15. How did John Wesley and George Whitefield vary in doctrine? In preaching style? In scope of ministry?

16. What was Jonathan Edwards' response to the effects of revival such as visions, trances, outbreaks of laughter, and bodily shakings?

17. How were African Americans affected by America's First Great Awakening?

18. What effect did the Great Awakening have on America and the American Revolution?

3

THE AGE OF PROGRESS

(c. 1801–1865)

THE FRENCH REVOLUTION

Though the American (1775–1783) and French (1789–1799) Revolutions were both struggles for freedom, one was a struggle between nations and the other, a war of ideas. For this reason, the French Revolution in particular marked the beginning of the "Age of Progress" or Modern Age. As the Renaissance gave birth to humanism and the Enlightenment gave birth to secularism, the Modern Age gave birth to liberalism. What began as a struggle for *liberty* in France quickly descended into a crusade for *liberalism*. Within a brief ten-year period, France had essentially formed a new republic, executed its king, established a revolutionary regime, permanently destroyed the Holy Roman Empire, eliminated all church courts and religious authority (including the pope), and sent some 40,000 priests into exile—and this was only the beginning. Revolutionaries enthroned a young actress on Notre Dame's cathedral altar, calling her "the Goddess of Reason," as parish churches were converted into "Temples of Reason" and other young women were decked out as living statues of "Liberty," "Reason," and "Nature" to symbolize the new religion of the republic. The reign of terror unleashed on the church looked like scenes from the book of Revelation and many Christians viewed it that way. If it was not the end, it was certainly the beginning of the end. The convulsions in France were reminiscent of pagan Rome— Europe had come full circle.

"Festival of Reason," Notre Dame, Paris (1792). The Cult of Reason was established during the French Revolution to replace Christianity. Churches across France were transformed into Temples of Reason. Notre Dame's cathedral altar was replaced with an altar to Liberty while "To Philosophy" was carved in stone over the entrance. Festive girls impersonating Liberty dressed up as Goddesses of Reason. Source: Bibliothèque nationale de France. Photo: Wikimedia/Tablar.

LIBERALISM

French Revolutionary leader Napoleon Bonaparte (1769–1821) said, "The peoples of Germany, as of France, Italy and Spain, want equality and liberal ideas," and liberalism is what they got.[1] Tyranny of the monarchy was soon replaced by "tyranny of the majority" as liberalism replaced traditional conservatism and absolutism in government with democracy and the rule of law laying the groundwork for the

---

1   Joel Colton and R.R. Palmer, *A History of the Modern World* (New York: McGraw Hill, 1995), 428: "Liberalism," *Wikipedia: en.wikipedia.org/wiki/Liberalism* (Accessed 21 February 2013).

separation of church and state.[2] As heirs of the Enlightenment, liberals believed strongly in a society built solely on human interaction apart from divine will. However, unlike humanism and secularism, which largely left Christianity alone, liberalism from its inception engaged in open hostilities against the Christian church. Apparently, "Liberty, Equality, and Fraternity" did not include Christians and "equal rights for all" meant that anyone except Christians could express their views on morality or public life and that liberty no longer meant the absence of governmental interference but the right of the individual "to do what one wills."[3] Sir Edmund Burke, a British statesman and observer of the French Revolution, wrote, "The French had shewn themselves the ablest architects of ruin that had hitherto existed in the world. In that very short space of time they had completely pulled down to the ground, their monarchy; their church; their nobility; their law ... and the danger of their example is no longer from intolerance, but from Atheism; a foul, unnatural vice, foe to all the dignity and consolation of mankind."[4]

According to Burke, the French Revolution was one "where the Elements which compose Human Society seem all to be dissolved, and a world of Monsters to be produced in the place of it."[5] Burke

---

2   "Tyranny of the Majority" was a section title in Alexis de Tocqueville, *Democracy in America* (1835): "Liberalism," *Wikipedia: en.wikipedia.org/wiki/Liberalism* (Accessed 21 February 2013).

3   Ben Wempe, *T. H. Green's Theory of Positive Freedom: From Metaphysics to Political Theory* (Exeter: Imprint Academic, 2004), 123: "Liberalism," *Wikipedia: en.wikipedia.org/wiki/Liberalism* (Accessed 21 February 2013).

4   Ibid., 66–67.

5   J.C.D. Clark, ed., *Reflections on the Revolution in France: A Critical Edition* (Stanford University, 2001), 61–62: "Edmund Burke," *Wikipedia: en.wikipedia.org/wiki/Edmund_Burke* (Accessed 21 February 2013).

also foresaw the dangers of a liberal democracy, noting that common people had dangerous and angry passions that could easily be aroused by gifted orators and manipulators if they had the vote. He feared that authoritarian impulses empowered by these passions could one day undermine cherished traditions and established religion.

THE VATICAN

Though Napoleon eventually restored Catholicism as the "religion of the majority" in France, the church would never regain her earthly power. Fifty years later when a similar revolution broke out in Rome, the papacy withdrew to the Vatican, holding on to its last remaining vestige of power—infallibility concerning spiritual matters. The pope's earthly reign was over. Surrounded by the new hostile forces of nationalism, socialism, and liberalism, the once mighty Roman Church retreated behind the walls of its Vatican fortress, essentially shutting itself off from the rest of the world. As far as the church was concerned, the only matters of importance lay within its walls, and within a few decades, liberalism had become the dominant world ideology. A Christian Europe was no longer the hope of the world.

St. Peter's Square at the Vatican in Rome by Viviano Codazzi at the Museo del Prado, Madrid, Spain (c.1630). The Vatican is a walled enclave city within the city of Rome; an ecclesiastical monarchy and city-state ruled by the pope. Situated on 110 acres, it is the smallest independent state in the world in both area and population. Source: Web Gallery of Art/Wikimedia.

PROTESTANT MISSIONARIES

Despite this massive retreat, the Age of Progress also became one of the greatest eras of expansion in the history of Christianity thanks, in large part, to the Protestant missionary societies. From Britain alone, which was now in the throes of its own Industrial Revolution and on its way toward becoming the greatest world empire, came hundreds of missionaries like William Carey (1761–1834), the father of modern missions to India, and David Livingstone (1813–1873), a pioneer in medical missions to Africa. While early Protestant missionaries saw themselves as tiny islands surrounded by a sea of heathenism, William Carey envisioned Christian missionaries who were firmly rooted in the culture where they were planted and capable of evangelizing entire nations. Carey believed, as it was the duty of all sinners to repent and believe the gospel, it was the duty of all Christians entrusted with the gospel to carry it to the ends of the earth. He further believed that, if no obstacle was too large to prevent merchants from traveling the world for profit, no difficulty should prevent Christians from traveling the world for the love of men's souls. Carey's vision created a new age in world missions. North American missionaries soon followed. Jonathan Edwards' prophetic vision that "all the earth would be filled with the knowledge of the Lord as the waters cover the sea" meant that America was destined by Providence to spread the gospel into all the world as a witness in preparation for the return and millenial reign of Christ.[6] This missionary march to convert the "heathens" around the world soon became the heart cry of every layperson, in every local congregation, in every city and town, and in every denomination in North America. By the end of the nineteenth century, almost every Christian body in

---

6   Habakkuk 2:14

the world had participated in worldwide overseas missions in some way as part of a larger Protestant missionary force that dotted the world's landscape. This same missionary zeal would soon be refueled by a Pentecostal outpouring and repeated by Pentecostal missionaries in the twentieth century. But in the nineteenth century, the greatest mission field of all was in America's own backyard.

THE AMERICAN FRONTIER

By the turn of the nineteenth century, America was again facing moral bankruptcy. An entire generation had come of age that knew little of George Whitefield or the Great Awakening. As Wesley had once warned, Whitefield's Great Awakening subsided because it lacked an effective discipleship and leadership structure. Eight years of war had also drained the nation dry. Only 5 to 10 percent of Americans were church members, and the negative influences coming out of Europe were turning America's colleges into hotbeds of rebellion. Many students began professing to be atheists, agnostics, or at best, skeptics, resulting in a general increase in profanity, drunkenness, gambling, and lewdness in America's cities and towns. The Presbyterians were among the first to sound the alarm, stating they were "filled with concern and awful dread" at what America was becoming and declared, "The eternal God has a controversy with this nation." Such prayers and concerns prompted a Second Great Awakening.

After the Revolutionary War, so many Americans moved west that the entire continent seemed to tilt. By mid-century, no less than half the population lived west of the Appalachians. Commissioned with the dual task of fighting Indians and taming the wilderness, frontiersmen quickly gained a reputation for being wild and lawless. Though the American frontier presented Christianity with its greatest opportunity to date to affect an entire nation, new trails of evangelistic methods would have to be blazed. The traditional European-style denominational church was no match for America's rugged frontier.

METHODIST CIRCUIT RIDERS

Methodist circuit riders like Francis Asbury (1745–1816) and "Pistol-Toting" Peter Cartwright (1785–1872) provided the perfect antidote for subduing the Western frontier. Their motto was "No family was too poor, no house too filthy, no town too remote, and no people too ignorant to receive the good news that life could be better."[7] So dedicated were these early circuit-riding preachers that a popular saying in inclement weather in those days was "There's nobody out today but crows and Methodist preachers." And while most seminary-trained ministers of the day spoke in dull, monotone voices and read prayers from books, these circuit-riding preachers spoke straight from the heart without notes and prayed as if God were in the room. Asbury himself believed in personally being led by the Spirit and preparing only a scriptural text. He also preferred preachers who were without credentials because they could relate better to the common person. But circuit preachers were not the only weapons in the church's frontier arsenal.

This woodcut illustration of Rev. Samuel E. Alford entitled "The Circuit Rider," by Alfred R. Waud, appeared on the cover of Harpers Weekly, October 12, 1867. It well portrays the difficulties circuit preachers encountered as they tamed the American frontier. Rev. Alford rode through northwestern Virginia, eastern West Virginia, and western Maryland. Source: Library of Congress Prints and Photographs Division.

---

7   Salter, *America's Bishop*, 167: GGR 191.

THE AMERICAN CAMP MEETING

In 1796, James McGready (1763–1817), a Presbyterian pastor of three small churches in Kentucky, led his congregations to sign a covenant to pray every Saturday and Sunday morning and to devote the third Saturday of each month to prayer and fasting for revival. Three years later, McGready invited some other denominational ministers to join him at their annual Communion gathering at the Red River church when the power of God came down. The following summer, they returned on the weekend of June 21–23, 1800, when the presence of the Spirit became so intense the congregation was reduced to tears. On the third and final day of meetings, the Spirit again lingered. John McGee, one of the Methodist ministers, started weeping and others soon followed. McGee then stood up and exhorted the crowd. Several women began shouting, and one in particular shouted above the others. McGee left the pulpit to go to her, but several warned him that the Presbyterians liked order. McGee described what happened as he headed toward the pulpit: "I turned to go back and was near falling; the power of God was so strong upon me. I turned again and, losing sight of the fear of man, I went through the house shouting and exhorting with all possible ecstasy and energy, and the floor was soon covered by the slain."[8]

When McGready announced a similar meeting at his Gasper River church in July, the response was overwhelming. Some came from as far away as a hundred miles, bringing their tents with them. The crowds grew so large they had to clear some underbrush near the church, build a pulpit, and set up log seats outdoors. The American

---

8   Charles A. Johnson, *The Frontier Camp Meeting* (Dallas: SMU, 1955), 35: CC 114.

camp meeting was born. Services lasted well into the night. When McGee preached that Sunday night, the Spirit again fell, and many who were seeking God were slain followed by cries and shouts of joy that seemed to drown out the preaching.

In 1801, Barton W. Stone (1772–1844), another Presbyterian pastor, who later cofounded the Churches of Christ and attended the Red River meetings, decided to use McGready's principles to start a similar series of meetings near his church in Cane Ridge, Kentucky. Crowd estimates were reported between 15,000 and 20,000. One minister who was present reported 3,000 slain in the Spirit at once with others breaking into loud laughter and still others running, shouting, barking like dogs, and making other strange sounds.[9] One eyewitness reported, "The noise was like the roar of Niagara. The vast sea of human beings seemed to be agitated as if by a storm. Some of the people were singing, others praying, some crying for mercy in the most piteous accents, while others shouted vociferously. A strange supernatural power seemed to pervade the entire mass of mind there collected. . . . At one time I saw at least five hundred, swept down in a moment as if a battery of a thousand guns had been opened upon them, and then immediately followed shrieks and shouts that rent the very heavens."[10] Another testified, "The like wonders have not been seen, except the Kentucky Revival last summer, since the Apostle's days."[11] Barton himself wrote, "Many things transpired there, which were so

9   Francis Asbury, "Letter to George Roberts," 18 August 1803, *Journal and Letters of Francis Asbury* 3:269, quoted in L.C. Rudolph, *Francis Asbury* (Nashville: Abingdon Press, 1966), 118: GGR 199–200.

10 Johnson, *The Frontier Camp Meeting*, 64–65: CC 116.

11 Quote by Aeneas McCallister in Richard M'Nemar, *The Kentucky Revival* (Cincinnati, 1808), 32: CM 83.

much like miracles, that if they were not, they had the same effects as miracles on infidels and unbelievers; for many of them by these were convinced that Jesus was the Christ, and bowed in submission to him."[12]

From Kentucky, the camp meetings soon spread into Tennessee, West Virginia, North and South Carolina, Georgia, and throughout the South. Some were as wild as the frontier itself. In North Carolina, yet another Presbyterian congregation held a similar series of meetings in 1801 in anticipation of revival, but nothing happened. Sorely disappointed, the pastor rose to conclude the last meeting when someone from the audience stood and shouted, "Stand still and see the salvation of God!" Immediately, "a wave of emotion swept over the congregation like an electric shock." The physical manifestations and speaking in tongues reportedly made it "like the day of Pentecost and none was careless or indifferent."[13] One University of Georgia student told of a meeting in which "they swooned away and lay for hours in the straw prepared for those 'smitten of the Lord,' or they started suddenly to flee away and fell prostrate as if shot down by a sniper, or they took suddenly to jerking with apparently every muscle in their body until it seemed they would be torn to pieces or converted into marble, or they shouted and talked in unknown tongues."[14]

---

12 "A Short History of the Life of Barton W. Stone Written by Himself" in *Voices from Cane Ridge*, ed., Rhodes Thompson (St. Louis: Bethany, 1954), Chap. 5–6: MM 223.

13 M'Nemar, *The Kentucky Revival*, 68: CM 83.

14 E. Merton Coulter, *College Life in the Old South* (New York, 1928), 194–195: HPT 13.

"Camp Meeting of the Methodists in N. America" by Jacques Gérard Milbert (c. 1819) aquatint engraving by M. Dubourg. Camp meetings became an American social and spiritual phenomenon of the Second Great Awakening in the early 1800s as many pioneer communities lacked established churches or resident pastors. Source: Library of Congress Prints and Photographs Collection.

One remarkable feature of the early camp meetings was the informal prayer groups that formed between the regular meetings. In these prayer groups, any man, woman, child, white or black, educated or not, could spontaneously exhort anyone within hearing distance. This earned the camp meeting its unofficial title "a carnival of preachers." In the regular meetings, Presbyterian, Baptist, and Methodist preachers took turns speaking as camp meetings were attended by all denominations, and all denominations experienced their fruit. In Kentucky alone between 1800 and 1803, the Baptists added 10,000 to their rolls, while the Methodists added 40,000. Peter Cartwright, an original convert of the Cane Ridge revival, wrote, "The work went on and spread almost in every direction gathering additional force till our country seemed all coming to God."[15]

THE SECOND GREAT AWAKENING

The Second Great Awakening served to create a vast spiritual and educational infrastructure across the American frontier that included a network of voluntary societies, Christian colleges, and Christian media

---

15   Peter Cartwright, *An Autobiography*, W.P. Strickland, ed. (New York: Hunt and Eaton, n.d.), 46: CC 116–117.

publications. Among these, the American Bible Society was founded in 1816. Women made up a large part of these societies as the Second Great Awakening produced, for the first time, at least three females to every two male converts between 1798 and 1826. Young people under the age of twenty-five also converted in greater numbers, as did an increasing number of common planters, plain folk, and slaves. On the Western frontier, camp meetings remained an important social venue for early settlers as many became exposed to Christianity for the first time through these outdoor meetings.

For many, the American frontier seemed pristine, untouched, and undefiled—the perfect place for recovering "pure, uncorrupted, and original Christianity."[16] Consequently, several new black and predominantly white Christian denominations as well as other religious groups developed out of the Second Great Awakening, including the Churches of Christ, Christian Churches (Disciples of Christ), Seventh-day Adventists, Church of Jesus Christ of Latter-day Saints (Mormons), African Episcopal, African Methodist Episcopal (AME), and AME Zion Church. Some southern cities like Charleston, Richmond, and Petersburg already had independent black congregations numbering in the hundreds. In fact, one of the most prominent figures to emerge out of the Second Great Awakening was the Negro preacher who, in many ways, represented the spirit of the American frontier revivals by dramatizing Bible stories and characters and relating them to the slavery experience.

---

16   C. Leonard Allen and Richard T. Hughes, *Discovering Our Roots: The Ancestry of the Churches of Christ* (Abilene, Texas: Abilene Christian University, 1988), 90: "The Second Great Awakening," *Wikipedia: en.wikipedia.org/wiki/Second_Great_Awakening* (Accessed 23 February 2013).

"A Negro Camp Meeting in the South," by Sol Ettinge, Harper's Weekly, August 10, 1872. America's Second Great Awakening produced many African-American congregations formed by slaves and freedmen alike, while others were welcomed as members and as preachers in traditionally white churches. The revival inspired many slaves to demand their freedom. Source: Library of Congress Prints and Photographs Division.

CAMPUS REVIVALS

Yet another ember that sparked the Second Great Awakening around the turn of the century was the New England campus revivals. Timothy Dwight IV, Jonathan Edwards' son-in-law and president of Yale College between 1795 and 1817, was among the first to sound the alarm by warning the citizens of New England of the "infidel philosophy" coming out of the French Revolution that he believed was threatening to destroy America's colleges and institutions. His series of chapel messages on "infidelity" not only resulted in one-third of the student body being saved but also led to similar revivals that swept through nearby cities and college towns. Dwight's book The Nature and Danger of Infidel Philosophy, published from his sermon series and aimed at "re-churching" America, allowed Yale and other New England communities to catch the spirit of the Second Great Awakening. But no one, north or south, would have a greater influence on America's Second Great Awakening than "the father of modern revivalism."

CHARLES GRANDISON FINNEY

Charles Finney (1792–1875) was raised in a non-Christian home in Upstate New York. As a teenager, he had learned just enough to teach school and considered joining the navy or attending Yale, that is until a teacher told him he could acquire the same knowledge in two years of independent studies. However, his parents finally persuaded him to become a lawyer, and he moved to nearby Adams, New York, where he became an apprentice to Judge Benjamin Wright. There in Adams, at Rev. George W. Gale's Presbyterian Church, Finney first became interested in spiritual matters though he readily admitted, "I was by no means in a state of mind to go to heaven if I should die."[17] Finney was particularly struck by the Presbyterians' Calvinistic prayers for revival, which he felt lacked the necessary faith for God to answer. Since Calvinists believed that God was sovereign and had predestined everything, they were afraid their prayers might have little effect. Thus, Finney concluded their prayers would have little effect on him and decided to seek God on his own. Then one morning in 1821, Finney heard an inward voice say to him, *What are you waiting for?* He wrote, "At this point the whole question of Gospel salvation opened to my mind in a manner most marvelous to me at the time. I think I then saw, as clearly as I ever have in my life, the reality and fullness of the atonement of Christ. I saw that his work was a finished work; and that instead of having, or needing, any righteousness of my own to recommend me to God, I had to submit myself to the righteousness of God through Christ. . . . Salvation . . . instead of being a thing to be wrought out, by my own works, was a thing to be found entirely in the Lord Jesus Christ." Again,

---

17   *The Autobiography of Charles G. Finney*, (Grand Rapids, Mich.: Baker, 1977), 10.

the inward voice said, *Will you accept it now today?* "Yes," he replied, "I will accept it today, or I will die in the attempt."[18]

FINNEY'S SPIRIT BAPTISM

Finney described what happened later that evening after Judge Wright left the office:

> *As I turned and was about to take a seat by the fire, I received a mighty baptism of the Holy Ghost. Without any expectation of it, without ever having the thought in my mind that there was any such thing for me, without any recollection that I had ever heard the thing mentioned by any person in the world, the Holy Spirit descended upon me in a manner that seemed to go through me, body and soul. I could feel the impression, like a wave of electricity, going through and through me. Indeed it seemed to come in waves and waves of liquid love; for I could not express it in any other way. It seemed like the very breath of God. I can recollect distinctly that it seemed to fan me, like immense wings. . . . I wept aloud with joy and love. . . . I literally bellowed out the unutterable gushings of my heart.[19]*

Though Finney admitted he had no prior knowledge about the baptism in the Holy Spirit, he later described it as an "indispensable qualification" for ministry, stating he was "surprised" and "pained" to learn how little attention had been given to it to date for preaching Christ to a sinful world.[20] Finney believed the grand purpose of

---

18   Charles Finney, *Memoirs of Charles Finney* (New York: A.S. Barnes, 1876), 14: GGR 291–292.

19   Ibid., 19–21: GGR 295.

20   Finney, *Autobiography*, 51.

Pentecost to be the salvation of souls and that the working of miracles and gift of tongues had merely been given to the apostles as signs to attest to the reality of this divine commission.[21] Once when asked what he thought of someone who had prayed for weeks for the baptism in the Holy Spirit and not received it, Finney replied, "I would think he was praying from false motives." His inquisitor retorted, "But from what motives should a man pray? If he wants to be happy, is that a false motive?" "Satan might pray with as good a motive as that," Finney replied. Then he quoted Psalm 51: "Uphold me with thy free spirit. Then will I teach transgressors thy ways; and sinners shall be converted unto thee." "See?" said Finney. "The Psalmist did not pray for the Holy Spirit that he might be happy, but that he might be useful, and that sinners might be converted to Christ."[22]

Finney awoke the next morning wondering whether his experience the night before had been real, but instantly, the baptism he had received the night before returned upon him in the same manner: "I arose upon my knees in the bed and wept aloud with joy, and remained for some time too much overwhelmed with the baptism of the Spirit to do anything but pour out my soul to God." Then the inward voice said, *Will you doubt?* He cried, "No! I will not doubt, I cannot doubt!"[23] From that moment on, virtually every person Finney came in contact with—including his parents and every church member except one—came under the same power and conviction of the Holy Spirit to receive salvation. It seemed no one could resist. Finney wrote, "Whenever I . . . let the Spirit take his own course with me, and gave

---

21   Ibid.
22   Ibid., 89.
23   Ibid., 24.

myself up to let him lead and instruct me, I universally found it in the highest degree useful. I found I could not live without enjoying the presence of God. . . . The Lord taught me, in those early days of my Christian experience, many important truths in regard to the spirit of prayer."[24]

One such truth learned in prayer came when Judge Wright's sister-in-law became seriously ill. Finney said, "It seemed to plant an arrow, as it were, in my heart. It came upon me in the sense of a burden that crushed me, the nature of which I could not at all understand; but with it came an intense desire to pray for that woman."[25] But as he went to the meetinghouse to pray, he could not say much except to "groan with groanings deep and loud."[26] Finally, after repeatedly groaning, agonizing, weeping, and making repeated trips between the office and meetinghouse, he prevailed in prayer and received the assurance that not only would the woman not die, but she would also not die in her sins. The woman fully recovered and soon found hope in Christ.

FINNEY'S PREACHING AND PRESENCE

After Finney's baptism experience, he wrote, "I had no desire to make money. I had no hungering and thirsting after worldly pleasures and amusements in any direction. My whole mind was taken up with Jesus and his salvation, and the world seemed to me of very little consequence. Nothing, it seemed to me, could compete with the worth of souls, and no labor, I thought, could be so sweet and no employment

---

24 Finney, *Memoirs*, 35–36: GGR 301.
25 Ibid.
26 Finney, *Autobiography*, 38.

so exalted as that of holding up Christ to a dying world."[27] When the presbytery arrived in 1824 to ordain him, his reputation had preceded him. However, having no desire to preach to Christians in churches, he decided instead to preach in public schoolhouses through the women's missionary society, traveling back and forth between Evans Mills and Antwerp, New York.

Borrowing from his years of training as an attorney, Finney preached using a lot of repetition, common speech, and practical illustrations—as if he were sitting in a parlor talking. Indeed, Finney was often asked why he talked instead of preaching. Instead of writing out his sermons, he would go out among the people to learn their needs and desires. Then, led by the Spirit, he would pray over the subject until his spirit was full and then pour out what God gave him on the people. He said that words and illustrations came to him as fast as he could deliver them and that if he ever wrote a sermon outline, it was afterward to preserve it, not before. He said, "If I did not preach from inspiration, I don't know how I did preach."[28] Finney's preaching was always blunt and direct, holding the people responsible for their sins as well as their salvation. Although Finney had once expressed opposition to the "ranting and excesses of the Kentucky frontier revivals," his own preaching produced similar results such as in Antwerp when 400 suddenly fell to the floor. He wrote, "I had not spoken . . . more than a quarter of an hour when all at once . . . the congregation began to fall from their seats in every direction and cry for mercy. . . . Nearly the whole congregation were either on their knees or prostrate in less

---

27 Ibid., 28

28 Basil Miller, *Charles Finney: He Prayed Down Revivals* (Grand Rapids, Mich.: Zondervan, 1951), 34: GGR 304.

than two minutes from this first shock that fell upon them. . . . I was obliged to stop preaching, for they no longer paid attention."[29]

Sometimes Finney's presence alone was enough to convict sinners, such as the time he toured a cotton manufacturing plant in New York Mills. As he passed through one of the departments where many young women were busy weaving, he observed two in particular who were looking at him and conversing. As he slowly walked toward them, one of the girl's hands started trembling until she could no longer work. When he was within eight to ten feet of her, she sank to the floor and burst into tears. Soon the whole factory fell under the power of God until the owner said to the superintendent, "Stop the mill and let the people attend to religion, for it is more important that our souls should be saved than that this factory run." So they gathered the workers in the spinning jenny room and had a revival. Within a few days, nearly everyone in the mill had been converted, and two new churches were formed from the three thousand converts.

Known as the "Father of Modern Revivalism," Charles Grandison Finney's revival methods combined with his teachings on a subsequent empowerment of the Spirit inspired the modern Holiness movement and laid the groundwork for Pentecostalism in the United States and abroad. Source: The International Church of the Nazarene.

In Evans Mills, Finney ran into one of the presbyters at his ordination, Father Daniel Nash (1775–1831). Father Nash had recently been confined to a dark room with an eye disease and, unable to read

29   MacNutt, *Overcome by the Spirit*, 110: MCH 351–352; Finney, Autobiography, 82.

or write, decided to dedicate the rest of his life to prayer. But now he was emerging spiritually transformed and doing much better. Finney noted, "He was full of the power of prayer" and "praying with him and hearing him pray in meetings, I found that his gift of prayer was wonderful and his faith almost miraculous."[30] The two quickly formed a partnership that would soon become legendary. Their goal, as stated by Nash, was simple: "When Mr. Finney and I began our race, we had no thought of going amongst ministers. Our highest ambition was to go where there was neither minister nor reformation and try to look up the lost sheep, for whom no man cared."[31]

One example of Nash's prayers, as shared by Finney, involved a local bartender whom he described as "a most violent and outrageous opposer" of revival and who delighted in cursing and swearing whenever Christians were around.[32] What's more, his tavern had become an oasis for everyone in the region who opposed Finney's revivals. But when Father Nash heard about this "hard case," he was much grieved and distressed and immediately added his name to his prayer list, praying for him several times a day. A few days later, Finney was holding an evening meeting when who should walk in but this bartender. His entrance made quite a stir as everyone feared the worst. But Finney, keeping an eye on him, soon realized he had not come to create trouble but seemed spiritually troubled instead and ready to receive Christ. Sure enough, the man soon stood, trembling, and asked if he could speak. Finney obliged, and the man proceeded

---

30 J. Paul Reno, *Daniel Nash: Prevailing Prince of Prayer* (Asheville, N.C.: Revival Literature, 1989), 7, 19.

31 Ibid., 7.

32 Ibid., 20.

to give one of the most heartbroken confessions ever heard, leading many others to repent. Soon all profanity and revelry in that town ceased as prayer meetings were held nightly at the tavern.

FINNEY'S REVIVALS

Finney's revivals happened as follows: "When God would direct where a meeting was to be held, Father Nash would slip quietly into town and seek to get two or three people to enter into a covenant of prayer with him. Sometimes he had with him a man of similar prayer ministry, Abel Clary. Together they would begin to pray fervently for God to move in the community."[33] Another wrote, "Charles Finney so realized the need of God's working in all his service that he was wont to send godly Father Nash on in advance to pray down the power of God into the meetings which he was about to hold."[34] Finney shared, "On one occasion when I got to town to start a revival a lady contacted me who ran a boarding house. She said, 'Brother Finney, do you know a Father Nash? He and two other men have been at my boarding house for the last three days, but they haven't eaten a bite of food. I opened the door and peeped in at them because I could hear them groaning, and I saw them down on their faces. They have been this way for three days, lying prostrate on the floor and groaning. I thought something awful must have happened to them. I was afraid to go in and I didn't know what to do. Would you please come see about them?' 'No, it isn't necessary,' I replied. 'They just have a spirit of travail in prayer.'"[35] Even after Finney's arrival, Nash rarely attended meetings but instead

---

33   Ibid., 7.
34   Ibid., 9.
35   Ibid., 8.

remained in a nearby house praying for the conviction of the Holy Spirit to melt the crowd.

Thus, between 1825 and 1827, Finney and Nash successfully filled town halls through the frontier communities of Western New York. This area had formerly been known as the "burned-over district" because so many itinerant preachers had previously come through, making its residents hardened to the gospel. However, Finney and Nash viewed it as just another opportunity to break up fallow ground.[36] Finney's revivals were also greatly aided by the completion of the Erie Canal in 1825, which connected the Great Lakes to the Hudson River and turned the cities along the canal into bustling centers of industry. Then between 1827 and 1829, the two men traveled through Pennsylvania and Delaware and finally to New York City between 1829 and 1830. Everywhere Finney and Nash went, the Spirit of God was poured out and the flames of revival spread. But as Finney's revivals grew, so did his enemies. They accused him of being a shameless self-promoter who stirred and manipulated crowds into emotional frenzies in order to attract larger and larger audiences. He was also criticized for what some considered coarse, irreverent, and barbaric speech and for allowing women to minister, such as in mixed-gender prayer meetings. However, by the fall of 1830, nearly all of Finney's critics had fallen silent.

THE ROCHESTER REVIVAL

After leaving New York City, Finney felt consternation about where to go next. He had received an urgent invitation to come to Rochester

---

36   Hos. 10:12

but had heard many reports about the division and strife among the churches there. Thus, after meeting with his top prayer leaders in Utica, New York, and after much discussion and prayer, he resolved not to go to Rochester and retired for the evening, fully intending to take a canal boat east in the morning and head south to New York or Philadelphia. But then the inward voice said, *What are the reasons that keep you from going to Rochester?* Finney divulged a list of reasons. *Ah! But are these good reasons?* the voice replied. *Certainly you are needed at Rochester all the more because of these difficulties. Do you avoid the field because there are so many things that need to be corrected, because there is so much that is wrong? But if all was right, you would not be needed.* The next morning Finney took a canal boat west to Rochester.

While in Rochester, Finney felt led to take "new measures," adopting for the first time the Methodist "anxious bench" on which those seeking God could be called forward to take special reserved seating. Many more came than expected, and between 1830 and 1831, Finney preached several nights a week and three times on Sunday. Soon all infighting stopped. Local businesses closed to let their employees attend the meetings, bars closed for a lack of business, crime rates dropped dramatically, and women went door-to-door praying for people and inviting them to the services. Even the entire student body at the local high school was converted after Finney was invited to speak to them. One student at Rochester Academy wrote, "The whole community was stirred. Religion was the topic of conversation, in the house, in the shop, in the office and on the street. The only theater in the city was converted into a livery stable; the only circus into a soap and candle factory. Grog [liquor] shops were closed; the Sabbath was honored; the sanctuaries were thronged with happy worshippers; a new impulse was given to every philanthropic enterprise; the fountains of benevolence were opened, and men lived to good."[37] The revival then spread into the neighboring communities as far as a hundred miles away.

Dr. Lyman Beecher (1775–1863), father of Harriet Beecher Stowe, the famous abolitionist and author of *Uncle Tom's Cabin*, who had previously been an outspoken critic of Finney, described the effects of the Rochester revival: "That was the greatest work of God, and the greatest revival that the world has ever seen in so short a time. One hundred thousand were reported as having connected themselves with churches as the results of that great revival. This is unparalleled in the history of the church."[38] Finney himself wrote, "At Rochester . . . the waters of salvation had risen so high, revivals had become so powerful and extensive . . . that men were afraid to oppose them."[39] One biographer wrote, "The Rochester revival would prove to be the height of the Second Great Awakening and a spark to light the fuse of a national revival that ran like wildfire throughout the United States in 1831."[40] Revival flames could be felt as far away as Ohio and New England. In New England alone, churches grew by one-third that year. One prominent foreign observer visiting the U.S. during this time noted, "There is no country in the world in which the Christian religion retains a greater influence over the souls of men."[41]

---

37   V. Raymond Edman, *Finney Lives On* (Minneapolis: Bethany House, 1971), 68: CC 127–128: GGR 318.

38   Finney, *Autobiography*, 164–165.

39   Ibid., 165.

40   GGR 319.

41   Alexis de Tocqueville, *Democracy in America* (1835).

A PREVAILING PRINCE OF PRAYER

Finney attributed it all to prayer, saying, "The key which unlocked the Heavens in this revival was the prayer of Clary, Father Nash, and other unnamed folk who laid themselves prostrate before God's throne and besought Him for a divine out-pouring."[42] Nash died later that same year, and Finney left itinerant preaching to go pastor in New York City. These were among Nash's last known written words: "I am now convinced, it is my duty and privilege, and the duty of every other Christian, to pray for as much of the Holy Spirit as came down on the day of Pentecost, and a great deal more. I know not why we may not ask for the entire and utmost influence of the Spirit to come down, and, asking in faith, see the full answer. . . . I have only just begun to understand what Jesus meant when He said, 'All things whatsoever ye shall ask in prayer, believing, ye shall receive.'"[43] At Father Nash's passing, Finney wrote, "He used to take the map of the world before him, and pray, and look over the different countries and pray for them, till he expired in his room, praying. Blessed man! He was the reproach of the ungodly, and of carnal, unbelieving professors; but he was the favorite of Heaven, and a prevailing prince of prayer."[44]

PASTORING IN NEW YORK

When Finney arrived at the Second Free Presbyterian Church in New York, he informed the brethren he did not intend to fill the house "with Christians from other churches." Instead, they would "gather from

---

42 Reno, *Daniel Nash*, 12.

43 Ibid., 24–25.

44 Ibid., 25–26.

the world" and "secure the conversion of the ungodly to the utmost possible extent."[45] The Chatham Street Garden Theatre was soon converted to this end. Upon completion, Finney preached to Sunday crowds of two to three thousand while leading revivals three times a week. Finney urged church members to spread out among the crowd, keeping their eyes open for anyone who seemed seriously affected by the preaching, and then try to detain them afterward for prayer in a nearby room. The church became so full they had to send out groups to start other churches—seven, in fact, by the time Finney left.

Finney left the Presbyterian Church in 1836 to pastor the new 2,400-seat Broadway Tabernacle Congregational Church, which he had helped design. Disillusionment over some of the presbyters' rulings led him to the decision. During this time, Finney denounced what he called "the abominable institution of slavery" while being ever so careful not to divert the church's attention from their primary work of converting souls.[46] Also during this time, he published his *Lectures on Revival* which sold quickly throughout North America and Europe—especially in England, Scotland, and Ireland, where he had also preached. They inspired George Williams to found the Young Men's Christian Association (YMCA) in London in 1844. In the lectures, Finney lambasted the Calvinistic idea of waiting on God for revival when God was clearly waiting on them. He declared, "People cannot do Satan's work more effectively than by using the sovereignty of God as a reason for not endeavoring to produce a revival."[47] And

---

45 Finney, *Autobiography*, 173.

46 Ibid., 174.

47 Charles G. Finney, *Lectures on Revival* (Minneapolis: Bethany House, 1988), 18

again, "Christians are more to blame for not being revived than sinners are for not being converted."[48]

"Preaching at Broadway Tabernacle" lithograph by F. Palmer & Co., 1850. Seating more than 2,400 people, Broadway Tabernacle was considered one of the most influential churches constructed in America in its day and was either the first or the forerunner of the American megachurch. Created for Charles G. Finney, (Finney personally influenced the design) it was also a center for anti-slavery spirit in New York City. Source: The New York Public Library Digital Collections. Photo: Wikimedia/Fæ.

TEACHING AT OBERLIN

Meanwhile, a controversy was developing at Lane Seminary in Cincinnati, Ohio, where the student body was made up almost entirely of Finney converts, while all the seminary trustees except one owned slaves. Therefore, when the trustees voted to allow slavery among its students and faculty, Asa Mahan, the lone opposing trustee, and a group of about fifty students known as the "Lane Rebels" left to begin a new school of theology at the Oberlin Collegiate Institute near Cleveland. The group invited Finney to join their faculty in the fall of 1835. Mahan became president, Finney, professor of theology, and the "Lane Rebels" were among its first theology students.

Before agreeing to join them, Finney stipulated there was to be no discrimination at the school based on color. Oberlin became not only America's first college to admit African-American students but also America's first coeducational institution, admitting four women

---

48   Ibid., 22.

in 1837. Oberlin's first black student, George B. Vashon, graduated in 1844 before becoming a founding professor of Howard University and the first black lawyer to be admitted to the New York State Bar. In 1850, the school became Oberlin College. In 1862, Mary Jane Patterson graduated from Oberlin, becoming the first black woman to earn a B.A. degree. Oberlin itself became a key stop along the Underground Railroad for runaway slaves, earning it the title "the town that started the Civil War."[49] President James A. Garfield would later tell a group of Oberlin students, "No college in the land had more effectively touched the nerve centers of the national life and thought and ennobled them than did this institution to which Finney devoted so many years of Christian service."[50]

THE SECOND BLESSING

Over the years, Finney grew increasingly alarmed over the number of converts from his revivals who had backslidden. Though an unprecedented 85 percent of those converted in Finney's revivals reportedly continued to live Christian lives years later—an astounding figure by any standard and in any age—Finney still grieved.[51] He concluded that a further work of the Holy Spirit was necessary for Christians to live holy lives and adopted Wesley's second work doctrine, which he called the "second blessing." Finney's revival methods, combined with his teachings on subsequent empowerment

---

49   Nat Brandt, *The Town that Started the Civil War* (Syracuse University Press: 1990): "Oberlin, Ohio," *Wikipedia: en.wikipedia.org/wiki/Oberlin,_Ohio* (Accessed 25 February 2013).

50   Miller, *Charles Finney: He Prayed Down Revivals*, 96–97: GGR 326.

51   Wesley Duewel, *Revival Fire* (Grand Rapids, Mich.: Zondervan, 1995), 92 [hereafter RF].

of the Spirit, would soon inspire the Holiness movement and lay the groundwork for modern Pentecostalism in the United States. Meanwhile, across the pond Pentecostal awakenings were also taking place.

GUSTAV VON BELOW

Gustav von Below (1790–1843), a Lutheran Pietist aristocrat and army officer in Prussia (part of modern-day Germany, Poland, and Russia), and his brothers began inviting nobles and commoners alike to join them on their estates in 1817 for informal study and worship. As worshipers began taking increasing roles in the meetings and patterning their practices after the early church, all the gifts of the Spirit including speaking and singing in tongues became common among them, affecting many high government and military officials. The movement quickly spread throughout Pomerania and eventually to the U.S. through immigration. Although the groups were temporarily suspended from the main body of Prussian Evangelical Christians because of their charismatic experiences, an ecclesiastical commission sent to investigate later declared the phenomenon to be "of God."[52]

EDWARD IRVING

In 1827, Edward Irving (1792–1834), pastor of Scotland's Caledonian Church at Regent Square in London, preached a series of messages using Acts 2:38 for his text: "Repent, and be baptized, every one of you, in the name of Jesus Christ for the remission of sins, and you shall

---

52 Karl Ecke, *Durchbruch des Urchristentums* (Nürnberg, n.d.), 13ff: CM 84–85.

receive the gift of the Holy Ghost." After noting that many had taught that this was an inward gift of sanctification because the outward gift of power had ceased with the passing of the apostles, he explained he could see no reason why the church could not still receive the complete gift of the Holy Spirit—including the gift of power.[53] Of course, this and other similar statements soon placed him at odds with church officials, to whom he replied: "If they ask for an explanation of the fact that these powers have ceased in the Church, I answer, that they have decayed just as faith and holiness have decayed; but that they have ceased is not a matter so clear. Till the time of the Reformation, this opinion was never mooted [doubted] in the Church; and to this day the Roman Catholics, and every other portion of the Church but ourselves, maintain the very contrary."[54]

WEST SCOTLAND REVIVAL

Then in 1830, Mary Campbell, who lived in West Scotland's Port Glasgow area and was dying of tuberculosis, spoke in tongues. Since Mary's sister Isabella had recently died of the same disease, many were clinging to hope for Mary's healing. On Sunday, March 28, one of Mary's sisters and a friend had been praying and fasting in the house all day for a restoration of the "Gifts." That evening, they entered Mary's room praying. Other family members joined in. Then "the Holy Ghost came with mighty power . . . as she lay in her weakness, and constrained her to speak at great length and with superhuman

---

53   C. Gordon Strachan, *The Pentecostal Theology of Edward Irving* (London: Darton, Longmann & Todd, 1973), 55: CC 118–119.

54   Ibid., 82: CC 119.

strength in an unknown tongue, to the astonishment of all who heard, and to her own great edification and enjoyment in God."[55]

A month later, James MacDonald, who lived on the other side of the river not far from the Campbells, also received the baptism in the Holy Spirit. After receiving this baptism experience, he went into the room of his sister Margaret, who was also nearing death, and commanded her to rise. She rose, miraculously healed. Acquainted with Mary Campbell's case, Mr. MacDonald then felt impressed to write her a letter commanding her to also rise. As the letter was read to Mary, "a power which no words can describe" came upon her, followed by a voice she described as "indeed the voice of Christ" directing her to rise, dress herself, and rejoin her family. She wrote, "I was verily made in a moment to stand upon my feet, leap and walk, sing and rejoice."[56] A few days later, James MacDonald and his brother George both began speaking in tongues. These events soon stirred the whole region as the MacDonalds house became filled with people from all over England, Scotland, and Ireland.

LONDON REVIVAL

As news of these events reached Edward Irving's church in London, he urged caution, realizing that if the reports were true, "it would revolutionize the Church and make such an upturning as the world had not seen."[57] However, after meeting personally with the MacDonalds

---

55 Jean Christie Root, *Edward Irving: Man, Preacher, Prophet* (Sherman, French, 1912), 69–81: MM 228.

56 Robert Norton, M.D., *Memoirs of James and George MacDonald of Port Glasgow* (n.p.: n.d.), 109–110; Strachan, *Edward Irving*, 68: CC 120.

57 Strachan, *Edward Irving*, 69: CC 120.

and Campbells and other eyewitnesses, he concluded the events were indeed a genuine work of the Spirit and began testifying publicly of them. Soon 6:30 a.m. prayer meetings were being formed throughout his church for the purpose of seeking such gifts. A year later, in 1831, Mrs. Cardale, a church member and wife of a prominent London attorney, spoke in tongues at a home prayer meeting. Six months later, Miss Hall left the sanctuary and ran into the church vestry speaking in tongues. The following Sunday, several spoke in tongues and prophesied during the morning worship, angering some of Irving's more sedate parishioners. This continued for three months.

THE CATHOLIC APOSTOLIC CHURCH

While most of the church supported Irving and the new manifestations, a few key leaders opposed him and reported him to the presbytery, who found him guilty of allowing individuals to lead public worship without official appointment or ordination. Irving was removed from his pastorate and locked out of his church. Now with no place to worship, Irving and about eight hundred members joined a new prayer movement and formed a new congregation of the "Catholic Apostolic Church" on Newman Street, which quickly became the "Central Church" of the new movement. Then, after being excommunicated from the Church of Scotland in 1833, Irving began formulating his views on the baptism in the Holy Spirit, which he believed to be an endowment of power subsequent to regeneration. He also spoke of a baptism "whose standing sign, if we err not, is the speaking in tongues" and the "root and stem" from which all the other gifts flowed.[58] To Irving, speaking in tongues was the "outward and visible sign of that inward and invisible grace which the baptism of the Holy Ghost conferreth."[59] Irving also understood tongues as a form of edification: "Therefore it is nothing to be doubted that tongues are a great instrument for personal edification, however mysterious it may seem to us; and they are on that account greatly to be desired."[60]

In an effort to fully restore early Catholic Apostolic Christianity, six persons were prophesied and declared to be "apostles." Among them were several from Irving's church, which then sent Irving to Glasgow to begin a new church. Already weakened by tuberculosis, however, Irving, traveling by horseback, soon died at the age of forty-two. Though the movement would quickly spread into continental Europe, America, and worldwide, Irving's untimely death left the young denomination entirely in the hands of laymen. In their attempt to infuse Roman and Eastern Orthodox liturgy, these laymen gradually choked out the Spirit and, void of any successors, the organization all but dissolved in 1868. Membership continued to decline after the death of their last "apostle" in 1901. However, a schism group called the "New Apostolic Church," broke off in Hamburg, Germany, in 1868. Though the New Apostolic Church today barely resembles the original, it boasts more than 11 million members worldwide (mostly Africans and Indians).

---

58   David Dorries, "Edward Irving and the Standing Sign," IE 49: CC 121.

59   Vinson Synan, *The Century of the Holy Spirit: 100 Years of Pentecostal and Charismatic Renewal* (Nashville: Thomas Nelson, 2001), 23 [hereafter CHS].

60   Dorries, Edward Irving, IE 51: CC 122.

Thus, seventy years before modern Pentecostalism began, Edward Irving formulated the classical Pentecostal doctrine, making him not only a Pentecostal forerunner but also among the first Protestants to acknowledge supernatural gifts as a permanent endowment of the church. Others like William Arthur, a British Methodist preacher and contemporary of Irving, concurred: "We feel satisfied that he who does expect the gift of healing and the gift of tongues or any other miraculous manifestation of the Holy Spirit . . . has ten times more scriptural ground on which to base his expectation, than have they, for their unbelief, who do not expect supernatural sanctifying strength for the believer."[61]

Seventy years before the modern Pentecostal movement began, Edward Irving formulated the classical Pentecostal doctrine of Spirit baptism as an endowment of power subsequent to regeneration "whose standing sign" is "speaking in tongues." This made him not only a Pentecostal forerunner but also among the first Protestants to acknowledge supernatural gifts as a permanent endowment of the church. Source: zosotruthtalk.wordpress.com.

American Baptist pastor A.J. Gordon described Irving as "a man of wonderful endowments" who "was accused of offering strange fire upon the altar of his church because he thought to relight the fire of Pentecost."[62] Irving's teachings represented a major milestone in the development of what would later become classical Pentecostal Christianity.

---

61   William Arthur, *The Tongue of Fire* (Columbia, S.C.: L.L. Pickett, 1891), 315: CHS 25–26.
62   A.J. Gordon, *The Ministry of Healing*, 102–103: CC 129.

JOHANN BLUMHARDT

Johann Christoph Blumhardt (1805-1880) was a Lutheran Pietist theologian and pastor in the tiny village of Möttlingen in Germany's Black Forest in 1842 when a young girl named Gottliebin Dittus and her family attended his church. Gottliebin struggled with many illnesses, was tormented by lights and sounds, and would often convulse in Blumhardt's presence. Finally realizing he had a case of demon-possession in his parish much like those recorded in the New Testament, Blumhardt tried many times to pray for the young girl, but to no avail. Finally crying out in desperation one day, he said: "Gottliebin, put your hands together and pray, 'Lord Jesus, help me!' We have seen enough of what the devil can do; now let us see what the Lord Jesus can do!" The attack immediately stopped, but then later returned. Over the next year, a series of prayer meetings ensued which came to a fevered pitch one evening when Gottliebin's sister (who herself had come under demonic attack) shouted, "Jesus is victor!" And from that moment on, Gottliebin and her family were completely restored.[63]

In the months that followed, prayer meetings continued every night as adults and youth alike confessed their sins, marriages were restored, addictions were broken, crimes confessed, and many received physical healings. Hundreds came from far and wide as Blumhardt's churchyard was filled to overflowing. The village could hardly accommodate the numbers of people streaming to it. Blumhardt said the people came from "from seven o'clock in the morning until eleven o'clock at night" for what he called the "Awakening."[64]

---

63 "Deliverance Leads to Healing and Revival," (2004) *Healing and Revival Press: healingandrevival.com/BioJBlumhardt.htm* (Accessed 15 May 2016).

64 Ibid.

Miracles and healings became daily occurrences. One mother came running to Blumhardt because she had spilled a pot of boiling oatmeal on her three-year-old child. The child was screaming in pain and covered with burns. Blumhardt picked the child up, prayed, and all pain immediately ceased and the burns were gone within days. Parents from another village brought their son who had an eye disease. Blumhardt prayed and his sight was fully restored within days. It was said, "Infirmities of all kinds vanished: eye problems, tuberculosis, eczema, arthritis, and more." One eyewitness said, "There were so many miracles that I can no longer recall the details. We felt the Lord's nearness so tangibly that they seemed natural, and no one made a great deal of it."[65]

In time, however, church and governmental leaders told Blumhardt he could no longer include healing as part of his pastoral duty, but would have to direct people to the medical profession. Blumhardt obliged, but when he saw apathy return to his parish and the Awakening being lost, he decided to purchase a run-down sulphur springs spa in Bad Boll, Germany, where he could continue to preach and minister to the sick without limitation. Again, the people flocked to Bad Boll, where as many as 150 at a time could stay and receive healing. Blumhardt, however, asked that healing not become the focal point of the ministry, asking instead that the people honor all of God's gifts. If someone made reference to Blumhardt being a hero who healed the sick, he would immediately

---

65   Ibid.

point to Christ as the hero and repeat his famous quote: "That I don't know, but this I do know; Jesus is the victor".[66]

After Blumhardt's death, his ministry was carried on for a season by his son, Christoph Friedrich Blumhardt who would later turn to politics. Today, the Blumhardts are best known for their "kingdom-now" or "kingdom-come" theology which would have great influence on other theologians like Karl Barth and Dietrich Bonhoeffer. Their theology may be summed up by the phrase "Jesus is Victor" as a means of God's kingdom and power breaking in on a situation to liberate humanity from spiritual and physical bondage.

SERAPHIM OF SAROV

Further east, a renowned monk, mystic, *starets* (elder), and wonderworker, Seraphim of Sarov (c. 1754–1833) in obedience to a vision decided to devote the rest of his life to helping suffering humanity. Hundreds of pilgrims a day came to visit him as Seraphim prophesied, healed the sick, spoke words of wisdom, and frequently told his guests what they were thinking before they could ask, making him one of the greatest *startsy* (elders) in the history of the Eastern Orthodox Church.

Seraphim, the son of a merchant in Kursk, Central Russia, became seriously ill at the age of ten. But after receiving a night vision, Seraphim was miraculously healed several days later. At eighteen, Seraphim cared little for the family business but loved to

---

66 "Johann Blumhardt," *Wikipedia: en.wikipedia.org/wiki/Johann_Blumhardt* (Accessed 15 May 2016).

pray, attend church, and read about the lives of the saints, and soon entered the Sarov monastery. As he withdrew to the forest to pray in the tradition of monasticism, he again became severely ill and was again healed after receiving a vision. Later taking his monastic vows at age twenty-seven, he was assigned the name "Seraphim," which in Hebrew means "fiery" or "burning-one." Seraphim soon became the priest and spiritual leader of his convent before again retreating to prayer in his log cabin in the woods, this time for twenty-five years.

One day while chopping wood, Seraphim was attacked by a gang of thieves, severely beaten, and left to die. But when the robbers were finally caught and brought to justice, Seraphim only pleaded for mercy, interceding on their behalf though he himself would remain hunchbacked the rest of his life. Also in monastic tradition and despite the pain from his injuries, Seraphim then spent a thousand consecutive days and nights with little rest, kneeling on a rock with his hands uplifted toward heaven in prayer.

Then in 1815, in obedience to yet another vision, Seraphim began admitting pilgrims to his hermitage. Thousands of people from all walks of life eventually came to visit the elder to receive healing and to partake of the rich spiritual treasures acquired over a lifetime of spending time with God in prayer. Seraphim greeted all his guests by falling prostrate on the ground, kissing their hands, calling them "my joy," and proclaiming, "Christ is risen!" One of Seraphim's most famous sayings to his guests was "Acquire a peaceful spirit, and around you thousands will be saved." Seraphim believed the purpose of the Christian life was to "acquire the Holy Spirit," saying, "It is necessary that the Holy Spirit enter our heart. Everything good that we do, that we do for Christ, is given to us by the Holy Spirit, but prayer most of all, which is always available to us."[67]

Thousands from all walks of life came to visit the elder Seraphim of Sarov to receive healing, prophecy, and words of knowledge and wisdom as he taught them the purpose of the Christian life—to acquire the Holy Spirit. Source: Wikimedia/KAK.

A CONVERSATION WITH SERAPHIM

One cloudy wintry November day in 1831 when the ground lay thick with snow and great flakes were still falling, Nikolay Motovilov (1809–1879), a Russian landowner, disciple of Seraphim, and proclaimed "Fool for Christ," was asked to sit on a stump in the woods near Seraphim's cabin as Seraphim sat across from him. As was often his custom, Seraphim preempted the conversation saying, "The Lord has shown me, that when you were a child you wanted to know the goal of the Christian life and that you had put this question to a number of eminent ecclesiastics. Yet no one told you anything definite. They instructed you to go to church, to pray, to do good works, telling you that there lay the goal of the Christian life. Some of them even said to you: 'Don't search into things that are beyond you.' Well, miserable servant that I am, I am going to try to explain to you what this goal is.

---

67   Bishop Alexander (Mileant), *St. Seraphim of Sarov: Life and Teachings*,
      Nicholas and Natalia Semyanko, trans.: "Seraphim of Sarov,"
      OrthodoxWiki: orthodoxwiki.org/Seraphim_of_Sarov (Accessed 18 September 2014).

Prayer, fasting, works of mercy—all this is very good, but it represents only the means, not the end of the Christian life. The true end is the acquisition of the Holy Spirit."

After Motovilov asked what he meant by the "acquisition of the Holy Spirit," Seraphim continued, "To acquire means to gain possession. You know what it means to earn money, don't you? Well, it is the same with the Holy Spirit. The aim of some men is to grow rich, to receive honours and distinction. The Holy Spirit himself is also capital, but eternal capital. Our Lord compared our life to trading and the works of this life to buying. 'Buy from me gold . . . that you may be rich' (Rev. 3:18). . . . In the parable of the virgins, it was said to the foolish virgins when they had no oil: 'Go to the dealers and buy. . . . ' The lack of oil is usually interpreted as the lack of good works, but this is not the real meaning. . . . Unworthy as I am, I dare to think that what they were lacking was the grace of the Holy Spirit. For the essential thing is not just to do good but to acquire the Holy Spirit as the one eternal treasure which will never pass away."

As Motovilov again expressed doubts as to how one could know he had acquired the Holy Spirit, Seraphim reiterated, "Friend of God, I've already told you that it's very easy: I've told you that some men found themselves filled with the Holy Spirit and were able to be convinced of his presence; what more do you want?" "I want to understand completely!" replied Motovilov. Then Seraphim grabbed Motovilov firmly by the shoulders and said, "My friend, both of us, at this moment, are in the Holy Spirit, you and I. Why won't you look at me?" "I can't look at you, Father," Motovilov replied, "because the light flashing from your eyes and face is brighter than the sun and I'm dazzled!" Seraphim replied, "Don't be afraid, friend of God, you yourself are shining just like I am; you too are now in the fullness of the grace of the Holy Spirit, otherwise you wouldn't be able to see me as you do."[68]

THE MOLOKANS

The Molokans were a sect of "Spiritual Christian" Russian peasants who, similar to Western Protestants, had broken away from the Russian Orthodox Church in the 1550s by rejecting religious icons and denying the Czar's divine right to rule. Their enemies called them "Molokans," which means "milk-drinkers," because they continued to eat meat and drink milk even on traditional Eastern Orthodox fasting days. The Molokans claimed to be direct descendants of the ancient Armenian Paulicians and, much like Western Anabaptists, were known for their pacifism, communal living, and spiritual worship. In the seventeenth century, the Molokans were severely ostracized for their refusal to take up arms or assist in military service. By the eighteenth century, the Czarist government had pushed them out of central Russia, forcing many to settle in the Transcaucasus mountains of Armenia and Azerbaijan near Mt. Ararat, where a revival broke out in 1833.

THE JUMPERS AND LEAPERS

The spiritual outpouring created a schism between the traditional Molokans known as "the Constants" and the new revivalists called "the Jumpers and Leapers" for their ecstatic worship and miracles, which they said rivaled even that of the apostles. In addition to their prophesying, speaking in tongues, raising hands in worship, jumping

---

68   Valentine Zander, *St. Seraphim of Sarov* (Crestwood, NY: St. Vladimir's Seminary Press, 1975), 84–86, 90: CP 187–88.

and skipping came in response to a prophecy given by their founder, Lukian Sokoloff, who declared that a time was coming when the righteous would "skip and jump like calves and lambs of the field." In 1854, the mantle of leadership was passed from Sokoloff to Maxim Rudometkin (c. 1818–1877), a popular charismatic leader who often traveled from village to village preaching repentance, declaring the millennial reign of Christ was at hand, and calling his followers "New Israelites" or "Children of Zion." Maxim also appointed two prophets and two prophetesses to represent him in spiritual matters in the community. During this time, many of the Jumpers and Leapers were betrayed by the Constants, who had them arrested.

In 1855, Rudometkin's spiritual leadership was confirmed by a twelve-year-old "Prophet Boy" named Efim Klubnikin, who also became prominent in the community as he prophesied of troubling times ahead. Soon some of the Molokans erected a public banner declaring an end to the Czarist reign and the beginning of the coming reign of Christ. Of course, this did not sit too well with government officials, who had determined by 1858 that Rudometkin's followers could pose a serious threat to the Czar's reign as well as to Eastern Orthodoxy. Rudometkin was soon arrested and imprisoned. Though he was eventually released to a monastery prison in 1869 after the minister of internal affairs found no basis for his life sentence, Rudometkin continued to be persecuted and beaten by the archpriest until he finally suffered a stroke and died in 1877. While in prison, Rudometkin wrote a series of spiritual manuscripts, which were smuggled out by friends and published in 1928 under the title the *Book of Spirit and Life*, which many Molokans use along with their Bibles to this day.

Rudometkin's writings affirmed the necessity of the baptism in the Holy Spirit and speaking in tongues:

> *We always stretch our innocent hands and pure hearts directly to Him in heaven single-mindedly, like children unto their father, and pray unto Him for the descent to us of the gift of the Holy Spirit in signs of the new tongues of fire and in measure as it pleases Him according to the diverse secrets of the will of His Father with whom we ever converse personally.... We have no need now of any teacher or preacher who himself is not baptized from on high with the Holy Spirit and fire, as we ourselves are always baptized in the manner of the holy apostles and all of those who are like them, who in that time all spoke in the new tongues of fire, of the mysteries of our God and His Lamb.... This baptism must always be within all of us who are of one mind. And everyone of us thus baptized must have on himself a spiritual sign, that is, the speech of the Spirit in the new tongues of fire.*[69]

Despite Rudometkin's imprisonment, the sect continued to grow rapidly, and by the end of the nineteenth century, there were between half a million and a million Molokans residing within the Russian empire. Meanwhile, Efim, the "Boy Prophet," continued reminding the people that great trouble was ahead and that the time to leave Russia was now. He declared, "soon the doors will close" and soon "leaving Russia would be impossible."[70] Early in the twentieth century, about 2,000 Molokans—mostly Jumpers and Leapers—left for North America. Many of them settled in the Los Angeles area and other parts of the west coast. Beginning in 1915, an estimated 1.5 million Armenian Christians

---

69   Maxim G. Rudmetkin, *Selections from the Book of Spirit and Life, Including the Book of Prayers and Songs* (Whittier, Calif.: Stockton, 1966), 61–76, 93–95, 119–210: CP 218.

70   "Molokan," *Wikipedia: en.wikipedia.org/wiki/Molokan* (Accessed 19 September 2014).

were slaughtered by Muslim and secular Ottoman Turks. Meanwhile, some of the Molokan immigrants who fled were said to have become influential in the famous Azusa Street Revival of 1906. Demos Shakarian, whose grandfather was among them, would one day help pave the way for America's postwar healing revival and charismatic movement. Demos often associated the Azusa Street Revival with the prophecies of Efim, the "Boy Prophet." Presently, about 25,000 Molokans reside in the U.S., and about 200 Molokan churches still exist in Russia and Azerbaijan. Molokans consider themselves true Pentecostals and their worship remains charismatic to this day.

Spiritual Christian Molokans in Los Angeles outside the Lorena Street "Big Church" in 1946. The sign reads "First United Christian Molokan Church of Spiritual Jumpers." Source: Paul Samarin, (ed.) The Molokan Review, v1.7, Los Angeles, California, August 1946, p. 17. Photo: Molokane.org.

PHOEBE WORRALL PALMER

The modern Holiness movement began in Phoebe Worrall Palmer's (1807–1874) parlor in 1835 as a movement within Methodism to recover Wesley's "second work of grace" doctrine. Phoebe and her husband, prominent New York physician Dr. Walter Palmer, were members of the Allen Street Methodist Church in New York City. Phoebe's sister, Mrs. Sarah A. Lankford, began holding the "Tuesday Meetings for the Promotion of Holiness," but by 1837, Phoebe, having experienced "entire sanctification" herself, began leading the meetings.

By 1839, men were allowed to come to the meetings and several Methodist bishops and other prominent theologians and ministers attended. Soon Phoebe and her husband were receiving invitations to speak at various churches, conferences, and camp meetings throughout the U.S., Canada, and Britain. Phoebe's first book, the *Way of Holiness* published in 1843, became a foundational book for the Holiness movement, and Phoebe went on to become a prolific author, later publishing a monthly magazine called the *Guide to Holiness*, which she edited until her death in 1874.

Borrowing from Finney's idea of protracted meetings, the Palmers' revivals ran anywhere from a few days to several weeks, with hundreds and sometimes thousands being converted and hundreds more receiving the "second blessing" of "entire sanctification" or "full baptism of the Holy Ghost." In her books, Phoebe described in colorful details some of their revival meetings in Great Britain. There was "weeping all over the house," and "the power of God" was "present to heal." "Girdings of almighty power" and "tokens of divine presence" were felt.[71] Phoebe spoke of one who came "seeking the endowment of power for which the one hundred and twenty were commanded to tarry. The baptism of fire descended; and, as in the early days of Christianity, utterance as a constraining gift was also given." She continued, "I might speak of many, very many, who have in a similar manner sought and obtained, with like results, the baptism of the Holy Ghost, and are working under the inspiration of this power."[72]

---

71 Phoebe Palmer, *Four Years in the Old World* (Boston: Foster & Palmer, 1865), 120, 111, 103: *Google Books: books.google.com/books/about/Four_Years_in_the_Old_World. html?id=WXo9AAAAYAAJ* (Accessed 22 February 2013).

72 Ibid., 126–127.

"A local preacher was the first to hasten to the communion-rail, and was the first to receive the 'tongue of fire.' Would that you could have heard his clear, unequivocal testimony, as with holy boldness, which perhaps scarcely was more than equaled on the day when the holy flame first descended on the Pentecostal morn, he spake as the Spirit gave utterance. . . . Surely now, as in the early days of the Spirit's dispensation, Pentecostal blessings bring Pentecostal power."[73] Note the replacement of traditional Wesleyan terminology with Pentecostal language. Phoebe Worrall Palmer's language would soon set a new precedence for generations to come.

The modern Holiness movement began as a movement within Methodism in Phoebe Worrall Palmer's living room in 1835 to recover Wesley's "second work of grace" doctrine. In addition to replacing traditional Wesleyan terminology with Pentecostal language in her book *Way of Holiness*, published in 1843, and her monthly *Guide to Holiness*, Phoebe and her husband, Dr. Walter Palmer, conducted protracted revival meetings throughout Great Britain, the U.S., and Canada. Source: The International Church of the Nazarene.

THE LAYMAN'S PRAYER REVIVAL OF 1857-58

In 1857, New York City businessman Jeremiah Lanphier, a convert at Finney's Broadway Tabernacle in New York who had been working tirelessly as a lay missionary to New York's inner-city residents, felt led to begin a weekly noontime prayer meeting. The meetings were to be held Wednesdays on the third floor of the old North Dutch Reformed Church on Fulton Street. They would be simple meetings that anyone could attend for a few minutes or the entire hour. Lanphier printed handbills entitled "How Often Should I Pray?" and dropped them off at nearby

---

73 Ibid., 96.

offices and warehouses and placed one on the church door. The first prayer meeting was held on September 23, 1857. Lanphier prayed alone for the first half hour. Soon, six other men from different denominations joined him. The following Wednesday, there were twenty, then forty. Before long, the meetings were daily. This did not alleviate the crowding as over a hundred—including many unsaved—kept coming. Within a month, the pastors who attended the Fulton Street meetings began holding similar meetings at their churches, and soon those meetings became overcrowded as well. Newspapers began reporting "an unusual spirit of prayer" as men and women, young and old alike, from every denomination came to experience the presence of God.

Within three months, similar meetings were springing up across America with thousands now praying in churches and homes. In New York, gospel tracts were distributed inviting others to attend. Three rooms at the Fulton Street Church were in overflow as hundreds more were being sent elsewhere in the city. The following March, a theater was opened for prayer, yet many more continued to be turned away. Now over 6,000 were coming to over one hundred prayer meetings in Manhattan and Brooklyn alone. Local shop signs read, "Closed; will re-open after prayer meeting." In Philadelphia, concert halls, fire stations, houses, and tents were filled to capacity. Some churches reported 5,000 new converts, and one tent meeting reported 150,000 in attendance over a four-month period. Soon similar noon prayer meetings were being held in Boston, Baltimore, Washington, D.C., Richmond, Charleston, Savannah, Mobile, New Orleans, Vicksburg, Memphis, St. Louis, Pittsburgh, Cincinnati, Chicago, and elsewhere. Even President Franklin Pierce started attending noon prayer meetings.

Jeremiah Calvin Lanphier, a simple New York City businessman and lay minister who received salvation at Finney's Broadway Tabernacle, organized a Wednesday noontime prayer meeting in 1857 that soon spread throughout the city and erupted into a major revival that lasted for years before going international. Source: bernielutchman.blogspot.com.

Noticeably absent from the revival were human organization and leadership. There were no preachers—just a revival built entirely on lay people, the Spirit of God, and miraculous answers to prayer. Also noteworthy was a most unusual display of unity among all social and denominational backgrounds. Even sinners felt comfortable attending the meetings to receive Christ. Others requested prayer for unsaved friends and loved ones. Telegraph companies allowed messages to be sent free of charge at certain times of the day as the flood of national testimonies seemed endless. One father requested prayer for his three unsaved sons living in another part of the country and soon received a letter stating that all three had been saved. Another requested prayer for his unsaved son on board a ship in the Pacific and soon received news of his conversion (which had occurred about the same time they prayed). Another group in Columbus, Ohio, prayed for their public schools, and all but two students in their high school were saved.

Those onboard ships heading for America reported sensing the presence of God when coming within 100 miles of the eastern shoreline. One ship felt God's presence so strongly they had a revival before landing. Before the ship could anchor, the captain had to request that a minister be brought onboard. A smaller commercial vessel reported everyone on board being converted within 150 miles of the eastern seaboard. Even the US battleship *North Carolina*, stationed in New York harbor, experienced a revival. Four Christians began holding prayer meetings on the lower deck when others heard them singing and began mocking and jeering them. But then the power of God hit them and they too fell on their knees crying for mercy. Hundreds on the ship were saved, and those transferred to other ships began holding revivals of their own.

A typical prayer meeting was opened by singing the first two stanzas of a hymn followed by a brief prayer from a lay leader or minister. The meetings were then opened to anyone who wanted to pray or speak, but for no more than five minutes. If someone went over the allotted time, a bell was rung and someone else would take a turn. Prayer requests and testimonies were often read and brief exhortations were given on prayer or revival, but all within the time limit. A leader would then close the meeting by pronouncing the benediction. Meetings were described as "so earnest, so solemn, the silence . . . so awful, the singing . . . so over-powering."[74]

Source: greatamericanrevivals.weebly.com.

"I recollect in one of our meetings in Boston that winter a gentleman arose and said, 'I am from Omaha, Nebraska. On my journey east I have found a continuous prayer meeting about two thousand miles in extent.'" – Memoirs of Rev. Charles G. Finney. In prayer meetings such as this one, there was no preaching—just lay people, the Spirit of God, and miraculous answers to prayer.

74   J. Edwin Orr, *The Fervent Prayer* (Chicago: Moody Press, 1974), 18: RF 128–136.

THE AMERICAN CIVIL WAR

Though many Americans in both the North and South remained bitterly divided on the issue of slavery in the years leading up to the Civil War, both sides claimed God was on their side. Nevertheless, the prayer revival that began in 1857 continued throughout the war. A strong prayer revival broke out among southern troops stationed in Richmond in 1861. It began in the hospitals among the wounded and then spread into the camps as the wounded returned to active duty. Prayer meetings were again organized as hundreds were converted. This soon spread to troops in Tennessee, Arkansas and throughout the Confederate armies. In fact, these revivals were encouraged by generals "Stonewall" Thomas J. Jackson and Robert E. Lee, both of whom were devout Christians. Chaplains and missionaries were allowed to distribute tracts and minister among the troops throughout the war. By the summer of 1863, Lee's Army of Northern Virginia had experienced what some have dubbed "the Great Revival of 1863" in which thousands were converted. By war's end, at least 150,000 southern soldiers had been converted, and at least one-third had become praying men. Others have described this as part of a "Third Great Awakening," which continued in America through the latter half of the nineteenth century.

In all, the prayer revival begun by Jeremiah Lanphier in 1857 led to the conversion of between 6 and 7 percent of the U.S. population and about 21 percent of the Confederate Army.[75] Then, as news of the Fulton Street revival spread to England, Scotland, Wales, Ireland, and other British settlements around the world, reports of a "continual Pentecost" or a "rushing mighty wind" continued to pour in—not a bad day's work for one layman.

---

75 RF 135–136.

STUDY QUESTIONS

1. Though both revolutions occurring within the same time period claimed "liberty," how was the French Revolution vastly different from the American Revolution?

2. What is liberalism and what sets it apart from both of its predecessors—humanism and secularism? Explain.

3. What were some of the conditions leading up to America's Second Great Awakening?

4. What were some of the weapons in the church's frontier arsenal used in America's Second Great Awakening?

5. How would you characterize Charles Finney's conversion and baptism in the Holy Spirit? What profound effects did these experiences have on both his life and ministry?

6. What were Finney's views on the baptism in the Holy Spirit subsequent to these experiences?

7. What was Charles Finney's working relationship with Father Daniel Nash?

8. What set Finney's Rochester revival apart from all other revivals to date? What circumstances led to the success of the revival?

9. Describe Finney's influence on America's Second Great Awakening? The Layman's Prayer Revival of 1857-58? The YMCA? The modern Holiness movement?

10. What makes Edward Irving a forerunner of modern Pentecostalism?

11. Who were the Spiritual "Jumpers and Leapers," and how were they able to influence three of America's greatest revivals—the Azusa Street Revival (Pentecostal movement), the healing revival, and the charismatic movement?

12. What were some of the unique features of the Layman's Prayer Revival? What effect did it have on the U.S.? The American Civil War? The world?

4

PENTECOSTAL PIONEERS

(C. 1866–1900)

After the American Civil War, all Americans were feeling the winds of change. Darwin's theory of evolution was gaining new inroads into society. The continued onslaught of liberalism and socialism from European-trained American college professors was also creating a new era of higher criticism of Christianity and the Bible. Moreover, modernism rejected all traditional forms of art, architecture, literature, faith, philosophy, social life, and activities in favor of a newly emerging economic, social, and political environment. Meanwhile, the Industrial Revolution, urbanization, and immigration were radically altering

America's landscape and presenting the church with an entirely new set of problems. But no one was feeling the winds of change quite like the Methodist Church in America. With America now in a state of postwar depression and an impoverished South desperately in need of reconstruction, many Americans once again turned to religion for answers. While one group of liberal Christians chose to embrace societal changes, believing society's ills could be remedied through volunteer efforts and a "social gospel," another group of conservative Christians chose to reject societal changes and, believing that a revival of "old-time religion" held the answer, began calling for a return to old-fashioned prewar camp meeting revivalism. As one southern Methodist bishop put it, "Nothing is so much needed at the present time throughout all these lands, as a general and powerful revival of scriptural holiness."[1] For some, even such innovations as robed choirs, organs, and seminary-trained ministers were considered much too modern and progressive.

THE HOLINESS MOVEMENT

In June 1867, a group of Methodist leaders called for a series of holiness camp meetings to be held in Vineland, New Jersey, for "the promotion of the work of entire sanctification," and The National Camp Meeting Association for the Promotion of Christian Holiness was born. It was hoped that through these meetings all would "realize together a Pentecostal baptism of the Holy Ghost" and return "with a view to increased usefulness in the churches of which we are members." The invitation went out in July: "Come, brothers and sisters of the various

---

1   Alexander Gross, *History of the Methodist Episcopal Church, South* (New York, 1894), 94: HPT 24.

denominations, and let us in this forest-meeting . . . make common supplication for the descent of the Spirit upon ourselves, the church, the nation, and the world."[2] Subsequent National Camp Meetings were held in Mannheim, Pennsylvania, and Round Lake, New York. The Round Lake meetings boasted 20,000 worshipers, including one president, Ulysses S. Grant. Particularly affected by these meetings were black Methodists and Baptists. In June 1877, a remarkable biracial, interdenominational, and mixed-gender revival was held at the Bethel African Methodist Episcopalian Church in Philadelphia. By the 1880s, the Holiness movement had gone nationwide as Holiness camp meetings, once again as in Whitefield's day, united Americans North and South under the banner of revival, helping to heal the breach caused by the Civil War.

American Pentecostalism is deeply rooted in the Holiness movement that swept the United States during the 1860s and 70s. Wesley's spiritual reformation in England developed into a full-blown revival in America as his belief in Christian Perfectionism was refined into a doctrine of "entire sanctification" or a "second blessing," which many believed to be the Pentecostal baptism. Holiness camp meetings were often emotional with zealous preaching and pre-Pentecostal manifestations that included shouting, dancing, running, shaking, and speaking in tongues. Source: Flower Pentecostal Heritage Center.

THE HIGHER LIFE MOVEMENT

Also by 1875, a similar series of "Higher Life" conventions being held in Keswick, England, were called "The Union Meeting for the

2   Delbert R. Rose, *Vital holiness: a theology of Christian experience: interpreting the historic Wesleyan message* (Minneapolis: Bethany, 1975), 52: HPT 25.

Promotion of Christian Holiness." The movement was based on William Boardman's 1858 book *The Higher Christian Life* and had a more Calvinistic tone than its American counterpart. William and Catherine Booth, founders of the Salvation Army, became a part of this movement, as did George Williams, founder of the Young Men's Christian Association (YMCA), some Quakers, South African Dutch Reformed minister Andrew Murray, and American ministers D.L. Moody, R.A. Torrey, A.B. Simpson, and A.J. Gordon. The Booths often preached in tandem, urging their audiences to be guided and directed by the promptings of the Spirit as they ministered. "You are to be a worker together with God for the salvation of your fellow man," General Booth exhorted.[3] The early Salvation Army meetings were every bit as charismatic as their American counterparts, with hands raised, outbursts of prayer, shouts, hysterical laughter, singing, dancing, and bodies swaying back and forth before falling backward into a common heap on the floor. No longer could Methodists claim exclusiveness to Holiness doctrine. The Higher Life movement was then brought back to America through A.B. Simpson (founder of the Christian and Missionary Alliance Church), A.J. Gordon (founder of Gordon College and Gordon-Conwell Theological Seminary), and D.L. Moody, forever linking the names Moody and Keswick. The American Keswick movement, however, differed slightly from its British counterpart in that Spirit baptism was considered more of an endowment of power than sanctification.

---

3   William Booth, *The Salvationist*, January 1879, quoted in Cyril Barnes, ed., *Founder Speaks Again* (London: Salvationist Publishing & Supplies, 1960), 45, 48: GGR 424.

Catherine Booth preaches at the Brighton Dome in 1869, as her husband, General William Booth, looks on. Well versed in Finney's *Lectures on Revival* and greatly influenced by Phoebe Palmer, Catherine became one of Britain's first women preachers at Gateshead in 1860, later recalling, "I have never yet been willing to be a fool for Christ. Now I will be one." Although her husband initially rejected the idea, he later wrote, "The best men in my Army are the women." Source: The Salvation Army International Heritage Centre, London.

THE METHODIST-HOLINESS SPLIT

By 1878, some leaders within the Southern Methodist Church in America began expressing concern over what they regarded as independence and obsessiveness with the Holiness movement. Some even began questioning the doctrine of sanctification itself as taught by these Holiness advocates. One leader wrote, "The holiness association, the holiness periodical, the holiness prayer meeting, the holiness preacher are all modern novelties. They are not Wesleyan. We believe that a living Wesley would never admit them into the Methodist system."[4] Even more disturbing were some of the more radical elements of the movement such as anti-denominationalism, called "come-outism." Daniel S. Warner formed the Church of God (Anderson, Indiana) in 1881 out of such beliefs, claiming to be "anti-denominational," yet with all the hallmarks of creating another denomination. In 1887, A.B. Simpson formed the Christian

---

4   John Leland Peters, *Christian Perfection and American Methodism* (Abingdon, 1956), 139: HPT 35.

Alliance in New York—another Holiness organization with the future makings of a denomination. Yet another radical element that developed within the Holiness movement by the 1880s was preaching against societal trends such as modern dress, fashion, jewelry, amusements, lodges, political parties, labor unions, doctors, medicine, liquor, tobacco, cola, and chewing gum. But nothing was considered more radical than the preaching of a so-called "third work" following sanctification called "the baptism of fire" or simply, "the fire."

The matter came to a head in 1894 when the General Conference of the Methodist Episcopal Church South, in an effort to stem the growing tide of controversy that threatened to engulf the church, disowned the entire Holiness movement, stating, "There has sprung up among us a party with holiness as a watchword; they have holiness associations, holiness meetings, holiness preachers, holiness evangelists, and holiness property. . . . We do not question the sincerity and zeal of these brethren; we desire the church to profit by their earnest preaching and godly example; but we deplore their teaching and methods in so far as they claim a monopoly of the experience, practice, and advocacy of holiness, and separate themselves from the body of ministers and disciples."[5] Suddenly, everyone who participated in the movement had to choose whether to stay with the old church or join the "come-outers." Many chose the latter, forming over twenty new denominations between 1895 and 1905.

---

5   *Journal, General Conference, M.E. Church, South,* 1894, 25–26: HPT 40.

THE FIRE-BAPTIZED HOLINESS CHURCH

Among the first to separate was the Church of the Nazarene (later, Pentecostal Church of the Nazarene) founded by Phineas Bresee in Los Angeles in 1895. But the most radical, by far, was the Fire-Baptized Holiness Church formed by Benjamin Hardin Irwin in Olmitz, Iowa, that same year. Irwin was most influenced by the writings of Wesley's colleague John Fletcher, who had taught that all who are sanctified should "enter the full dispensation of the Spirit" until they live in the "Pentecostal glory of the church . . . baptized with the Holy Ghost" or "baptized with fire."[6] After receiving his own baptism of fire, Irwin traveled throughout the Midwest drawing large crowds to his meetings, which resembled early camp meetings complete with screaming, shouting, jerking, dancing, laughing, falling into trances, and speaking in tongues. All over the Midwest people were claiming to fall "under the power" and experience "the fire." By 1897, Fire-Baptized Holiness Associations were being formed in Florida, Georgia, South Carolina, North Carolina, Virginia, and Canada. By 1899, Irwin had even taken steps to form a national headquarters near Cleveland, Tennessee, with plans to establish a missionary training school and "school of the prophets." Though many leaders within the Methodist Church and Holiness movement rejected Irwin's teachings on the "third blessing," Irwin's churches continued to gain wide acceptance. Irwin even took preaching against extravagant dress for women to the next level by stating it was also a sin for men to wear neckties. In 1900, Irwin confessed to "open and gross sin," which shook the young denomination to its core, leaving it in the hands of his thirty-one-

---

6   John Fletcher, *The Works of the Reverend John Fletcher* (New York, 1851) vol. 2, 356, 632–69; vol. 4, 230–232: HPT 52.

year-old successor, Joseph Hillery King. By teaching the baptism in the Holy Spirit as a separate and subsequent experience to salvation and sanctification, the Fire-Baptized Holiness Church became an important link and "direct precursor" to modern Pentecostalism.[7]

Joseph Hillery King believed his views on Holy Spirit baptism and speaking in tongues represented the best and clearest expression of the Christian faith. Originally a Methodist "circuit walker" (his parishes were too poor to afford a horse), he later joined the Fire-Baptized Holiness Church, becoming its overseer, and ultimately led the young denomination into Pentecostalism and its merger with the Pentecostal Holiness Church. Source: Flower Pentecostal Heritage Center.

THE CHURCH OF GOD IN CHRIST

Another church, which began in 1895, would soon become the largest African-American Pentecostal denomination in the nation. The Church of God in Christ (COGIC) was founded by Charles Harrison Mason, a Missionary Baptist minister who had been influenced by the writings of former slave and Holiness evangelist Amanda Berry Smith (1837-1915). Mason met with several men in 1895 who had strong ties to the Holiness movement, including C.P. Jones of Jackson, Mississippi, J.E. Jeter of Little Rock, Arkansas, and W.S. Pleasant of Hazelhurst, Mississippi, all of whom became founding elders of the church. The four men began working together, holding their first miracle deliverance revival in Jackson, Mississippi, in 1896. But reports coming from these meetings, combined with their Wesleyan-Holiness doctrine, soon led to all Calvinist-Missionary Baptist doors being closed to them.

---

7   HPT 59.

Consequently, when they returned to Jackson for a second revival in 1897, Mason had to preach from the south entrance of the courthouse. Wishing the meetings to continue, however, a Mr. Lee let them use his living room the following night. But they quickly outgrew that space, and by the third night, a Mr. Watson was graciously letting them use his abandoned cotton gin warehouse, which became the original meetinghouse for the Church of God in Christ. At the close of the meetings, "a church which would emphasize the doctrine of entire sanctification through the outpouring of the Holy Spirit" was organized, making it the first legally chartered Southern Holiness denomination. This subsequently led to many white independent Holiness ministers seeking ordination through the young denomination, giving it an interracial flavor.[8] Mason believed the church's name was biblically inspired and divinely revealed, saying that the Lord told him, "If you take this name, 'Church of God in Christ,' there will never be a building large enough to house the people whom I will send to you."[9] Today, the Church of God in Christ is the largest Pentecostal denomination in the U.S. and fifth largest denomination overall in the U.S. with over 12,000 churches and more than 5 million members. Worldwide, it has between 6 and 8 million members, making it also the largest black Pentecostal denomination in the world.[10]

---

8   "The Founder & Church History," *The Church of God in Christ: www.cogic.org/our-foundation/the-founder-church-history* (Accessed 24 February 2013).

9   "Our History," *The Reformed Churches of God in Christ International: www.reformedcogicintl.org/ourhistory.htm* (Accessed 24 February 2013).

10 "Our Foundation," Church of God in Christ (Retrieved February 24, 2013); National Council of Churches (February 2, 2010) "Catholics, Mormons, Assemblies of God growing; Mainline churches report a continuing decline" (Retrieved March 8, 2010); Melton, J. Gordon, *Religions of the World Second Edition: A Comprehensive Encyclopedia of Beliefs and Practices*, 2010, 681: "Church

Bishop C.H. Mason, founder of America's largest Pentecostal church, the Church of God in Christ (COGIC), traveled the length and breadth of the country and to many foreign lands preaching to interracial audiences in COGIC and non-COGIC churches alike, licensing several white Pentecostal ministers and preaching at the founding meeting of the Assemblies of God in 1914. Source: Harvey Burnett/Bethel COGIC.

THE CHURCH OF GOD

In 1896, after B.H. Irwin's failed attempt to organize a Fire-Baptized Holiness Association in the state of Tennessee, three evangelists who had left their Baptist and Methodist churches to join the movement crossed the state line to hold a revival in the Shearer Schoolhouse in Cherokee County, North Carolina. In doing so, the three evangelists— William Martin, Joe Tipton, and Milton McNabb—formed a nucleus for what would soon become the Church of God (Cleveland, Tennessee).[11] In addition to laughing, rejoicing, praising, and dancing, one outstanding feature of this revival was that some one hundred men, women, and children who received sanctification also fell under the power of God and began speaking in other tongues. Of course, this caused no small stir in the community. Several of the worshipers' homes were pillaged and destroyed by sheriff-backed Baptist and Methodist leaders, and one of their meetinghouses was burned to the ground.

Nevertheless, the group continued to meet for the next six years in the home of W.F. Bryant, who had assumed leadership of the group.

of God in Christ," *Wikipedia: en.wikipedia.org/wiki/Church_of_God_in_Christ* (Accessed 24 February 2013).

11   L. Howard Juillerat, ed., *Book of Minutes, General Assemblies, Churches of God* (Cleveland, Tenn., 1922), 7–14: HPT 72.

Occasionally, other evangelists such as R.G. Spurling, Jr., an itinerant Baptist preacher who had been expelled from his denomination for preaching Holiness, came and spoke, as well as mystical Quaker A.J. Tomlinson from Indiana, who sold Bibles and literature for the American Bible Society. Finally, on May 15, 1902, the first local church was organized under the name The Holiness Church at Camp Creek. Then in 1903, Tomlinson was invited to come and permanently lead the group. As Tomlinson prayed and agonized over the decision, he received a vision that it would indeed become a "True Church of God" of the Bible in the last days. Tomlinson agreed and was immediately elected pastor, as Spurling and Bryant were sent out to evangelize other communities. Within three years, three more churches were established—two in Tennessee and one in Georgia.

The Shearer Schoolhouse in Cherokee County, North Carolina, became the site of the initial outpouring of the Holy Spirit in the Church of God in 1896. The revival, which included speaking in other tongues, occurred ten years before the Azusa Street Revival. Source: Dixon Pentecostal Research Center.

Tomlinson's, Spurling's, and Bryant's meetings often produced the same results as early frontier camp meetings. Reports of shouting, weeping, clapping, jerking, and shaking of hands were frequent. Others fell to the floor in trances for four or five hours. Like the early camp meetings, these meetings attracted large crowds of between five and seven hundred. By 1905, it was felt that the four churches needed to organize, and in 1906, the first General Assembly convened. Though the group did not intend to start a new denomination, by the time the Second General Assembly convened in 1907 at their Union Grove church near Cleveland, Tennessee, the designation "Church of God" had been given with A.J. Tomlinson as its first general overseer in 1909. Today the Church of God has over 7 million members in over 170 countries, making it one of the largest Pentecostal denominations in the world.[12] Some trace the church's roots even further back to 1886 when R.J. Spurling and eight others were first barred from their Baptist church and organized The Christian Union at the Barney Creek Meeting House on the North Carolina-Tennessee border. Though the group later disbanded and returned to their original churches, if included, this would make the Church of God the oldest Pentecostal denomination in the U.S.

Ambrose Jessup Tomlinson, a mystical Quaker, joined the Holiness Church at Camp Creek and was elected first general overseer of the Church of God (Cleveland, Tennessee). He later became the first president of Lee College (now Lee University) and founded the Church of God of Prophecy. Source: Dixon Pentecostal Research Center.

THE PENTECOSTAL HOLINESS CHURCH

Yet another major player in early Pentecostalism was the Pentecostal Holiness Church founded by Rev. A.B. Crumpler, a Methodist minister from North Carolina. Crumpler began preaching sanctification in his home state in 1890 after being exposed to Holiness teaching in Missouri. At the height of the 1896 Holiness revival, Crumpler preached to

---

12   "Brief History of the Church of God," *Church of God:*
www.churchofgod.org/ about/ a-brief-history-of-the-church-of-god (Accessed 25 February 2013).

thousands in churches, tents, and brush arbor meetings across North Carolina. He also wrote articles for national Holiness magazines such as the *Way of Faith* in Columbia, South Carolina, and *Living Words* in Pittsburgh, Pennsylvania, forming the North Carolina Holiness Association that same year. In 1898, he formed the first Pentecostal Holiness Church in Goldsboro, North Carolina. But in 1899, Crumpler was tried for insubordination within the Methodist Church for refusing to stop preaching the doctrine of sanctification. Crumpler immediately withdrew, stating he had been tried for "preaching the glorious doctrine of Methodism."[13] Undeterred, Crumpler published the Holiness Advocate in 1900 and met with several other former Methodist ministers in Fayetteville, North Carolina, to form the Pentecostal Holiness Church. Its purpose was simple: to provide "a congenial church home" where those who had been saved and sanctified could be free to worship, free to dance, free to shout, and free to proclaim the message of holiness without fear.[14] Today the Pentecostal Holiness Church has an international presence with over a million members with such notables as Oral Roberts, Charles Stanley, and C.M. Ward having been on their membership role. In the 1960s, the denomination affiliated with other Pentecostal churches around the world to form the International Pentecostal Holiness Church (IPHC) and increased its membership to over 3 million.[15] One of those affiliate churches is the 350,000-member Jotabeche Pentecostal Methodist Church in Santiago, Chile—considered the second largest congregation in the world.

---

13   G.F. Taylor, "Our Church History," Feb. 17, 1921, 8–10: Joseph E. Campbell, *The Pentecostal Holiness Church 1898–1948: Its Background and History* (Franklin Springs, Georgia: Life Springs, 1951), 217–232: HPT 63.

14   Ibid.

15   "24th General Conference Highlights," *International Pentecostal Holiness Church: iphc.org/gso/home/archives/iphc-timeline* (Accessed 25 February 2013).

Abner Blackman Crumpler, a Methodist minister, conducted an interracial revival at a Goldsboro, North Carolina, tobacco warehouse in 1896, emphasizing the experience of sanctification through baptism in the Holy Spirit. Two years later, he conducted a similar tent revival that resulted in the first Pentecostal Holiness Church. Ten years later, he would be forced out of his own denomination for refusing to accept tongues as the initial evidence of Holy Spirit baptism. Source: NC Conference Archives & Research Department of the IPHC.

OTHER SANCTIFIED STREAMS

Though the Methodist-Holiness movement was the largest, it was certainly not the only stream to contribute to modern Pentecostalism. Other "sanctified" streams of Baptists, Presbyterians, Congregationalists, evangelical faith cure, and healing evangelists also participated. Evangelical faith cure was a late-nineteenth-century divine healing movement that affected a wide variety of Protestant leaders in the northeastern U.S. and elsewhere. This included A.J. Gordon, A.B. Simpson, William Boardman, Dr. Charles Cullis, Sarah Mix, Carrie Judd Montgomery, Andrew Murray, and E.W. Kenyon. Rev. N.J. Holmes, pastor of the Second Presbyterian Church in Greenville, South Carolina, after hearing D.L. Moody's emphasis on holiness and having a long talk with him one day, obtained the Holy Ghost sanctification experience for himself in 1896. In 1898, Holmes inaugurated Holmes Theological Seminary in Greenville, South Carolina, and soon joined the Holiness movement, bringing his school with him. Though the school initially had ties with the Fire-Baptized Holiness Church, it later became part of the Pentecostal Holiness Church, making

Holmes Bible College the oldest continuously running Pentecostal school in the world.

D.L. MOODY

Dwight Lyman Moody (1837–1899), a Congregationalist who later refused any denominational ties, received his Spirit baptism in 1871 prior to joining the Higher Life movement in Britain between 1873 and 1875. According to Moody, his spiritual encounter began when two Methodist ladies who sat in the front pew of his Illinois Street Church in Chicago, kept telling him, "We are praying for you." After they repeated this several times, Moody lost patience with them and asked, "Why are you praying for me?" "Because you need the power of the Spirit," they replied. Moody wrote, "I thought I had the power." But sometime later, Moody asked these ladies to come and talk to him. He wrote, "They poured out their hearts in prayer that I might receive the filling of the Holy Spirit. There came a great hunger into my soul. I did not know what it was. I began to cry out as I never did before. I really felt that I did not want to live if I could not have this power for service."[16] Though nothing happened that day, later when Moody was in New York collecting funds for the Chicago fire victims, he said, "My heart was not in the work of begging. I could not appeal. I was crying all the time that God would fill me with His Spirit." Moody's associate, R.A. Torrey, recounted what happened next as Moody walked up Wall Street: "In the midst of the bustle and hurry of that city his prayer was answered; the power of God fell upon him as he walked up the street and he had to hurry off to

16   James Gilchrest Lawson, *Deeper Experiences of Famous Christians* (New Kensington, Pa.: Whitaker, 1998), 352–353: CHS 31.

the house of a friend and ask that he might have a room by himself, and in that room he stayed alone for hours; and the Holy Ghost came upon him, filling his soul with such joy that at last he had to ask God to withhold his hand, lest he die on the spot from very joy. He went out from that place with the power of the Holy Ghost upon him."[17]

Both Moody and Torrey mentioned a marked difference in Moody's revivals from that day. Moody wrote, "I went to preaching again. The sermons were not different; I did not present any new truths, and yet hundreds were converted. I would not now be placed back where I was before that blessed experience if you should give me all the world."[18] Shortly thereafter, one Baptist minister wrote after attending one of Moody's London meetings, "When I got to the rooms of the Young Men's Christian Association, Victoria Hall, London, I found the meeting on fire. The young men were speaking with tongues, prophesying. What on earth did it mean? Only that Moody had addressed them that afternoon."[19] Many years later, an American Pentecostal evangelist, Lester Sumrall, was praying in tongues at a meeting in Liverpool, England, when an elderly gentleman approached him asking, "Can you do that all the time?" Sumrall replied, "Yes, as the Spirit moves, I can." The man responded, "I was in this city with Dwight L. Moody. As I knelt in prayer with him, he did the same thing you are doing. He spoke in some words that I could not understand."[20]

---

17   Ibid., 367.

18   William R. Moody, *The Life of Dwight L. Moody* (New York: Revell, 1900), 149: GGR 367.

19   Gordon Lindsay, "The Speaking in Tongues in Church History," *Voice of Healing* (August 1964), 3: CC 130–1.

20   Lester Sumrall, *Pioneers of Faith* (Tulsa: Harrison House, 1995), 184–185.

D.L. Moody preaches at Her Majesty's Opera House in London in 1874. Ira Sankey is seated beside him at the organ. Dubbed "Crazy Moody" for his boldness in sharing the gospel, after receiving the filling of the Holy Spirit, Moody remarked that while his preaching remained the same, the results differed— "hundreds were converted." Source: D.L. Moody, W.H. Daniels, ed., *Moody: his words, work, and workers* (New York: Nelson & Phillips, 1877). Photo: Wikimedia/Internet Archive Book Images.

R.A. TORREY

Rueben Archer Torrey (1856–1928), who joined D.L. Moody's evangelistic work in 1889, and popularized the doctrine of Spirit baptism as superintendent of Moody's Bible Institute and pastor of Moody's church through his books and sermons, boldly declared: "The baptism with the Holy Spirit is an operation of the Holy Spirit distinct from and subsequent from His regenerating work, an impartation of power for service . . . not merely for the apostles, not merely for those of the apostolic age, but for . . . every believer in every age of the church's history."[21]

A.B. SIMPSON

Albert Benjamin Simpson (1843–1919), Canadian preacher and founder of the Christian and Missionary Alliance, alluded to recent occurrences of speaking in tongues in India and Africa to assert that speaking in tongues as recorded in Acts was not limited to apostolic times. He said, "There appears to be no reason why this gift should

---

21   Reuben A. Torrey, *The Person and Work of the Holy Spirit* (New York: Revell, 1910), 176–210: CHS 30.

not appear at any time in the history of the Church. It was not always employed in the Apostolic Church as the vehicle of preaching to people of other languages, but rather as a channel of direct worship and adoration." Though Simpson's denomination wholeheartedly embraced Spirit baptism and all spiritual gifts—including tongues— even training many early Pentecostal pastors and missionaries and influencing Pentecostal denominations, a severe rift would later develop over the doctrine of tongues as the only initial evidence.[22]

A.J. GORDON

Adoniram Judson Gordon (1836–1895), pastor of the Clarendon Street Baptist Church in Boston who had also participated in the Higher Life movement, showed his Pentecostal tendencies in his books *The Ministry of Healing*, *The Two-Fold Life*, and *The Ministry of the Spirit* published in 1882, 1884, and 1894 respectively. In *The Two-Fold Life*, Gordon declared, "It is still our privilege to pray for the baptism of the Spirit and to tarry in supplication until we be endued with power from on high."[23] In *The Ministry of the Spirit*, he wrote, "It seems clear from the Scriptures that it is still the duty and privilege of believers to receive the Holy Spirit by a conscious, definite act of appropriating faith, just as they received Jesus Christ." And "We hold indeed, that Pentecost was once for all, but equally that the appropriation of the Spirit by believers is always for all."[24] In *The Ministry of Healing*,

---

22   Christian and Missionary Alliance Pamphlet, "The Gift of Tongues: seek not, forbid not" (n.d.): CM 100.

23   A.J. Gordon, *The Two-Fold Life* (Boston: Howard Garnett, 1884), 75–76: CC 129.

24   A.J. Gordon, *The Ministry of the Spirit* (New York: Revell, 1894), 76, 80: *Gordon College Archives:* *xythos.gordon.edu/Archives/Gordon_Herritage/Ministry%20of%20the%20Spirit.pdf* (Accessed 27 February 2013).

Gordon not only affirmed the present-day ministry of healing but also declared, "The gifts of tongues and of prophecy therefore do not seem to be confined within the first age of the church."[25] The latter went on to become one of Gordon's most revered books and a standard among early Pentecostals. Gordon also influenced the founding of Rochester Bible Training School—an important center in the early days of Pentecostalism and, according to one Pentecostal historian, "the first permanent school to make a genuine impression on the movement."[26]

While A.J. Gordon's books *The Two-Fold Life*, *The Ministry of the Spirit*, and *The Ministry of Healing* became standards among early Pentecostals, his Clarendon Street Baptist Church in Boston was described as "one of the most spiritual and aggressive in America." He later founded Gordon College and Gordon–Conwell Theological Seminary. Source: *Adoniram Judson Gordon*, by Ernest B. Gordon. Photo: Wikimedia/Magnus Mankse.

MARIA WOODWORTH-ETTER

Yet another important stream to emerge out of the late nineteenth-century Holiness movement and play a major role in the development of modern Pentecostalism was the healing evangelists. One of them, Maria Beulah Woodworth-Etter (1844–1924), was raised in a non-Christian home in New Lisbon, Ohio. After being converted in a Disciples of Christ church at thirteen, Maria heard the voice of God

---

25 A.J. Gordon, *The Ministry of Healing, or Miracles of Cure in All Ages* (New York: Revell, 1882), 53: *Gordon College Archives: xythos.gordon.edu/Archives/Gordon_Herritage/Ministry%20of%20Healing.pdf* (Accessed 27 February 2013).

26 Carl Brumback, *Like a River* (Springfield: Gospel Publishing, 1977), 79: CC 129.

say, "Go out in the highways and hedges and gather the lost sheep."[27] Confused because her church did not allow women preachers, she thought maybe one day if she married a missionary they could go into ministry together. A few years later, Maria fell in love and married injured Civil War veteran Philo Horace Woodworth. They soon took up farming and had six children, but sadly, five out of six died of disease, and Maria herself also became sickly. Only their oldest, "Lizzy," survived. Yet, Maria wrote, "In all this, I could see the hand of the loving Father calling me to leave all and follow Him." Still feeling unqualified to do the Lord's work, Maria attended a mystical Quaker meeting where she asked God to anoint her for service. She later shared her experience: "The power of the Holy Ghost came down as a bright cloud. It was brighter than the sun. I was covered and wrapped up in it. My body was light as the air. It seemed that heaven came down, I was baptized with the Holy Ghost, and fire, and power which has never left me. Oh, Praise the Lord! There was liquid fire, and the angels were all around in the fire and glory."[28]

Now empowered, she made herself ready for ministry. However, the more she studied and read about how God used women in the Bible, the more condemned she felt for doubting her own calling. She wrote, "The dear Savior stood by me one night in a vision and

---

27   Wayne E. Warner, "Neglect Not the Gift That Is in Thee," Etter Sermon from *The Woman Evangelist* (Metuchen, NJ and London: Scarecrow, 1986), 7: Roberts Liardon, *God's Generals: Why They Succeeded and Why Some Failed* (New Kensington, Penn.: Whitaker, 1996), 47 [hereafter GG].

28   Maria Woodworth-Etter, *Marvels and Miracles: God Wrought in the Ministry of Mrs. M.B. Woodworth Etter for Forty-Five Years*, (1922), 11: *Revival Library: www.revival-library.org/catalogues/pentecostal/woodworthetter.html* (Accessed 1 March 2013).

talked face to face with me, and asked what I was doing on earth. I felt condemned, and said, 'Lord, I am going to work in Thy vineyard.' The Lord said, 'When?' and I answered, 'When I get prepared for the work.' Then the Lord said to me, 'Don't you know that while you are getting ready souls are perishing? Go now, and I will be with you.'"[29]

A MINISTRY OF HEALING

Maria's first opportunity to preach came at a Quakers' meeting. While preaching, she had a vision of hell in which she saw souls perishing. Now, day and night, she felt a need to call sinners to repentance as she began preaching locally. Then after their farm failed, she became licensed through John Winebrenner's Churches of God in Ohio and she and her husband began traveling in ministry together throughout the Midwest. Soon Maria gained a reputation for having the power of God manifested in her meetings. In another vision, she saw angels come into her room and take her out West over prairies, lakes, forests, and rivers. Then she saw a wide open field of golden grain and saw herself preaching. As she began to preach, the stalks fell like sheaves. The Lord said to her, "Just as the grain fell, so people would fall" when she preached.[30] The first time it happened, she reported, "Fifteen came to the altar screaming for mercy. Men and women fell and lay like dead. I had never seen anything like this."[31] In Alexandria, Indiana,

---

29 Ibid., 12.

30 Warner, *The Woman Evangelist*, 10: GG 49.

31 Maria Woodworth-Etter, *A Diary of Signs and Wonders* (Tulsa, OK: Harrison House, n.d.), 37: MCH 374–375.

Maria reported five hundred falling to the ground all at once. Then in 1884, she felt led to start praying for the sick. Though reluctant at first, thinking it might hinder the work of evangelism, the Lord assured her it would only result in more being saved. Soon Maria was a national phenomenon, even having to buy a large tent to hold the crowds.

The years between 1890 and 1900 were both challenging and rewarding for Maria as she was attacked on every side by both the religious crowd and secular press. In Framingham, Massachusetts, she was placed on trial for practicing medicine without a license and for hypnotizing people by placing them in trances. But many, including a young minister named E. W. Kenyon, came and testified on her behalf, and she was released. In St. Louis, a local psychiatrist filed charges of insanity against her for her repeated visions. In Oakland, California, in 1890, a man prophesied in one of her meetings that a terrible earthquake would hit San Francisco that April. Though one finally did hit San Francisco in April—sixteen years later—the press had a field day in 1890. In 1891, Maria became aware of her husband's infidelity, which resulted in a bitter divorce. After making threats against her ministry, her husband died a year later.

By 1894, Maria had crossed America three times coast to coast proclaiming Christ in churches, theaters, opera houses, and under her famous tent. Maria had no itinerary and often changed plans as directed by God. Once while on her way to California, she felt led to turn east instead and head for St. Louis. Those St. Louis meetings ended up being among her most dramatic and powerful as hoodlums came with pistols and clubs and tried to overthrow her meetings. Maria told her coworkers to pray and that the God of Elijah would answer. One sister knelt at the altar and prayed that God would save and bless the hoodlums. Another followed. Then Maria raised her hand in the name of the Lord and commanded the hoodlums to listen to her. She said the Lord had sent her there to do "good," and that she was not leaving until she had finished doing what the Lord told her to do. Then she said the Lord would strike dead the first one who tried to harm or strike any of them. As she spoke, the power of God fell, and the hoodlums froze. Some fell to the ground as if dead. Others just stood with their mouths hanging open and tears streaming down their cheeks. Most just stood as if afraid to move and then quietly left. Maria wrote, "After that, the hoodlum element always respected me."[32]

Tent for Mrs. Maria Woodworth-Etter. Sign reads, "Mrs. M.B. Woodworth-Etter, Evangelist, Bestowed with Gift of Divine Healing, Meetings Daily at 2 & 7:30 P.M., Admission Free, All Welcome." Source: Missouri History Museum, St. Louis, Swekosky-MHS Collection.

Finally, in 1900, after bowing to pressure from even her own denomination, Maria withdrew her license with the Churches of God and launched out on her own. In 1902, Maria married Samuel Etter and the two traveled together in ministry until 1905 when Maria suddenly and mysteriously disappeared from public ministry. But in 1912, Maria reemerged and continued ministering until her death in 1924.

---

32 Colin Melbourne, "Maria Woodworth-Etter: Strength Perfected in Weakness," *Born Again Christian Info: www.born-again-christian.info/ maria.woodworth.etter.htm* (Accessed 1 March 2013).

A TRAILBLAZER FOR GOD

Maria Woodworth-Etter publicly proclaimed Christ across the nation in a time when women had neither voice nor vote. She ministered to hundreds of thousands with little formal training. She pitched a tent and prayed for the sick before healing revivals existed. She often preached to crowds of 25,000 without a microphone. She stood against death threats, explosions, mobs, storms, the press, and persecution among false brethren—even another healing evangelist—but emerged victorious through it all. Yet in many ways, Maria was a typical nineteenth-century Midwestern woman who had married a Civil War veteran, worked a farm, and raised children. One historian described her as "like your grandmother" but with a "tremendous spiritual authority over sin, disease, and demons."[33]

Before modern Pentecostalism existed, Maria had effectively mapped out a theology of the Spirit that included salvation, holiness, the baptism in the Holy Spirit, healing, and the imminent return of Christ. Ten years before Charles Fox Parham's Bible School in Topeka, Kansas, Maria conducted a meeting in Topeka, Kansas in which "a number of bodies were healed of different diseases, and a number laid out as dead under the power of God."[34] Thirteen years before the

---

33 Carl Brumback, *Suddenly . . . From Heaven* (Springfield: Gospel, 1961), 27: Wayne E. Warner, "Maria Woodworth-Etter: A Powerful Voice in the Pentecostal Vanguard," *Assemblies of God Enrichment Journal: enrichmentjournal.ag.org/199901/086_woodsworth_etter.cfm* (Accessed 2 March 2013).

34 Maria Beulah Woodworth, *The Life, Work, and Experiences of Maria Beulah Woodworth* (St. Louis: by author, 1894), 437–438: Wayne E. Warner, "Maria Woodworth-Etter: A Powerful Voice in the Pentecostal Vanguard," *Assemblies of God Enrichment Journal: enrichmentjournal.ag.org/199901/086_woodsworth_etter.cfm* (Accessed 2 March 2013).

Azusa Street Revival, Maria conducted a five-month-long meeting in Los Angeles. She commented on the meetings, "While we stood between the living and the dead, preaching the gospel on the apostolic line, earnestly contending for the faith once delivered to the saints, proving to the people that Christ is the same yesterday, today, and forever, according to the Lord's promise, He was with us, confirming His Word with mighty signs and wonders following."[35] For these reasons and more, Mariah Woodworth-Etter has been called "the grandmother of the Pentecostal Movement."[36]

Known as "the grandmother of the Pentecostal Movement," Maria Woodworth-Etter effectively mapped out a theology of the Spirit and conducted Holy Ghost tent revivals across America that included salvation, holiness, Holy Ghost baptism, healing, and the imminent return of Christ—ten years before Parham's Bible School and thirteen years before the Azusa Street Revival. Source: Flower Pentecostal Heritage Center.

In Maria's autobiography published in 1894, she told a nineteenth-century audience that if they would only believe, test God, and meet his conditions, "a mighty revival would break out that would shake the world, and thousands of souls would be saved. The displays of God's power on the Day of Pentecost were only a sample of what God designed should follow through the ages. Instead of looking back to Pentecost, let us always be expecting it to come, especially in these days."[37]

---

35 Ibid., 428.
36 GG 47.
37 Ibid., 437–438.

JOHN ALEXANDER DOWIE

John Alexander Dowie (1847–1907) was born in Scotland, became sickly as a child, developed a great love for reading the Bible, and felt called to ministry. At thirteen, his parents moved to Australia, where he experienced some early successes in business. However, still feeling the tug of ministry, he returned to Scotland at twenty-one where he enrolled in Edinburgh University. There he studied theology and political science and became exposed to the writings and teachings of former student Edward Irving on the present-day gifts of the Spirit. While serving as honorary chaplain at the Edinburgh Infirmary, Dowie also became exposed to some of the primitive practices of nineteenth-century medicine and was shocked to learn that physicians and surgeons were only guessing or experimenting on people. Dowie became infuriated that doctors publicly offered great hope to their patients while privately admitting how little they knew. After his studies in Edinburgh, Dowie returned to Australia in 1872, where he was invited to pastor a small Congregational church. But he soon grew restless with the church's lethargy, resigned, and was offered a larger church at Manly Beach until his heart again grew weary.

THE WAY OF HEALING

In 1876, Dowie received an invitation to pastor the much larger Newton Congregational Church in Sydney, but within weeks of taking the position, a plague had swept through the area and Dowie suddenly found himself presiding over forty funerals. Feeling totally dejected, he cried out to God for an answer: "And there I sat with sorrow-bowed head for my afflicted people, until the bitter tears came to relieve my burning heart. . . . Then the words of the Holy Ghost inspired in Acts 10:38 [how God anointed Jesus of Nazareth with the Holy Ghost and with power who went about doing good, and healing all who were oppressed by the Devil] stood before me all radiant with light, revealing Satan as the Defiler, and Christ as the Healer. My tears were wiped away, my heart was strong, I saw the way of healing. . . . I said, 'God help me now to preach the Word to all the dying around, and tell them how 'tis Satan still defiles, and Jesus still delivers, for He is just the same today.'"[38]

No sooner had Dowie finished praying that prayer than he heard a rap at the door. Mary, a little girl in the church, was dying. Dowie rushed from his house, ran down the street, and entered the girl's room. As he saw her in her agony, anger burned within him. The doctor tending to her said to him, "Sir, are not God's ways mysterious?" "God's way!" Dowie exclaimed. "No sir, that is the devil's work and it is time we called on Him Who came to 'destroy the work of the devil.'"[39] Offended at his words, the doctor left the room. Dowie then asked Mary's mother why she had sent for him. Upon learning that she wanted the prayer of faith, Dowie bowed down by the girl's bedside and cried out to God: "Our Father, help! And Holy Spirit teach me how to pray. Plead thou for us, oh, Jesus, Savior, Healer, Friend, our Advocate with the Father. Hear and heal Eternal One! From all disease and death deliver this sweet child of thine. I rest upon the Word. We claim the promise now, The Word is true, 'I am the Lord that healeth

---

38   Gordon Lindsay, *John Alexander Dowie: A Life Story of Trials, Tragedies, and Triumphs* (Dallas: Christ for the Nations, 1986), 23: GG 25.

39   Ibid., 24: GG 26.

thee.' Then heal her now."[40] Instantly, the girl stopped moaning and lay still. Her mother asked if she was dead. Dowie replied, "No, Mary will live. The fever is gone."[41] Soon Mary sat up in her bed and started eating. Dowie then went to her brother's and sister's rooms and prayed for them, and they too were healed. In fact, not another member of Dowie's church died from that epidemic. Dowie wrote, "I found the sword I needed was in my hands, and in my hand, I hold it still, and never will I lay it down."[42]

John Alexander Dowie. After forty members of Dowie's Newton Congregational Church in Sydney, Australia, died in an epidemic in 1876, Dowie received a revelation based on Acts 10:38 of Satan as defiler and God as healer. Dowie prayed and not another member died. Dowie then left the pastorate to launch an international healing ministry. Source: *Three Thousand Years of Mental Healing* by George Barton Cutten (1911). Source: Project Gutenberg.

DOWIE IN AMERICA

In 1878, overwhelmed by this new revelation and repelled by the rampant skepticism in the churches, Dowie left the pastorate and secured Sydney's Theater Royal, where he began preaching to hundreds Christ's message of salvation and divine healing. Then after a brief failed attempt at politics, Dowie returned to preaching and moved to Melbourne, where he established a large church, built a tabernacle,

---

40 Charles A. Jennings, "Life & Ministry of John Alexander Dowie," *Truth in History: www.truthinhistory.org/life-ministry-of-john-alexander-dowie.html* (Accessed 5 March 2013).

41 Ibid.

42 Ibid.

and founded the International Divine Healing Association. Dowie believed God healed in four scriptural ways: 1) the direct "prayer of faith," 2) the intercessory prayer of several, 3) anointing with oil by elders, along with the "prayer of faith," and 4) the "laying on of hands of those who believe, and whom God has prepared and called to that ministry."[43] Then in 1888, Dowie felt God leading him to go to the United States. So after completing a preaching tour in New Zealand, he sailed for San Francisco. Local newspapers carried the story that Dowie was coming to America, and people from all over California came to be healed.

In those early days, Dowie prayed for only one person at a time, and only if they were repentant of any former lifestyle, believing that "sin" was "the cause" and "disease, death, and hell" were "the inevitable effects and consequences."[44] Thus, he did not pray for many, but those he did pray for were healed. One elderly woman from Sacramento came with her crutch to the Palace Hotel where Dowie was staying. With tears in her eyes and ready to yield her heart to the Lord, she looked at Dowie. "Now, will you trust Jesus as your Healer?" Dowie asked. The woman said she knew Jesus was present that very moment in spirit and power. Without another word, Dowie knelt at her feet, placed the diseased foot in his hand, and prayed for her saying, "In

---

43   John A. Dowe, "God's Way of Healing," *Leaves of Healing* 15 (1904), 308: "The Christian Catholic Apostolic Church and the Apostolic Faith: A Study in the 1906 Pentecostal Revival": Cecil M. Robeck, Jr., ed., *Charismatic Experiences in History* (Peabody, Mass.: Hendrickson, 1985), 128 [hereafter CE].

44   John A. Dowie, "Wilt Thou Be Made Whole," *Bread of Life* 6 (March, 1957): 10: Edith L. Blumhofer, "The Christian Catholic Apostolic Church": CE 128.

Jesus' Name, rise and walk." She arose and walked several times across the room. As they were leaving, Dowie said, "You have left something behind, your crutch." "I don't need it anymore," she replied. "I am healed." Then she walked more than eight blocks to her daughter's house.[45] Soon Dowie was holding healing meetings up and down California's coast.

THE WORLD'S FAIR

As Dowie expanded his meetings to other parts of the country, Chicago newspapers declared him an imposter and made it clear he was neither needed nor wanted in their city. Yet Dowie felt strongly God wanted him to start a new work there. He just needed a sign. Then just as he was about to close one of his divine healing conventions in Chicago, he received a prayer request for a Mrs. Jennie Paddock, who had been abandoned by doctors and was lying on her deathbed with a fibroid tumor. Perhaps this was the sign he needed. Kneeling right then and there, Dowie prayed for the dying woman and she was instantly healed. A Chicago newspaper ran the story. Dowie, now convinced God wanted him to build a mission there, knew the 1893 Chicago World's Fair and Columbian Exposition was scheduled to open soon. The timing could not have been more perfect.

Just outside the fair gates, Dowie built a wooden tabernacle and erected a sign and flag. The sign read "Zion Tabernacle" and the flag "Christ is All." As crowds gathered for the fair, Dowie conducted

---

45   Jennings, "John Alexander Dowie," *Truth in History: www.truthinhistory.org/life-ministry-of-john-alexander-dowie.html* (Accessed 5 March 2013).

services day and night. Many who attended testified of being healed and attendance quickly grew. Almost immediately, lines of people formed outside waiting to see the miraculous cures taking place inside. At one point, Dowie's services even rivaled that of Buffalo Bill's Wild West Show across the street. Before long, Dowie had more publicity—both good and bad—than he could possibly imagine. Hundreds came from around the country to attend Dowie's services and receive divine healing until there was not enough available lodging. In response, Dowie opened several large boarding houses around the city called "healing homes" where people could come to receive training, counseling, and healing between services. His own residence was called "Divine Healing Home Number One." Of course, the local papers called them "Lunatic Asylums."[46]

Dowie built this small, unpretentious wooden Zion Tabernacle just outside the doors of the 1893 Chicago World's Fair and Columbian Exposition. As crowds thronged the fairgrounds, many passed by the little wooden hut, while others attended or stood in line to view the miraculous healings taking place inside. Soon large crowds had gathered, bringing to the attention of the world the great truth that Jesus Christ is the same yesterday, today, and forever. Source: *Leaves of Healing* vol. 1 no. 1, August 31, 1894, p. 1. Photo: courtesy of the Clendening History of Medicine Library, University of Kansas Medical Center.

NOTABLE HEALINGS

During this time, several notable people were healed through Dowie's ministry, including Sadie Cody, niece of Col. W. F. "Buffalo Bill" Cody,

---

46 Lindsay, *John Alexander Dowie*, 109: GG 33.

who was brought by ambulance to one of Dowie's Healing Homes to be prayed for. Many of her friends expected her to be brought home a corpse because of her spinal tumor, but after Dowie prayed for her, she was able to stand for the first time in eight months. Within five weeks, she returned home and resumed her normal duties, completely restored. Miss Amanda Hicks of Clinton, Kentucky, president of a local Bible college and cousin to President Abraham Lincoln, was also brought to Chicago on morphine, lying on a stretcher in the final stages of terminal cancer. Though doctors had given up on her, Dowie prayed for her and her terrible agony instantly departed as she was able to walk for the first time in months. But later after she returned home entirely well, her denomination dismissed her from her position because she had been divinely healed.

Also in 1894, Dowie began his own Zion Publishing House, printing his periodical *Leaves of Healing* in Dutch, German, and English which he eventually distributed to 40,000 subscribers in the U.S., Europe, Australia, and South Africa. The newsletter was packed with testimonies and teachings on divine healing. By then, Dowie's church, Zion Tabernacle, had also acquired a spacious facility for its ongoing services.

CONTROVERSIES DEVELOP

By 1895, however, Dowie became embroiled in a number of controversies, lawsuits, and arrests for taking a stand against unscrupulous medical doctors, the pharmaceutical industry, crooked politicians, corrupt corporations, liberal clergymen, Freemasons, and so on. Thousands flocked to his meetings acclaiming him as their spokesman, and Dowie never minced words. Many applauded him for his straightforward talk against the evils of society and for saying what they themselves were afraid to say. Dowie even spoke publicly against fellow Chicago evangelists R.A. Torrey and D.L. Moody, as well as any other minister who refused to directly condemn the use of medicine. As far as Dowie was concerned, God had "but one way of healing." The Devil had "a hundred so-called ways," and there was "no fellowship between the blood of Christ and medicine."[47] Some within the medical community tried to stop him by filing a lawsuit against him for practicing medicine without a license. Choosing to represent himself, Dowie lost a lower court decision before appealing to a higher court and winning. Hoping to wear him out, however, city officials had him arrested a hundred times that year—almost daily at one point—causing him to spend $20,000 of his own money in his defense, but Dowie never backed down and even seemed to thrive on the publicity as his crowds grew ever larger.

Later that year, Dowie organized the Christian Catholic Apostolic Church to grant them protection under the state constitution to pray for the sick without medical interference, and soon other affiliated churches were springing up all over Illinois, Indiana, Ohio, and elsewhere. Now unable to arrest him and recognizing his newsletter as a major lifeline to his ministry, an editor of the *Chicago Dispatch* plotted to revoke his mailing privileges by digging up a transcript of a Dowie sermon in which he denounced the infallibility of the

---

47 John A. Dowie, "The Everlasting Gospel of the Kingdom of God Declared and Defended," *Leaves of Healing* V (1899), 713: Blumhofer, "Christian Catholic Apostolic Church": CE 131.

pope and showing it to the local Postmaster General—a devout Catholic! In a fit of rage, the postmaster revoked Zion's second-class mailing privileges, forcing them to pay fourteen times the regular cost. Dowie paid the postage increase, urging his readers to petition Washington, and was soon granted an audience with the Postmaster General in Washington, D.C. The *Chicago Dispatch* was denounced by the federal government and its editor imprisoned. During his visit to Washington, Dowie was also granted an audience with President William McKinley. Upon leaving the White House, he sensed something was wrong and commented to some of the president's staff that he feared for McKinley's life. Six years later, President McKinley would die of an assassin's bullet wound in Buffalo, New York.

ZION'S HEALING LEGACY

By 1896, Dowie practically managed the city of Chicago. All his enemies were either dead, in prison, or silenced. Chicago's police force, which had once arrested him over a hundred times, was now his friend and protector. Most of Chicago's political figures, including the mayor, had been voted in by Dowie's people. Dowie had even divided the city into sections, commissioning teams of seventy to go preach the gospel of salvation and healing in every district. Hardly a soul remained in Chicago who had not heard the gospel. For six months, Dowie leased Chicago's largest auditorium and moved his services there, filling it each time as thousands received healing.

"God's Hand on the Walls of Zion—Showing also the Platform and Choir Gallery of Zion Tabernacle." The "trophy wall" (background), full of crutches, canes, trusses, bandages, and braces, served as an enduring testimony to God's healing power. Source: *Leaves of Healing*, vol. 5 no. 2, November 5, 1896, p. 1. Photo: courtesy of the Clendening History of Medicine Library, University of Kansas Medical Center.

Zion also attracted a number of other ministers and evangelists who had been healed or had family members who had been healed through Dowie's ministry, many of whom would go on to lead prominent and influential healing ministries themselves. This hall of fame included John G. Lake, F.F. Bosworth, John R. Richey, Raymond T. Richey, Lillian B. Yeomans, Charles Fox Parham, and Gordon Lindsay, as well as Fred Vogler, and J. Roswell Flower. The latter two would become instrumental in founding the Assemblies of God. John G. Lake, an elder and deacon in Dowie's church, would later impact South Africa for Christ. F.F. Bosworth, conductor of Dowie's award-winning Zion City Band, would later preach in great cities across North America. Both were introduced to Pentecost at Zion. Lake wrote, "Were it not for Zion I should be the most unhappy of men," and no wonder.[48] Lake's brother, who had been an invalid for years, was healed under Dowie's ministry. Lake's sister, who had had five cancers, was also healed. Lake's wife was instantly healed of a heart disease, and two months later, their son was healed. Lake later wrote, "We did not know how to pray the prayer of faith then as well as we do now. We had not made everything right, and the Lord did not answer our prayer.

---

48   Jennings, "John Alexander Dowie," *Truth in History: www.truthinhistory.org/life-ministry-of-john-alexander-dowie.html* (Accessed 5 March 2013).

We went to Zion and the boy was healed. He is now a healthy, happy boy."[49] Even Lake himself, who had recurring arthritis pain in his legs that nearly crippled him, went to one of Dowie's Healing Homes, had an older gentleman pray for him, and the power of God went into his legs, instantly healing them.

African Americans were also welcomed members of Dowie's church—a phenomenon virtually unheard of in those days. Indeed, some two hundred or so were eventually sent out as missionaries to South Africa, where they established churches and became very influential. Those churches eventually proliferated into several African Zionist denominations, which now represent the largest grouping of Christian churches in South Africa.

ZION CITY

As a diversionary tactic in 1899, Dowie declared an all-out war against "Doctors, Drugs, and Devils." The press swarmed as Dowie secretly negotiated on a 6,600-acre plot of land forty miles north of Chicago on Lake Michigan. And the plan worked! Before the press knew what had happened, a deal had been struck. As the New Year's Eve Watch Night Service introduced the year 1900, Dowie unveiled his plans for the building of Zion City. Zion was to be fully Christian—a closed theocratic community complete with its own factories, stores, generating plant, college, hotels, auditoriums, and banks—all controlled by the church. They would even print their own postage stamps. Notably absent would be doctors, surgeries, drugs, tobacco, liquor, swine, dance halls, and theaters. The city would have three

---

49   Ibid.

branches—the Christian Catholic Apostolic Church would be the ecclesiastical branch, Zion College its educational branch, and stores and factories would comprise its commercial branch. At the center of town would be an 8,000-seat wooden tabernacle. Chicagoans could ride the train to Zion City for all-day Sunday services. Subdivisions would soon be allotted and leased. And this was only the first of many Zions to come—all for one purpose: to restore the last days' ministry of the Holy Spirit and his gifts in preparation for the return of Christ. "Zion stands for Salvation, Healing, and Holy Living" was the oft-repeated phrase.[50]

By 1901, plans had materialized and construction of Zion City was well underway. In the meantime, Dowie had secured a two-year lease on the 12,500-seat Chicago Coliseum, where he spoke weekly before capacity crowds. Though 10,000 people would eventually settle in Zion City, Dowie failed to consider the multitude of details involved in managing a city and how it would tax his strength and affect his health, leaving little time to preach or pray for the sick.

"Welcome Home of the General Overseer Rev. John Alexander Dowie, July, 1904, Zion City, Ill." This aerial photo was taken by George R. Lawrence with 17 kites and a 49-pound camera. The shutter was triggered by an electric signal through a 2,000-foot wire. Source: Library of Congress Prints and Photographs Division.

---

50 John A. Dowie, "God's Witness to Divine Healing," *Leaves of Healing* 8 (1900), 97; F.F. Bosworth, "Bosworth's Life Story," (Toronto, n.d.): Blumhofer, "Christian Catholic Apostolic Church": CE 131–32.

DOWIE'S FINAL YEARS

Sadly, Dowie's later years were characterized by pompous and erratic behavior as he succumbed to the trappings of power. He began wearing a high-priestly outfit, calling himself "Elijah the Restorer" and "The First Apostle of the End-Times Church" and making all sorts of other false and grandiose claims. He lived extravagantly, taking world tours to places like Hawaii, Australia, New Zealand, Mexico, France, Italy, Germany, and England. He established other Zion Churches, a second Zion Publishing House in London, and Zion Plantation—a paradise colony in east central Mexico. His questionable moral practices and lavish lifestyle soon left Zion bankrupt and in financial ruin. Wilbur Voliva, whom Dowie had brought in from his Australian branch to oversee his headquarters in his absence, during one of those absences led the charge to have Dowie removed from office. Even the *Chicago Tribune*, which had once been so critical of Dowie, now sounding sympathetic, noted that Zion's new general overseer seemed to "lack an important ingredient essential to his position—a check upon bitterness, a saving element of mercy and kindness."[51] When Dowie returned after suffering a stroke in 1906, he became locked in a court battle with Voliva over ownership of the city. But the courts soon sided with Voliva and, after a citywide election was held in September, Voliva's leadership was confirmed. Dowie suffered a second stroke before his death in 1907. After his death, many of those who faced financial ruin from Zion's declining real estate values, still believed the rich legacy of faith and healing they inherited from Dowie's ministry far outweighed any temporary financial losses. One reporter wrote at

---

51 *Chicago Tribune*, 29 April 1906: Blumhofer, "Christian Catholic Apostolic Church": CE 135.

his passing, "No man of our time has ever secured anything like the personal following he has."[52]

John Alexander Dowie dressed in his high priestly robe (c. 1904). Sadly, Dowie's later years were characterized by pompous, erratic, and eccentric behavior that included a "Prayer Duel" with a Muslim leader who claimed to be the Messiah and a botched "New York Visitation" showdown with a Methodist bishop at Madison Square Garden. Source: www.james-joyce-music.com. Photo: Wikimedia/Sirius86.

DOWIE'S LEGACY

Perhaps Gordon Lindsay, who was raised in Zion City, best summed up Dowie's legacy when he wrote, "Tens of thousands testified of healing under this man's ministry and his work was without a parallel in his day. . . . Like a clap of thunder out of a clear sky, John Alexander Dowie started on his worldwide mission of setting forth from the Word of God, and putting into practice, the ideas, ideals and principles of the coming Messianic Kingdom; and thereby succeeded in making 'Zion' a household word throughout the world. It has been said in him were treasured up the rarest gifts and talents ever given to man. As an iconoclast, he denounced evil in high and low places, tore off the mask of hypocrisy from unfaithful shepherds behind the pulpit, protested against the shams and fads of a giddy world, and heralded the death-knell of the dying age."[53]

---

52 "The Passing of Dr. Dowie," *Word To-Day* 10 (April, 1906), 359: Blumhofer, "Christian Catholic Apostolic Church": CE 126–27.

53 Gordon Lindsay, ed., *Voice of Healing*, May, 1949: Jennings, "John Alexander Dowie," *Truth in History: www.truthinhistory.org/life-ministry-of-john-alexander-dowie.html* (Accessed 5 March 2013).

Despite his character flaws, Dowie truly was "the father of healing revivalism" and a pioneer of modern Pentecostalism.[54] Hanging from the walls of Dowie's huge tabernacles in Chicago and Zion City were "crutches, canes, trusses, bandages and braces" left behind by those who had been healed.[55] Dowie was a firm believer in the last days restoration of all spiritual gifts. Once when asked what he thought about the gift of speaking in tongues, Dowie replied, "I don't know. I think some of you are getting a new tongue. You are getting a tongue that gives praise to the Lord, for a new blessing that has come into your homes, and He is giving us new tongues. We have not everything yet, that is true, but He gives the Word of Wisdom, and the Word of Knowledge, and Faith, and Gifts of Healing, and Workings of Miracles, and Prophecy and Discernings of Spirits, and He will give us in due time Tongues and Interpretation of Tongues. He will. That is coming in its right time."[56]

A CENTURY CLOSES

Many echoed Dowie's sentiments. C.I. Scofield, editor of the Scofield Bible, stated that more books had been written on the Holy Spirit in the 1890s than in all of previous Christian history. Pentecostal historian Vinson Synan wrote, "In a sense, the entire 19th century

---

54 David Edwin Harrell, Jr., *All Things Are Possible: The Healing and Charismatic Revivals in Modern America*, (Bloomington: Indiana University, 1975), 13 [hereafter ATP].

55 Kenneth Mackenzie, *Our Physical Heritage in Christ* (New York: n.p., 1923), quoted in *Bread of Life* 6 (1957), 11: Blumhofer, "Christian Catholic Apostolic Church": CE 131.

56 Jennings, "John Alexander Dowie," *Truth in History: www.truthinhistory.org/life-ministry-of-john-alexander-dowie.html* (Accessed 5 March 2013).

was like a Pentecost novena—the church waiting in the Upper Room, tarrying for power, and praying for and expecting an outpouring of the Holy Spirit with a renewal of the gifts of the Spirit from the new century that was about to dawn."[57] Charles Haddon Spurgeon (1834–1892), the "Prince of Preachers," proclaimed this from his London Metropolitan Tabernacle in 1857: "In a few more years—I know not when, I know not how—the Holy Spirit will be poured out in a far different style from the present. . . . For the hour is coming, and it may be even now, when the Holy Ghost will be poured out again in such a wonderful manner, that many will run to and fro and knowledge shall be increased—the knowledge of the Lord shall cover the earth as the waters cover the surface of the great deep; when His kingdom shall come, and His will shall be done on earth as it is in heaven. . . . My eyes flash with the thought that very likely I shall live to see the out-pouring of the Spirit; when 'the sons and the daughters of God shall prophesy, and the young men shall see visions, and the old men shall dream dreams.'"[58] Spurgeon did not live to see it, but he was oh, so close.

---

57   CHS 36.

58   Charles H. Spurgeon, *Spurgeon's Sermons* (Grand Rapids, Mich.: Zondervan, reprinted from 1857), 129–130: CHS 25.

STUDY QUESTIONS

1. How were the modern Holiness and Higher Life movements similar; different?

2. What were some of the causes and effects of the Methodist-Holiness split?

3. Name some of the Holiness denominations and how they were founded.

4. Why is Maria Woodworth-Etter called a trailblazer, forerunner, and "grandmother of the Pentecostal Movement"?

5. Why was Maria reluctant to pray for the sick? What was the result of her obedience?

6. What led John Alexander Dowie to begin a worldwide healing ministry?

7. What led to Dowie's publicity (both bad and good) in the city of Chicago?

8. For what purpose(s) was Zion City, Illinois founded?

9. What factors do you think led to Dowie's bizarre and erratic behavior later in life?

10. How would you describe John Alexander Dowie's legacy?

INDEX

acquire the Holy Spirit, 188-90

Acts of the Apostles, 15, 78, 135, 179, 221, 231-32

Africa, 50, 76-77, 107, 109, 155, 183, 208, 221, 236, 239-40

African Americans, 134, 139-42, 161-63, 177-78, 207, 212-13, 240

African Episcopal Church, 162

African Methodist Episcopal Church (AME), 162, 207

Agitations. *See* jerking

Aldersgate, 113-14

Alumbrados, 40

AME Zion Church, 162

American Bible Society, 162, 215

American colonies. *See* United States

American frontier, 100, 145, 156-62, 168, 172, 215

American Keswick movement, 208

American Revolution, 140, 142-44, 151, 156

Amish, 23

Anabaptists, 13, 17-23, 53-54, 61, 191

Andalusia, 42

angels, 101, 125, 224-25

Anglican. *See* Church of England

Anne Boleyn, 35-37

baptism in the Holy Spirit, 12, 18, 22, 124-25, 137, 165-67, 180-84, 193, 195, 206-08, 210-12, 218-22, 228-29. *See also* acquire the Holy Spirit; filled with the Spirit; Holy Spirit, receive the

baptism, water. *See* water baptism

Baptists, 13, 17-23, 31, 37, 53-54, 58, 61, 137, 139-40, 142, 145, 161, 184, 191, 207, 212, 214-16, 218, 220, 222-23

Barbados, 74

Barclay, Robert, 70

barking, 92, 159

Barney Creek Meeting House, 216

Bastille, 85

Beecher, Dr. Lyman, 174

Below, Gustav von, 179

Bernard of Clairvaux, 2

Bethlehem Chapel, Prague, 4

Bethlehem, Pennsylvania, 108

Bible, the Holy, 3, 15-16, 18-19, 22, 36, 53-54, 57, 61, 79, 85, 88-90, 92, 95, 103, 110, 112, 122, 141, 162, 192, 205, 215, 224, 230, 244. *See also* Scriptures; Word of God, the

blacks. *See* African Americans

Blumhardt, Christoph Friedrich, 187

Blumhardt, Johann Christoph, 185-87

Boardman, William, 208, 218

Bohemian Church, 4-6, 103-09

camp meetings, xvi, 100, 158-63, 195, 206-07, 211, 215

Campbell, Mary, 180-82

Canada, 195-96, 211

Cane Ridge revival, 159-61

Canon Law, 8, 15

Capet, Hugh, King of the Franks, 77

Cappadocian Fathers, 124

Carey, William, 155

Carmelite Order, 44-47

Carolinas, the, 75, 108, 130, 137, 140-41, 160, 211, 214-18

Cartwright, Peter, 157, 161

casting out demons, 13-15, 30, 58, 70, 73, 89, 119, 228, 240

Cathars, 2, 38

Catherine of Aragon, 35-36

Catholic Apostolic Church, 182-83

Catholicism, xvi, 1-11, 13, 15-21, 23-25, 31-32, 36-53, 60-61, 65, 66-67, 77, 83-86, 90-91, 94, 103, 151-54, 180, 238

Cévennes, 77

Charles II, King, 57, 76

Charles V, Emperor, 9, 35

Chicago, 197, 219, 234-44

Chicago Dispatch, 237-38

Chicago Tribune, 242

Global Wakening

Inform. Inspire. Ignite.

www.globalwakening.com

Visit www.globalwakening.com and help us inspire and equip a new generation with a supernatural Christian worldview that will help ignite a global wakening of God's church!

You can also download companion study tools including a free timeline and summary of the complete trilogy, glossary, sources, pronunciations, abbreviations, and more.

ALSO AVAILABLE FROM JEFF OLIVER

From Pentecost to the Present: The Holy Spirit's Enduring Work in the Church

Book 1: Early Prophetic and Spiritual Gifts Movements

Jeff Oliver

Contrary to popular belief, miracles did not pass away with the twelve apostles. If anything, the Pentecostal sparks that were lit by them continued to spread throughout the known world.

This first installment explains how Jesus and the apostles established the concept of the Holy Spirit's abiding presence in the church laying the groundwork for a Christian initiation that included salvation and Spirit baptism. How spiritual gifts operated through the twelve apostles as they spread Christianity into the known world. How bold witnesses, supernatural signs, and practical love resulted in massive expansion of the early church despite extreme persecution. How Montanism tried to revive the church from moral decay through strict living and prophetical gifts before it was rejected. How Emperor Constantine I reunited the Roman Empire under a new Christian-friendly regime. How the new state-run churches, overrun with sin, caused many to flee to the wilderness resulting in another intense spiritual revival. How the Middle Ages featured the mass conversion of much of northern Europe through miracle-working missionary monks, followed by a period of great jubilation, mystical faith, and charismatic revivals, and ending with the incredible healing ministry of Vincent Ferrer.

From Pentecost to the Present: The Holy Spirit's Enduring Work in the Church

Book 3: Worldwide Revivals and Renewal

Jeff Oliver

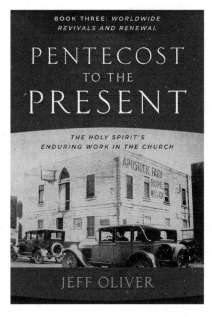

Without knowing the Holy Spirit's work in history, we cannot possibly understand what He is doing today, much less prepare for what He will do.

This third and final installment illustrates how Charles Parham founded the modern Pentecostal baptism with speaking in tongues, how Evan Roberts gained worldwide attention through the 1904-05 Welsh revival, and how William Seymour spearheaded an international Pentecostal movement from Azusa Street in Los Angeles in 1906. How Pentecostalism spawned new denominations, national and international ministries, global renewal movements, and inspired innovators to take modern revivalism to a whole new level. Then when Pentecostalism penetrated American Middle-class Protestantism, many observers began speaking of a "third force" in Christianity. Meanwhile, revolutionary changes in the Catholic Church opened the door for the Catholic Charismatic Renewal. Then, just as the charismatic movement was beginning to subside in America, it went global, as charismatic mega churches, Bible schools, and television networks took the message of renewal to the world. The twenty-first century has witnessed a dramatic shift in Christianity to the Southern Hemisphere fueled, in part, by the global rise of Pentecostalism, with many new movements on the horizon.

THE JOHN BUNYAN COLLECTION

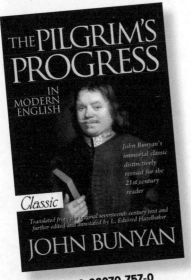

978-0-88270-757-0
528 pages / TPB

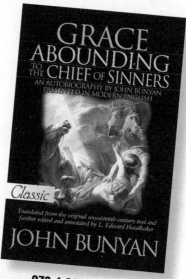

978-1-61036-133-0
248 pages / TPB

978-1-61036-153-8
400 pages / TPB

Pure Gold Classics
Timeless Truth in a Distinctive, Best-Selling Collection

An Expanding Collection of the Best-Loved Christian Classics of All Time.
AVAILABLE AT FINE BOOKSTORES.
FOR MORE INFORMATION, VISIT WWW.BRIDGELOGOS.COM

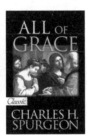
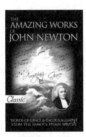

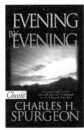
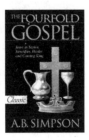

More *Pure Gold Classics* on next page ...

978-0-88270-754-9	978-0-88270-948-2	978-088270-402-9	978-0-88270-888-1
Audio Download	488 pages / Audio CD	Audio Download	Audio Download
312 pages / $15.99	$15.99	312 pages / $15.99	816 pages / $16.99

978-0-88270-763-1	978-0-88270-947-5	978-0-88270-473-9	978-0-88270-854-6
Audio Download	Audio Download	Audio Download	Audio Download
264 pages / $14.99	288 pages / $14.99	360 pages / $14.99	144 pages / $12.99

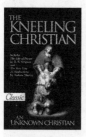

978-088270-397-8	978-0-88270-873-7	978-0-88270-821-8	978-088270-400-5
Audio Download	256 pages / Audio CD	480 pages / $16.99	Audio Download
372 pages / $15.99	$14.99		424 pages / $16.99

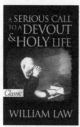

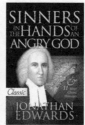
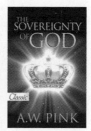

978-0-88270-453-1	978-0-88270-504-0	978-0-88270-949-9	978-0-88270-424-1
Audio Download	Audio Download	Audio Download	Audio Download
326 pages / $15.99	326 pages / $15.99	376 pages / $15.99	328 pages / $15.99

More *Pure Gold Classics* on next page ...